Knucklehead Kid

— to —

College Professor

Stories I Sometimes Tell My Friends

ROBERT ERIC BEASLEY

Knucklehead Kid to College Professor: Stories I Sometimes Tell My Friends

By Robert Eric Beasley

 REZINE Publishing
Franklin, IN
rezinepublishing@gmail.com

Disclaimer: The publisher reserves the right to revise this publication and make changes to its content without notice. To report typos or other erratum or to suggest improvements, contact the publisher.

Cover design by Bailey Jo Stamper.

10 9 8 7 6 5 4 3 2 1

ISBN-13: 9798336210842

To Elizabeth, Zachariah, Isaac, Nathanael, and Elijah
I Love You

Contents

Preface

50 72 65 66 61 63 65

On Christmas morning, 2023, I received a book titled *Tell Me Your Life Story, Grandpa* (Questions About Me, 2021) as a gift from Nathan and Abby (my son and daughter-in-law). As I held that little baby blue book in my hands, it brought to mind, once again, that maybe I should write a short book that includes some of the stories from my life that I sometimes hear myself telling others—usually for humorous effect. I had been thinking about writing a book like that for a couple of years because two of my other sons had mentioned to me that I should write an autobiography.

I was reluctant to do that, however, because I knew the enormous amount of work that goes into writing a book, and I just didn't think I could write another one at this point in my life. I knew that if I started such a project, I would dive into it and wouldn't come up for air until it was finished. Besides, it's not like I didn't have other things to do. I still had a full-time job and plenty of other life responsibilities to fulfill. Writing another book just didn't seem like something I wanted to do.

But a couple of weeks later, after the dust had settled around the Christmas holiday, and all the decorations had been put away, I picked up that little baby blue book again. As I looked through it and read all its probing questions (and other prompts), I knew I had an important choice to make. Either I put the book on my bookshelf, where it might never be looked at again, or I make the effort to help my grandchildren know me as a person—when they're old enough to care.

As I typed my answers into a word processing document, it became clear that answering *all* the questions in the book would require a *lot* of effort—especially if I wanted to be thorough. So, I began thinking that maybe I should answer the questions and compile them into a short book. And if I was going to do that, I might as well include the stories that I sometimes hear myself telling others—placing everything into the context of a life story.

I even began to think of a few reasons why I might actually *enjoy* writing such a book.

First, although I've written a number of books already, they've all been college textbooks that are very technical in nature and in my area of expertise—software engineering. I've always enjoyed writing when working on those projects, but the process has always been very slow, very tedious, and intellectually taxing—all in an effort to be precise. So, I thought I might enjoy writing a book where I could just think, write, and let the ideas flow without worrying much about perfection.

Second, although I'm not a famous actor, war hero, athlete, rock star, politician, or notorious something, I *have* lived an interesting life, and I have some good stories to tell. I love autobiographies myself. In fact, that's my favorite literary genre—followed by biographies and history. I read those kinds of books all the time. For some reason, I love seeing life through the eyes of others. That's just interesting to me. So, I thought I might enjoy writing a book that I could share with other people who like reading autobiographies or who just like hearing good stories.

And third, although three of my sons read some of my textbooks in college (supposedly), no one else in my family has read anything I've written—at least not that I know of. So, I thought I might enjoy writing a book that the other people in my family could read—especially my children, grandchildren, great-grandchildren, and so on.

One of the things that was interesting about the experience of writing this book was how so many memories returned to the forefront of my mind as I wrote—memories that I hadn't thought about in a very long time and had almost forgotten. As I sat at my desk typing, I often had to stop and think hard about the details of the story I was telling. When I couldn't remember the details, I had to reach out to someone who did—without letting them know what I was up to. I just didn't want to tell anyone I was writing a book until it was done.

Another thing that was interesting about the experience was that, as I wrote, it was almost like I was reading a book about someone else. As I typed, there was always a "movie" playing inside my head—except *I* was the central character. I really enjoyed reading about that central character in this book. I hope you enjoy reading about him too.

The 1960s

54 68 65 20 31 39 36 30 73

I was born Robert Eric Beasley at 9:07 pm on September 18th, 1962, at Paris Hospital in Paris, Illinois to Bobby Lee Roy Beasley and Judith Katherine (McCumber) Beasley. I was a healthy, 8-pound 8-ounce boy. At the moment of my birth, I possessed an intellectual blank slate—I knew *nothing* about *anything*. Think about that. I knew nothing about time. I knew nothing about object permanence (the fact that objects continue to exist even when you can't see them). I knew nothing about cause and effect. I knew nothing about numbers or mathematics or logic. I knew nothing about culture or tradition or religion or etiquette. I knew nothing about language. I knew nothing about work or play. I knew nothing about joy or love or pride. And I knew nothing about myself. I had a lot to learn.

Now, I'm not into numerology or anything, but I'd like to share something interesting about the details of my birth—before I get too far into my story. I think this is pretty unusual. If you group the numbers in my birthdate just right, while preserving the order of the numbers, and if you apply some basic mathematical operators to the groups of numbers, you get an interesting result. So, if you group 9-18-1962 like (91) (8) (19) (62), and you apply some basic addition and subtraction operators like (9-1) (8) (-1+9) (6+2), you get 8 8 8 8. And, if you consider the fact that I was 8 pounds 8 ounces when I was born, you get 8 8 8 8 8 8.

Pretty crazy, huh? The thing is, I never noticed that until I finished the first draft of this book. As a matter of fact, it occurred to me on the *very* night I finished the draft. For some reason, I woke up in the middle of the night thinking about the first paragraph of this chapter, including the numbers in my birthdate, and all of a sudden, it popped into my head. I'm not sure why I was thinking about the first paragraph of the chapter. Perhaps I was starting to replay the whole story from the beginning. But for whatever reason, Eureka! There it was! I hope eight isn't some kind of unlucky number or something. I'm kind of afraid to google it.

* * *

My parents moved to Paris when my dad took a job as Assistant District Landscape Architect for the Illinois Division of Highways. My mom and dad were 17 and 18 years old, respectively, when they got married, 18 and 19 years old, respectively, when they had my sister, Dawn Reneé, and 21 years old when they had me. That's pretty young by today's standards. But back then, it was relatively common for people to get married right out of high school and have children soon after. Today, the median age for a first-time marriage is around 30 years old for men and 29 years old for women. I can't even imagine being married at 18 years old. I knew virtually *nothing* about women at that age—or about the world for that matter.

My mom told me that the moment I was born she yelled, "Praise the Lord!" That's interesting because she wasn't particularly religious at the time, and that phrase wasn't part of her normal language. Later in her life, however, she would become "religious," and that phrase would become a common expression for her.

Mom told me that she had always prayed that I would be a tall man, which I did eventually become—6'2" to be precise. Being 6'2" has had its advantages in my life. I've always been able reach things way up high at home, on store shelves, and so on. It has also been an advantage in many of the sports I've played over the years, including basketball and tennis. So, thanks Mom for praying that for me.

She also told me that she wouldn't let anyone else hold me when I was born. I'm not sure how long that went on, but for some reason, she was very possessive of me. It could have been the cuteness factor. I know it didn't go on for too long, though, because I remember seeing a picture of my grandfather, Jack Beasley, holding me when I was a baby. I guess she *had* to let him hold me. After all, he was my grandpa.

* * *

My dad told me that I was partly named after him (Bobby) and partly named after his uncle, Robert—my grandma Sadie's brother. He didn't want to name me Bobby, which I appreciate, and he didn't want to pass down the middle names Lee and Roy, which I doubly appreciate. As for the Eric part, my mom just liked the name. I like the names Robert (a German name that means "bright fame") and Eric (a Norse name that means "sole ruler") not because of what the names mean but because they're nice, masculine names. Plus, Robert can be shortened to Bob.

Most of the people that know me call me Bob, but I've always signed my name Robert. Only two people in my life called me Rob— my mom and my first boss after college. I have no idea why they called me that. Maybe my mom called me Rob to distinguish my name from my dad's. Of course, when I got into trouble, it was always Robert Eric—but really loud. When I was in high school, virtually all my friends called me Beas. However, in college and afterward, no one ever called me that. Interestingly, all my sons were called Beas in college, and my dad is still called Beas by his friends and relatives. These days, a few of my tennis buddies call me Bobby, and a couple of other people I know call me Bobber. So, Robert has been a pretty versatile name.

But I've not always *looked* like a Robert to everyone. I know this because there have been a number of times in my life when someone thought my name was something else—for whatever reason. At least a couple of people thought my name was Steve. I don't know why. I mean, do I look like a Steve? I've also had Dave and Richard and Bill.

Back in high school, some of my friends and I would sometimes call each other Jack. You know, like "What's up, Jack?" or "You saw it here, Jack!" So, this one time, when my friends and I were playing pond hockey, which we did a lot in the winter months, the brother of one of the regulars played with us. The newcomer's name was Tim. During the game, my friend John skated around me and scored a goal, after which he swooshed by me and said something like, "Take that, Jack!" You know, the kind of harmless trash talk boys engage in sometimes. This kind of thing happened a few more times as well, which, by the way, is *not* a good commentary on my hockey-playing skills. Anyway, later in the game, someone finally referred to me as Bob, at which point Tim skated up to me and said with a puzzled look on his face, "Bob? I thought your name was Jack."

* * *

In 1965, my family moved to Springfield, Illinois, where my dad took a job as an assistant to the State Landscape Architect for the Illinois Division of Highways. In Springfield, we lived in a little light green house—which is still there by the way. I know that because, a year or so ago, I looked it up on Google Maps. It's a different color now, but it's still there and has been very nicely maintained.

My very earliest memories take place in and around that little light green house. Those memories include making pea-size mud balls in the back yard and playing with our white cat, Casper, whom we named after the cartoon character Casper the Friendly Ghost.

I also saw my first rock band around that time. One day, my mom and dad took my sister and me to visit their friends at their home on Lake Springfield. The couple had two boys who were probably around six and eight years old. Of course, to me, they were big kids. All I can remember is that the boys and their friend were singing and playing instruments to the song *Day Tripper* by the Beatles—a song that had only recently come out on the radio. I just thought that was so cool! In hindsight, however, I wonder if they were just an air band. But to me at that age, it seemed so real.

Another song I can remember hearing and singing around that time was *The 59th Street Bridge Song (Feelin' Groovy)* by Simon and Garfunkel. That song came out in 1966. For the longest time I thought the lyrics said, "Just kicking down *Chicago* stones…looking for fun and feeling groovy." Of course, the actual lyrics are "Just kicking down *the cobble* stones…looking for fun and feeling groovy." As you can tell, I was an early adopter of the "misheard lyrics" approach to learning lyrics. Even now, I sometimes look at the lyrics of songs I've known for years and am surprised to find out that I've been saying them wrong for decades.

I also had my first career aspirations while we lived in that house. I knew exactly what I wanted to be when I grew up. I wanted to be a garbage man. So, when the garbage truck came around on trash day, I put on my work gloves, grabbed the garbage can from the bathroom, hoisted it onto my shoulder, took it out to the curb, and watched the men chuck it into the back of the truck. As I stood there watching the garbage truck get smaller and smaller as it drove away, I dreamed that, one day, I would be the guy hanging off the back of the truck throwing people's trash into the hopper.

My favorite toys at the time were Hot Wheels and Matchbox cars and trucks. I spent endless hours lining up those vehicles on the edge of the couch—pretending to drive them all over the place. In my mind, I imagined all kinds of realistic scenarios—a dump truck picking up a load, a cop car stopping a speeding motorist, a fire engine rushing to a fire, a crash on the road. I guess I could keep myself entertained pretty easily.

Some of those cars had the most magical colors. The purples, deep blues, reds, rose golds, and gold chromes were amazing. To this day, when I see some of those colors, especially the rose golds and gold chromes, it takes me back to my childhood and produces a feeling in me that I probably couldn't describe. It's sort of like nostalgia mixed with euphoria.

On my fourth birthday, I learned to ride a two-wheeler. I remember it like it was yesterday. My mom made tacos for dinner that evening because that's what I wanted. She always made tacos using Old El Paso refried beans and taco seasoning packets—you know, the ones with the yellow and red labeling. After dinner, I had a very sudden, out-of-the-blue realization that I no longer needed the training wheels on my bike. It was like an epiphany or something. So, I asked my dad to take my training wheels off. After he took them off, I hopped on my bike and boom! I could do it! Right there on my fourth birthday. I felt like a big kid.

It was also while we lived in that house that I first exhibited signs of being a real knucklehead. I was a smart aleck for sure—maybe even a little defiant. Those traits would cause me a lot of trouble as a kid. Fortunately, I grew out of them eventually—for the most part anyway.

One night, when I was supposed to be in bed going to sleep, I just wouldn't shut up. I kept yelling questions to my parents who were in the living room watching TV. They were obviously getting annoyed with me and telling me to be quite and go to sleep. When my dad had

had enough, he came into my bedroom and, with this terrifying look on his face, said, "If I hear one more *peep* out of you…." He probably went on to warn me that I'd get a spanking or something. Then he was like, "Do…you…under…stand…me?" To which, of course, I said, "Yes." But right after he left the room, I thought it would be a good idea to respond to his warning with a very quiet little "Peep." Well. I guess it wasn't quiet enough. I always had to have the last word.

This other time, someone came to our house and told my mom that I was throwing rocks at cars as they drove by. To be honest, I don't remember doing that. I guess I was just being a little boy. Maybe I thought it was *my* street, and they had no right to drive on it. If that was the case, I think I was just practicing for later in life when I would need to tell kids to stay off my lawn.

Although my mom and dad were loving parents, who I'm sure were concerned about my safety, people just didn't keep a close eye on their kids like we do today. Evidently, at three or four years old, I could just stand by the street and throw rocks at cars, and Mom wouldn't even know it—unless someone told on me, of course. So, when I tell other stories like that in this book, please know it was a different era.

* * *

In 1967, we moved to Marseilles, Illinois, where my dad took a job as Assistant District Landscape Architect for the Illinois Division of Highways—this time for a different state district than the one he had worked in when we lived in Paris. In Marseilles, we lived in a big white house on a wooded lot that had a lot of chipmunks and spiders. Daddy longlegs spiders to be specific. One time, when my cousin Jim was visiting, he decided to see how many legs he could pluck off a daddy longlegs spider before it could no longer walk. Jim was a knucklehead too evidently. Even today, I wouldn't think of touching one of those things. They're hideous. As are all spiders.

While we lived in Marseilles, my dad grew frustrated and unhappy in his job with the State of Illinois. So, my parents decided that we should take a trip to visit my aunt Bev and uncle Art and my cousins Danny and Julie in Downey, California (a suburb of Los Angeles) to see if there might be something out there that he would like to do in terms of a career. Since my grandma Virginia wanted to go as well, we drove down to her house in Tuscola to pick her up. When we got to my grandma's, we transferred our luggage to her yellow 1966 Chrysler 300 because there would be five of us making the long trip, and her car was more spacious than ours.

On our way to California, we stopped in Normandy, Missouri (a suburb of St. Louis) to visit my aunt Brinda and uncle Jim. Uncle Jim, my mom's twin brother, was in his second year at the Logan College of Chiropractic (now Logan University) and wanted to show my dad around campus and talk to him about chiropractic. Dad had already had some conversations with a few other folks about chiropractic, and he had seen how it had helped some of his family members and friends, so he was interested in hearing more about the profession.

When our visit with my aunt Brinda and uncle Jim was over, we traveled the rest of the way to our destination in California. The trip was grueling as my dad liked to get where he was going as quickly as possible. We drove the entire trip in three days, which meant we only stayed overnight in a hotel twice on our way out there. During the trip, I collected all the carbon-copy gasoline receipts my dad was given after paying for gas, and I attached them to this little brown clipboard I had. There were a lot of them on that trip because the roundtrip was more than four-thousand miles long, and my grandma's car got 10 miles per gallon.

As we traveled for hours and hours down the interstate highway, I often stood on the floor between the back and front bench seats of my grandma's car asking questions. (Seatbelts weren't on our radar back then). I'm not sure of the nature of my questions, but I *do* know there were a lot of them. The only questions I actually remember asking were "Are we there yet?" and "How much longer?" and "Where are we?" One time, as we drove through the blazing hot desert, I asked my dad that last question. Without skipping a beat, he pointed to a great big billboard by the side of the highway and said, "See that sign? We're just this side of it?" Well. He wasn't wrong.

While we were in California, after giving it a good deal of thought, my dad decided that he wanted to become a chiropractor. So, when we got back to Marseilles, he told his supervisor that he would be leaving his job with the Illinois Division of Highways after three months and would be moving to Missouri to begin chiropractic school.

* * *

When the three months came to an end, we moved into one side of a duplex home in Normandy, where my dad began his studies at the Logan College of Chiropractic. One day, as I rode my bike in our new neighborhood, I got into a fight with a neighborhood kid about whose bike was faster. Hearing the ruckus, my sister and the boy's sister came running to break up the fight. And that's how we met Jeff and Sherry. Soon after that event, Dawn and I became good friends with Jeff and Sherry. Their house was just down the hill from ours. Maybe a hundred yards or so. It could have been closer, but when you're that age, a short distance can seem much greater.

I was good friends with Jeff until we moved away from the St. Louis area a few years later, but Dawn and Sherry remained best friends their whole lives. Sherry was the first girl I ever had a crush on. I was only four or five at the time, so maybe "crush" is too strong a word. But I do remember thinking she was *very* cute. I also remember sitting in Jeff and Sherry's house one day and figuring out how old I'd be in the year 2000. I'd be 38 years old on my birthday. (Wow! That came and went!) I was excited for that time in the future because I knew we'd all be driving to work in our flying cars. Uh-huh.

Similar to the epiphany-like experience I had when I all of a sudden knew I could ride a two-wheeler, I had another sudden realization in the driveway of the duplex we lived in. I was either playing with Jeff or Joey (the kid who lived in the duplex directly across from ours). All of a sudden, I *knew* that I could catch a baseball with ease. The thing that was strange about it was that it wasn't a gradual thing. It happened in an instant. I had been playing catch for a while by that point in my life, but catching the ball just hadn't become natural to me yet. Now it was. Very cool.

By the way, here's something wild. Several years later, on July 23rd, 1973, well after we had moved away, and Jeff and Sherry's family had moved out of their house in Normandy, Ozark Air Lines Flight 809 crashed into a ravine across the street from their old house killing most of the people on board. Some of the wreckage even clipped their house causing some minor damage to it.

* * *

In 1968, we moved to a different place in Normandy, where my dad took a job as the property manager of a small townhouse complex. The townhouses were brand new, and each one had an upstairs, main floor, and basement. In addition to working as the manager of the townhouse complex, my dad worked as a drummer to make additional money for chiropractic school. On Saturday mornings, he sometimes worked as a studio drummer making records and TV commercials. On Saturday afternoons, he occasionally worked as the drummer for a live radio program. And on Saturday nights, he sometimes worked as a drummer in the nightclubs of St. Louis. I remember when my dad would come into my room at night to give me a kiss before going to work in one of the nightclubs. He always wore a dark green paisley dinner jacket, and he smelled like Old Spice. To this very day, when I smell Old Spice, it conjures up that scene in my mind. I can see it like it was yesterday.

Between the buildings of our small townhouse complex were some beautiful white concrete fixtures, like bird baths and benches. One day, I got the brilliant idea of taking the ball-end of a ball peen hammer and chiseling a semi-circular shape into the side of the seat part of one of the concrete benches. When I was all done, it looked like a horse had taken a huge bite out of it. I'm not sure what was I thinking. You know, permanently damaging someone else's brand-new property. But that's what I did, and I had fun doing it. Anyway, at the tail end of my project, someone (an adult) saw what I was doing and told me they were going to call the police on me. As you can imagine, I was scared to death. I stayed inside our townhouse for days until I figured the cops had given up looking for me.

It was during this time in my life that I first started liking music. My parents had a record player and some Elvis records in the basement of our townhouse, and I remember going down there and playing their Elvis records for hours. I still love Elvis. I mean, he's not my favorite or anything, but I still listen to his music sometimes. He had a great voice. I'll even watch an Elvis movie on occasion. They really take me back to a simpler time.

In the late summer of 1968, I began kindergarten at Thomas Jefferson School in Normandy. My teacher was Mrs. Eickhoff. Mrs. Eickhoff was a nice middle-aged woman who I liked a lot. I distinctly remember walking up to the heavy wooden and leaded glass doors of my kindergarten classroom for the very first time and walking in with my mom. I didn't feel any kind of fear on that day. However, I must have developed a fear of failing during that school year because, when the school year was over, I was super worried that I hadn't passed and wouldn't get to move on to the first grade. I was so relieved when my parents got my report card and told me that I had passed kindergarten and would be attending first grade the following school year.

* * *

In 1969, we moved again because the townhouse we were renting got purchased by someone. The apartment complex that we moved to wasn't too far away, and I soon made friends with two brothers who lived in the next apartment building over. Jim and Rick were pretty close in age, and I'm pretty sure they were both older than me.

Right behind our apartment building, and I mean no more than 50 to 100 feet away, was a train track, and every day, trains would creep by—probably going no more than two or three miles per hour.[1] Somehow, someone got the idea of climbing on a train while it was moving and taking a ride. I'm almost certain that the idea wasn't mine, and I think Jim and Rick had done it before. So, probably three or four times, we "hopped a train" and rode it for a couple hundred yards or so. We usually hopped on flatbeds, but I recall hopping into an empty boxcar as well. In hindsight, I'm horrified that we did that. We could've been maimed or killed! Although I'm a "safety first" nerd now, I just had no regard for safety back then. I was basically an idiot.

While we lived in the apartment by the tracks, my grandma Virginia called and said she was coming for a visit. On the phone, she told me that she had a *very* special surprise for me. I…could…not…wait! So, I daydreamed about her arrival for days. Really. I knew my grandma was going to bring me something that I would absolutely love. When she finally got to our apartment, I begged her for my gift. Of course, she

---

[1] The train track is no longer there, by the way. I googled it. Somewhere along the way, it was converted into a trail called the Ted Jones Trail.

told me to be patient and that we'd open presents after dinner. When I finally got to open my surprise, it was a 5" x 7" framed picture of her. I can still see it in my mind's eye today. Although I probably tried not to show it, I was *so* disappointed. I thought she was going to bring me a fabulous toy or something—a new Hot Wheels truck, a water pistol, or maybe some GI Joe stuff. I was seven years old, and I got a framed picture of my grandma. Can you believe it? God bless you Grandma, but next time, just give me the money. I'll buy the gift.

Around this time, my mom and dad met another young married couple—Bob and Linda. Bob was in chiropractic school with my dad, and Linda stayed home to raise their kids. So occasionally, Linda would come over to our apartment to hang out with my mom. She was very funny and fun to be around, but she liked to smoke cigarettes. In those days, people just torched one up—right in their friend's apartment. I don't think they even had to ask. Anyway, whenever Linda came over, she'd say to me, "Hey, Little Beas. Want a puff?" Well. Yes, I did. And I puffed on that cigarette like a pro too (except for the inhaling part) as I mimicked what I saw the adults do. Linda thought that was so funny! I don't know if my mom did though. It's kind of hard to say. I mean, she didn't tell me I couldn't do it. I don't think we knew all the risks associated with cigarette smoking back then.

* * *

In the late summer of 1969, I began the first grade. My teacher was Mrs. Ropulewis. Mrs. Ropulewis was probably 22 or 23 years old at the time and was *very* pretty. My grades that year were all A's, B's, and S's, but it appears that I was a little difficult to deal with. Here is the dialog between Mrs. Ann Ropulewis (AR), and my mom, Judy Beasley (JB), as it appeared on my kindergarten report card.

AR: "Bobby is capable of—and is making—decent strides academically. Sometimes, I feel as though he could try a bit harder. The result here would be less carelessness, I feel. He enjoys attracting attention to himself, but this trait is gradually being overcome. He is doing better disciplining himself—but could learn to use free time more wisely."

JB: "I'm so happy Bobby is doing better. He really loves school and his teacher. Thank you for your patience and time."

AR: "Bob is beginning to see that we want to be fair with him—but he has certain things he must conform to. The 'battle of our wills' is subsiding. I am helping him to see the necessity in your work and that you love him very much—but little ones need more attention. He has shown more of a desire to [do] good work. This is very important and certainly something to be proud of."

JB: "Bobby seems to have improved at home also. Thank you for making such an effort to help him."

AR: "It's been quite a year!!! Times weren't always smooth, but I really feel that Bobby has improved in self-control. If this is true—then all the knocking of our heads together was worth it!!! He remains capable academically and I have really 'enjoyed' the experience of having him in school. Thank you for your extreme concern in his progress."

Well, that says quite a lot about the little boy I was back then. Mrs. Ropulewis said I needed to work harder. I needed to be more careful. I needed to stop drawing attention to myself. I needed to be more self-disciplined. I needed to be more conforming. And I needed to be less stubborn. Tough words from the woman I loved. Yes, I had a pretty big crush on Mrs. Ropulewis. I think my attitude ruined my chances with her.

The 1970s

54 68 65 20 31 39 37 30 73

In the late summer of 1970, I began the second grade. My teacher was Mrs. Hamilton. Mrs. Hamilton was a relatively young woman. I'd say she was probably in her middle to upper 20s at the time. When I sat in her classroom, I frequently daydreamed about flying around it in my wood-and-steel chair-desk combo. You know, the kind where you could dispose of your used chewing gum inside the hinged desktop or under the seat. I just couldn't keep my mind on the lesson at hand when there were dogfights to be won.

One day, someone came to our classroom to give us a talk about all the horsing around that was going on in the hallways of the school. I think it was Mr. Finley—the school principal. Evidently, the rowdiness had gotten out of control, and it was time to put an end to it. Mr. Finley told us the story of a boy who was running in the hallway, ran into a water fountain, went down over it at the waist, and hit his eye directly on the splash guard—that part of the fountain that some kids put their cheek against when they take a drink. He went on to tell us that, when the kid stood back up, his eye had popped out and was dangling from its socket by the vein that connected his eye to its blood supply in his head. I never ran in a school hallway again.

In late September of that year, my dad graduated with his Doctor of Chiropractic degree from the Logan College of Chiropractic. After the graduation ceremony, my mom and dad took a road trip through a few different parts of the country to find somewhere they both liked and where my dad could start a new chiropractic clinic. Eventually, they settled on a small town just outside of Lexington, Kentucky called Winchester.

After they had made their decision, they told their parents that we were moving to Winchester and found out that we had relatives who lived there. The only relatives I remember, though, were my grandma Virginia's cousin Gertrude and her husband Bluford Earl. I don't know how old they were, but they seemed ancient to me. I just remember feeling the need to let Gertrude know that she had a mustache—like the kind you see on a 15-year-old boy. And since I hadn't yet grown a filter between my brain and my mouth, I made her aware of that fact. I thought she should know so she could improve her looks and stop confusing little kids.

In addition to our relatives in Winchester, I also found out that my second-grade teacher, Mrs. Hamilton, was from Winchester. What a coincidence! It was cool that Mrs. Hamilton and I had Winchester in common. I think it made the transition to our new town a little more comfortable for me.

* * *

When we got to Winchester about a month later, we moved into a small house a block from Hannah McClure Elementary School, where I began the remainder of my second-grade year. My new teacher was Mrs. Wiley. Mrs. Wiley hated me for some reason. I say, "for some reason," but in hindsight, I'm sure it had something to do with my inability to behave. All I know is she used to smack me on the back of my hands with a wooden ruler fairly frequently and make me write stuff like "I will not put my hands on other people" or "I will not talk out of turn" a hundred times as a homework assignment. Of course, if I knew then what I know now, I would've written a computer program in two minutes to complete the task.

In Mrs. Wiley's classroom, we had what was called a "cloakroom." Ooo…a cloakroom! How about calling it something modern and not evil sounding like "coat closet?" Anyway, sometimes I would sneak in there and go through everyone's coat pockets looking for sandwiches. No. I didn't really do that, but my friend and I *did* sneak in there one time, take the paper off a cigarette he had brought from home, and put the delicious-smelling tobacco into the space between our bottom lips and teeth—just like our grownup role models on TV did. Let's just say it didn't taste as good as we thought it would.

* * *

While we lived in Winchester, I got a brand-new bicycle as a present from my parents. My sister, Dawn, got a new bike as well. My bike was a dark green stingray-style bike with a black and white checkered-flag banana seat. I loved that bike and kept it clean and polished. Dawn's bike was a white stingray-style bike with a white banana seat. I loved her bike as well—but for different reasons. More on that later.

Right across the street from our house was a small college called Southeastern Christian College. It was great living next to that college because my friend Doug and I pretty much had the run of the place. There was no security to speak of, so we could walk into any building we wanted, and no one would bat an eye. I remember going into this one building and seeing dozens of animal skeletons encased in glass-enclosed cabinets. Squirrels. Cats. Snakes. Pretty much everything. I'm guessing that building housed the Biology Department.

But the building that Doug and I spent the most time in was the gymnasium, which was two blocks down the street from my house and directly catty-cornered to Doug's. Having a gymnasium like that at my disposal was great because I was just starting to develop an interest in basketball. Sometimes I'd even go there by myself just to shoot around. Back then, the American Basketball Association was still a thing, and they used red, white, and blue basketballs. I had a red, white, and blue basketball as well, and it was magical watching that ball spin on its way to the hoop. Just like the pros.

* * *

The most significant event of my life occurred in the winter of 1970. It was an event that would *eventually* affect every aspect of my life. One night, as I was lying in bed, I felt prompted in my spirit to go into my mom and dad's bedroom and ask my mom how to be "born again." I have no idea why I was thinking about that, but the Jesus Movement *was* in full swing, so maybe I overheard my mom and dad talking about Christianity with family or friends. I *do* know that several of my aunts and uncles had become born again prior to that, so maybe that's what it was. Or maybe I heard something on TV about it.

Anyway, I felt the need to be born again that night, so I got out of bed, walked into my mom and dad's bedroom, went over to my mom's side of the bed, and asked her how to be born again. She told me that I needed to "ask Jesus into my heart," which I immediately did after returning to my room. Of course, at eight years old, I didn't know what all that meant. My faith was very simple, but I at least understood that God had forgiven my sins and that I was now "saved" from the result of those sins. Although one only needs to be saved once, I must have asked Jesus into my heart every night until I was in about the fourth grade. I must have really meant it.

I didn't have an exciting conversion experience like some people have. I mean, I was only eight years old. It wasn't like I was weighed down by years of paralyzing guilt that was miraculously lifted off my shoulders. No. My conversion experience was much less dramatic— but just as real. All I know is, before that night, I really hated going to church. And after that night, I loved it. It was a clear change of heart that came from somewhere outside of me. Besides that, I didn't really change that much—from what I can remember. I was still an ornery kid. But there *would* be some small spurts of spiritual growth over the next several years.

* * *

In the summer of 1971, my boyhood fascination with setting things on fire began. It started when my aunt Barb and uncle Dale and their kids, Jim, Todd, and Angie, were staying with us as they passed through Kentucky on their way back home to Illinois after visiting Opryland in Nashville, Tennessee. I'm almost certain that it was shortly before the Fourth of July because they had purchased a suitcase full of fireworks while they were in Tennessee—some of which I'm sure were illegal in Illinois.

In addition to the boxes of Black Cats, Cherry Bombs, M-80s, and Roman Candles, which we didn't play with while they were visiting, they had these handheld fireworks that produced a welding torch-like fire on the end that changed colors from red to blue and everything in between. I don't remember what they were called. But I was able to find some similar ones on YouTube recently, so I know they still make them.

The fact that they produced a flame that looked like a welding torch gave me the idea that I should weld some stuff. At first, I began using the "torch" on the big tree that stood in our front yard. But that didn't do much. So, I moved on to the great big roll of black asphalt roofing felt that sat between the two sawhorses next to our house. Evidently, our house was getting a new roof. After using my torch on the roofing felt for a few seconds, it started on fire. Of course, Jim and Todd and I were horrified and began to panic. But, instead of running inside and telling our dads that the roofing felt (and subsequently our house) was about to go up in flames, the three of us walked into the house in rapid succession to get little 12-ounce cups of water to put out the flames— all the while pretending to be calm and collected like nothing out of the ordinary was going on.

After making several trips in and out of the house with our opaque, pastel-colored, plastic Tupperware cups, one of our dads asked us what was going on out there—to which I replied, "Nothing." You know, as if everything was *just* fine. But of course, it wasn't. There was a *fire* going on out there! Luckily, we got the fire put out pretty quickly. But wow! We could have burned the whole house down!

Strangely, I don't remember getting into trouble for that. I'm sure someone wanted some answers as to why their roofing supplies had been damaged while they were away from the worksite. Surely my dad knew that it was likely one of us boys. I'm sure he knew that Jim and Todd and I had been out front playing with fireworks when they were visiting. And he probably connected the dots when he thought back about how nervous we boys looked going in and out of the house with those Tupperware cups in our hands.

I don't know. Maybe he covered for us when the roofers inquired about the damage to their stuff knowing that boys just do stupid things sometimes. But since I've never known my dad to be less than honest, that probably wasn't it. Or it could have been that I outright lied about our involvement in the episode. That could be. I can imagine myself *at that age* saying something ludicrous like, "Black roll of roofing felt in our front yard? I've never even seen a black roll of roofing felt in our front yard!" Or maybe I just blocked the getting-in-trouble part out of my mind. It's hard to say. I guess I'll never know.

* * *

Later that summer, we moved to St. Charles, Missouri, where my dad went into practice with two of his friends from chiropractic school who were taking over the large practice of a doctor who had recently passed away. We moved into a house on a small farm on the outskirts of town that had a lake, some woods, and a red barn that housed some Shetland ponies. One of the ponies was named Pierre. Pierre was gray and spotty and very cantankerous. I think it was because he was old. The owner of the farm told us not to ride Pierre because he was known to bite people. But we could ride any of the other ponies whenever we wanted. Although riding horses wasn't my thing, Dawn and her friend Sherry took advantage of the perk regularly.

While we lived in St. Charles, I attended the third grade at Becky-David Elementary School. At Becky-David, I had two teachers. One was Mrs. Priest, an older woman who was a saint. And one was Mrs. Means, a middle-aged woman who was, well, mean. At least that was my *perception* of her at the time. I'm sure she was a lovely woman, and I probably had something to do with her attitude toward me. I seemed to have that effect on some teachers.

There are two other things I remember about being at that school. One was that we had a nine-weeks-on-three-weeks-off academic cycle. I really liked that because we had three-week vacations all year round. The other was that the girls were bigger than me and the other boys. I don't remember any of the kids at that school—except for the guy who tried to pick on me one day. I'm pretty sure his name was Mark. Mark had straight blonde hair, and he aways had an angry look on his face—at least when he was looking at me. He was also much smaller than me, so I'm not sure what he was thinking. After I beat him up, he never bothered me again. Problem solved.

* * *

It was in that farmhouse that I began building models. One of the models I built was the Apollo 11 Saturn V Rocket from Estes. It was probably the largest model I ever built—with its main engines, its first, second, and third stage fuel segments, its lunar, service, and command modules, and its launch escape system on the top. When finished, it stood over three and a half feet tall. It took me quite a while to build because I was determined to follow all the directions to a tee, including painting everything the correct color and putting on all the decorative stickers. It looked remarkably realistic.

Unfortunately, it was also the time in my life that I started blowing things up. Setting things on fire was fun, of course. But blowing stuff up just added that extra dimension of enjoyment. As it turned out, my Saturn V Rocket was the first in a long line of models, including cars, trucks, and airplanes, that I built and then completely destroyed by fire or explosion—usually after I had proudly displayed them on my shelf for a while.

* * *

In St. Charles, I started watching reruns of *The Rifleman*, starring Chuck Connors. He was very cool. He had this great squint in his eyes when he got serious, and he would spin his rifle like most guys would spin their pistols. So, one day, I asked my parents for a BB gun for my birthday or Christmas or something. Since we lived out in the country, they obliged, probably thinking, "What could he possibly damage out here?" The gun was awesome! It was a Crosman that basically looked like your standard Winchester rifle—like the Winchester Model 1894. (No. I don't know anything about rifles. I just googled it.)

When I played with my rifle, I would squint my eyes and spin it just like Chuck Connors. I would also stand on the dock at the pond and shoot at dragon flies. When luck was on my side, I would shoot those hideous purple and green metallic-looking insects right in half. I would also shoot at birds as they perched above my head in the trees. The first time I actually killed one, I felt really horrible about it. I don't think I ever did that again.

One night, Bob and Linda, my parents' friends from chiropractic school, were at our house visiting. They had parked their yellow VW microbus in front of our house about 20 feet from our front door and about the same distance from the big tree in our front yard. To the tree, I had attached a brown paper bullseye target that I was using for target practice. After practicing my shooting skills for a while, I went indoors. When it was time for Bob and Linda to leave, they walked out to their microbus and noticed that the back passenger-side window of the it had been completely shattered—with a BB size hole right in the middle. Of course, I was the immediate suspect. I understood why, but I *didn't* do it—at least not deliberately. I'm sure no one ever believed me, but it's true. All I can think of is that one of my BB's ricocheted off the tree and hit the window. It was really strange.

* * *

It was in St. Charles that I heard the Carpenters for the very first time. My sister had some Carpenters records and a record player in her bedroom, and I would sometimes go in there and take a listen. (I was really fortunate because I not only could use my own stuff whenever I wanted, but I could also use my sister's stuff when she wasn't looking.) The Carpenters were very popular at the time, and I really liked their music. I still listen to them on occasion. I think Karen Carpenter had one of the most magical voices of all time. If you don't know what I mean, take a listen to the Carpenters when you get a chance.

* * *

In 1972, we moved to Creve Coeur, Missouri. The two doctors my dad had been practicing with just couldn't seem to get along, and the conflict drove my dad crazy. While in practice with those guys, my dad had met another doctor who practiced in Creve Coeur. The guy was very nice, and he really liked my dad, so Dad jumped at the opportunity to go into practice with him.

In Creve Coeur, I attended Weber Elementary School, where my fourth-grade teacher was Mrs. Mullins. Mrs. Mullins was probably in her early to middle 40s and was a very kind woman. I really liked her. For some reason, I would sometimes trip up and address her as "mom" before quickly correcting myself. It would just slip out. In Mrs. Mullins class, I earned the position of class president by bribing every single student in my class with, "If you vote for me, I'll vote for you." I literally went around to each student before the day of the election and *quietly* made my "campaign pitch."

Of course, I won the election overwhelmingly, and Mrs. Mullins thought I was the most popular kid ever. She was pretty proud of me. I found out later that the person I *actually* voted for, a girl named Molly, didn't even vote for me. The way I saw it, we had an agreement, and she lied to me. What a loser. Being the president of my fourth-grade class might sound impressive, but the only prestige associated with the position was that I got to turn off the lights and close the door after everyone else in the class had left the room—like when we went to the cafeteria for lunch or outside to recess.

* * *

In the fourth grade, I became concerned about the environment for the first time—more specifically about the need to preserve our natural resources, like oil, coal, and natural gas. I'm not sure where my concern came from, but I'm guessing someone came and spoke to our class on Earth Day, or we watched a movie on the topic or something. But my concern wasn't an alarmist type of concern or anything—you know, the kind that comes complete with political motives. Instead, it was all about being good stewards of the natural resources we were given by God. If I *did* learn about environmental issues in school, I'm almost certain that *that* wasn't the message conveyed to us in class. But that's definitely what I got out of it.

So, armed with my new convictions about energy conservation, it wasn't long before I began nagging my parents and sister about turning the lights off in the house when they weren't being used. I mean, I had learned that, once we burn a barrel of oil, a ton of coal, or a cubic foot of natural gas, it was gone forever. Such natural resources were just *not* renewable. By the way, my ability to nag people about turning off lights and not wasting energy in general would come in quite handy later in life when I was raising children.

* * *

The cool thing about the house that we moved into in Creve Coeur was that it was like two or three blocks away from the public ice-skating rink. On many days after school, I would walk there and go ice skating. The beauty was it only cost $0.25 to get in. That was pretty cheap. So, my mom and dad bought me a pair of black figure skates—yes, *figure* skates. I guess they didn't know that *hockey* skates would have been a better choice for a boy like me. And evidently, I was too unaware to be embarrassed by them. I was just grateful to have my own skates.

At the ice rink, I skated for hours as awesome classic rock music blasted over the speakers above the rink. To this very day, when I hear the songs *Roundabout* by Yes and *Do It Again* by Steely Dan, it takes me back to my childhood—ice skating in that rink.

Another cool thing about our house was that it had a long driveway that ran all the way from the street to the garage behind the house. I'd say the driveway was a hundred feet long. At least that's what it seemed like to me at the time. Our driveway was perfect for performing bicycle stunts. My friends and I would build these elaborate ramps and then jump them on our bikes—Evel Knievel style. When I say, "our bikes," I mean my friends would jump the ramps with their bikes, and I would jump the ramps with my sister's bike—you know, the white stingray-style one. Of course, I cared far too much for the condition of my own bike to tear it up jumping ramps, so I used hers. Over time, I pretty much tore up Dawn's bike jumping ramps and doing other stunts. But my bike was fine.

* * *

One winter day, after a pretty good snow, I shoveled our driveway, set up a ramp, and made a few jumps with Dawn's bike. I must have gotten bored or something, so I decided to pull a little prank on my mom to break the monotony. In the ditch at the end of the driveway near the garage, I placed my body face up in the snowbank, bent my leg backward into an "L" shape to give the illusion that it was broken, and pretended to be dead.

I waited and waited for what seemed like an eternity when my mom finally came to the back door and yelled, "Bobby, it's time to come in!" She saw me there in the snow, but I didn't move. She yelled the same thing again. But still no movement. She probably tried something else a bit firmer like, "Robert Eric! Get into the house right now!" But I still didn't move a muscle. Then, all of a sudden, she started running down the stairs of the back porch screaming hysterically, "No, Bobby! No, Bobby! No, Bobby!" When she got to me, I jumped up laughing. But when I saw the devastated look on her face, I was struck with grief. I had scared my mom like no parent should ever be scared. This story still breaks my heart when I think about it. I never should have done that.

* * *

Our next-door neighbors were a couple who were probably in their 70s at the time. Julius and Helen were very sweet and would let me and Dawn ice skate in their driveway whenever any standing water on it had frozen over. Helen told me many, many years later that I was a very ornery kid and that I drove Julius crazy because I would go over to their house and ask him a million questions.

One day, Julius passed away, and my family attended his visitation at a funeral home. It was the first time I had ever attended an event like that, so I had no idea what to expect. I remember standing in line with my parents and sister as we waited to go to the front of the chapel for some reason. I also remember the place smelling like Easter lilies. When it was our turn to go, we walked up to the front of the chapel. And there was Julius, lying perfectly still inside a big brown coffin with bright lights shining on him. I was shocked. I had no idea that I would be seeing a deceased person in real life. It was surreal. Although I love the smell of Easter lilies now, the smell of them always brings back visions of Julius's visitation that day.

* * *

At some point, I got a bunch of Hot Wheels track—the kind that had the orange track segments that you connected together using little pink connectors that looked like tongues. My friends and I would build custom racetracks that usually started at the top of a table and ended up somewhere on the floor. Hours of fun. Cars and trucks were still some of my favorite toys in the fourth grade, but they were beginning to lose their appeal as I got a little older.

Since I really loved to build stuff, my parents bought me an Erector Set for Christmas or my birthday or something. It was an amazing gift because I really like to build things. The Erector Set was made of metal and included all kinds of beams, wheels, pulleys, and nuts and bolts. I built all kinds of stuff with that set, but I distinctly remember building a crane that could hoist a payload. When it was complete, I could attach something to the hook on the end of the cable and crank the handle that I had connected to a couple of pulleys that created leverage.

While we lived in that house in Creve Coeur, I had a neighborhood friend named Doug. Doug and I weren't friends for very long because my family would soon be moving across town, and we would never see each other again. I would sometimes go over to Doug's house, and we would make each other pass out. I'm not going to tell you how we did it because it was such a stupid thing to do. What I *will* tell you is that, as I was passing out, everything faded from color to white. Then, as I was waking up, everything faded from white to color. And when I was fully conscious again, I usually saw Doug looking at his watch to determine how long I had been out. Although I didn't know it then, I *do* know now that that stunt was dangerous. So, don't do it. Seriously.

* * *

In the summer of 1973, we moved to a different house in Creve Coeur. My dad said we moved there because it was a nicer place. The cool thing about this house was that it was only a block away from a Lion's Choice restaurant, where I could get ice cream cones for $0.05. That was super cheap—even back then. Luckily, the move didn't affect the school I attended.

In the fifth grade, I got a new teacher. His name was Mr. Brinks. I really liked Mr. Brinks. He was probably in his middle to late 30s, he was tall and lanky, and he always wore a brown suit and matching tie. He also had a dark five o'clock shadow on his face even though he was always clean shaven. He basically looked like the astronomer, Carl Sagan, with black horn-rimmed glasses. I think what I liked about Mr. Brinks the most was that he was much more scientific than any of the other teachers I had had to that point.

During the school year, I began playing the trombone. Although my dad had tried to get me to play the drums in the second grade, I just wasn't interested. For some reason, I was much more attracted to the shininess of the trombone and how you changed the pitch that the instrument produced by moving the slide up and down.

It was in our new house that I built a computer for the first (and only) time. Computers weren't really on my radar back then, but for some reason, I decided to build one. Maybe Mr. Brinks introduced the concept to us at school or something. He *did* look like the computer programmer type. To build the computer, I used a shoebox, some bare copper wire, some masking tape, 18 three-inch construction nails, a light bulb and socket that I took out of one of those handheld utility lanterns, and a big 6-volt Eveready lantern battery that had those big positive and negative copper springs on the top and weighed like two pounds.

Of course, the computer was extremely primitive. In fact, now that I know how computers work, I can say with confidence that it wasn't *really* a computer at all. It was more of a box of circuit breakers. But to my rather undeveloped fifth-grade mind, it fit my understanding of how a computer worked—you asked it a question, and it gave you an answer. That's all I knew.

To make the computer, I punched eight nails through the top of the shoebox down its left side and eight of the nails down its right side so that there was an eight row by two column array of exposed nail heads. Next to the nail heads on the left side, I wrote some simple mathematical expressions like $1+5$, $2-3$, $4x2$, and $6/3$, and next to the nail heads on the right side, I wrote corresponding answers like 6, -1, 8, and 2. Of course, I made sure that the mathematical expressions and their corresponding answers weren't directly across from each other. That would be entirely too easy. Then, on the inside the shoebox, I ran a copper wire from each expression nail to its corresponding answer nail and covered it with tape so that it wouldn't touch any of the other wires.

Next, I cut a hole in the top of the shoebox, where I secured the light bulb socket and light bulb. Then, I connected the positive spring of the battery to the positive post of the light bulb socket and attached a wire from there to another construction nail. This nail became my "expression wand." And finally, I attached a wire from the negative spring of the battery to another construction nail. This nail became my "answer wand." That was it. So, when I touched my expression wand to an expression nail head, and I touched my answer wand to the corresponding answer nail head, an electrical circuit was created, and the light bulb lit up. It was simple but effective. I know it wasn't rocket science, but at least I wasn't twiddling my thumbs.

* * *

I also built a solar heater that year. I guess the creative juices were flowing in my eleven-year-old head at that time in my life—first the computer and now this. Although I built the heater in the fifth grade, the idea for it had occurred a few years back—in early 1970 to be exact. Back then, I had noticed that it was very warm inside our yellow 1964 Ford Galaxie 500—even when it was very cold outside in the middle of winter. Although the outside of the car was yellow, the inside of the car was completely black, and as long as the windows were closed, and the sun was shining in on the black interior, it could get pretty warm in there. So, even though I didn't act on it then, that's when I got the idea of a heater that didn't use electricity. It would just use sunshine. The interesting thing is, I don't think solar heating was even a thing back then. But if it was, I certainly didn't know about it. I thought I had an original idea.

I hung on to the idea of a solar heater for the next few years until I got into the fifth grade. To build the heater, I got this, say, 3' x 3' x 3' box from somewhere, cut it so that one side of it had an angle that faced toward the sky when it lay flat on the ground, lined the entire inside with Styrofoam, and then covered the Styrofoam with black construction paper. I then attached a piece of clear plexiglass to the angled side of the box so that the sun could shine in, and I put a 1" hole in two sides of the box so that the heated air inside could escape. And voila! It worked! Well, sort of. I mean, the air inside the heater got pretty warm, but not much of it was coming out of the holes I put in the sides. So, to help expel the heated air, I put a small *electric* fan up to one of the holes. Of course, since most of the air from the fan wasn't actually going into the hole, this was pretty inefficient. It did, however, move a little bit of the heated air out of the opposing hole.

Of course, now that I think about it, the electric fan pretty much ruined my idea of not using electricity. Also, why didn't I just put two additional holes in the top of the heater? If I had done that, I think the unheated air would have been sucked in through the two original holes, and the heated air would have been expelled through the two new holes naturally. Maybe I didn't yet know that hot air rises. But I doubt that. I probably just wasn't connecting the dots.

* * *

At this point in my life, I started to feel a sense of competitiveness when it came to sports. During recess at school, a classmate and I started playing tetherball together, and I began getting very serious about winning. As I got ready to play a game, I remember feeling the desire to win welling up in my soul. I was only 11 or 12 years old, but

I worked up a big sweat, so much so that it was difficult to concentrate in the classroom afterward because I was so hot and sweaty.

It was also around this time that my dad taught me how to play tennis. I don't remember whose idea it was, but we went to some local courts, where he taught me the basic rules of the game and showed me how to hit a tennis ball. I can still see it in my mind's eye. I think we only played tennis once while we lived in Creve Coeur. We might have played more than that, but I don't recall playing tennis together again until several years later. Although I didn't take tennis seriously then, I would get much more into it in high school.

Although tennis wasn't my thing at the time, my friends and I would play baseball, basketball, football, pro wrestling, or whatever any time we had the chance. Sometimes, we'd watch a game on TV and then go outside and mimic what we had just seen the pros do. That's basically how we learned to play all those sports—by watching the pros.

It was a great time in life because I wasn't concerned at all about what I ate. On a lot of days in the summer, I'd go outside for a couple of hours to play some football and then run home and eat a huge bowl of Lucky Charms, Cap'n Crunch, or whatever other sugary cereal my mom had brought home from the store. Then, I'd go back outside for a couple more hours to play something else. I'd then run home and eat some more cereal. And the cycle continued. Of course, I don't eat junk like that anymore. Well…maybe once in a *great* while. Instead, I usually eat Grape Nuts, Raison Bran, and Steel Cut Oats—good stuff like that. Lucky for me, I like the taste of those cereals as well. But I would have to say that, in terms of taste, Lucky Charms is still my all-time favorite sugary cereal. And when I eat them, it takes me back to my childhood.

In the summer of 1974, I started playing Little League baseball. It was my very first taste of *organized* baseball, and I loved it—especially wearing the uniform. At one of our practices, the outfield was covered with thousands of tiny frogs that you couldn't help but step on while you walked. I pretty much stepped on a frog with every step I took as I played my position in left field. Every time I stepped on one, it would crunch under my feet, its little mouth would open wide, and its pink innards would bulge out like it was blowing bubbles with a mouthful of Bubblicious. It was gross. I can't remember how long we practiced that day, but I would imagine our practice was cut short.

The only other thing I remember about that baseball season was my coach telling us to eat a "good breakfast" before our first game. His recommendation? A big ol' bowl of sugary cereal. I could get on board with that!

* * *

When we lived in the St. Louis area, our family would sometimes take trips to Tuscola, Illinois. Tuscola is where my mom and dad were from, so we had family there. One time, at my grandma Virginia's house, my cousins Jim and Todd were over, and we were having a great time together—as usual. Jim, who was about a year and a half older than me, convince me to let him give me a "swirly." Swirlies were a big thing then—the epitome of humorous fun for boys. If you don't know what a swirly is, it's when you take someone's head, push it down into a toilet, and flush. The beauty is, when the victim comes up from the toilet, his hair looks like the swirl on top of a Dairy Queen Soft Serve ice cream cone. I know our parents were proud that day because we had not only created some wonderful (and cheap) entertainment for ourselves, but Jim had vaccinated me from many future diseases.

* * *

In February of 1974, in the middle of my fifth-grade year, we moved again. This time to Tuscola. We moved to Tuscola because my parents wanted to get involved in a home church there called The Assembly. A number of our family members were already involved in the home church, including my aunt Brinda and uncle Jim and their kids Scott and Steve and my aunt Barb and uncle Dale and their kids Jim, Todd, and Angie. I was very excited about moving to Tuscola, where I would be close to my grandparents, aunts and uncles, and cousins.

When we arrived in Tuscola, we moved into a nice stone house in a subdivision called Southland Acres on the outskirts of town. Since I was a huge Pittsburg Steelers fan at the time, my mom and dad painted my room Steelers yellow for me. After the paint dried, I hung all kinds of Steelers paraphernalia on the walls, like pennants and posters of my favorite players—Terry Bradshaw, Franco Harris, "Mean" Joe Green, and a few others on the team. It was *very* cool.

One time, when my sister and I were at home alone on a *really* cold night, she dared me to run to our mailbox and back in nothing but my "tighty whities." I'd say the mailbox was about 50 feet from our front door. Regrettably, I took the bait. By the time I got back to the house, she had closed and locked the door and was flipping the porch light on and off in an attempt to draw the attention of the neighbors to me. After a couple of minutes of discreetly demanding that she open the door (so I wouldn't draw even more attention to myself), she let me back in. Yep. She got me *good*. Probably one of her proudest moments.

Since my dad didn't yet have his Chiropractic license for the State of Illinois, he couldn't go into practice right away. In fact, the process of getting his license turned out to be a huge bureaucratic fiasco, and it took him nearly three years to finally get it. So, while he studied for his license and sat for his exams, he had to work a few other jobs to make ends meet.

Sometimes, he drove an 18-wheeled coal truck for my uncle Dale, and sometimes I rode with him. The route was between the coal mine in Murdock, Illinois to the coal-fired power plant in Springfield. I always enjoyed riding in that truck with my dad and listening to the chatter on the citizen ban radio. I loved the "Breaker 1-9", "What's your 20?", and "10-4 good buddy" code-speak. In fact, I eventually set up a CB radio in my bedroom and spoke with truckers and other folks myself. My "handle" was The Silver Bullet—as in "Breaker 1-9. You've got the Silver Bullet. Come on." My dad also drove an over-the-road 18-wheeler for a company that picked up freshly brewed beer from the major breweries in the region and delivered it to locations all across the country. Dad's CB radio handle was The Back Cracker. Get it? Chiropractor? Back Cracker? Much more original than mine.

My dad also worked in the Murdock coal mine for a while, but I'm not sure how long that went on. I just remember that he would come home completely covered in coal dust. Eventually, he started a dry wall business with a friend, and, later on, a third friend joined the business. My dad has always been a hard worker, and he always did whatever it took to provide for us when I was a kid.

Although it took a while, my dad finally got his chiropractic license for the State of Illinois, and he went into practice. This time by himself.

* * *

The elementary school that I attended in Tuscola was called North Ward Elementary School. At North Ward, I made a lot of friends right off the bat. But, for some reason, I fell into the crosshairs of the class bully. The interesting thing about the class bully was that she was a girl. I won't say her name because I wouldn't want to embarrass her. As I tell this story, please keep in mind that, when you're 11 years old, some of the girls in your class *are* bigger than you—and she *was* bigger than me. Every day at recess, she would wait outside for me (along with her sidekick, of course, who was *also* a girl) and pick on me for no reason. Of course, there may have been a reason, but I certainly didn't know what it was. My wife says she probably liked me.

Unfortunately for the class bully, she didn't know that I knew how to fight. Up to that point in my life, my friends and I had watched a lot of boxing and pro wrestling on TV, and we had practiced all the moves we had learned from that. But, more importantly, I had some real-life experience. In fact, I had gotten into several *real* fights (often fistfights) before moving to Tuscola. It just seems like that's how boys resolved their issues back then.

So, at recess one day, she came at me. I guess I had pushed her over the edge or something. Anyway, I turned and ran, and she chased me. But after a dozen steps or so, I turned around and punched her in the mouth—right there on the playground blacktop by the jungle gym and steel swing set. Of course, that stopped her in her tracks. As she stood there stunned, she dipped her fingers in the blood from her mouth to determine the damage that had been done.

I don't remember if we got into trouble for fighting that day, but I *do* know that she didn't pick on me after that. And if she *did* like me, I'm pretty sure she didn't want me to be her boyfriend anymore.

So, in the fifth grade, I beat up a girl. Not too impressive. But before you judge, you should know that I've beaten up girls a *lot* bigger than her. I'm just kidding—unless you count my sister. When Dawn and I were a little younger, I'd sometimes have to take her to the ground, sit on her, and tap on her chest bone with the knuckle of my middle finger until she cried and surrendered to my will. I'd be watching a TV show or something, and she'd just walk in and change the channel! What else was I supposed to do? Although I had to do that on occasion, I don't remember her tattling on me for it. She probably knew better. When I texted her recently to ask if she remembered me doing that to her, her reply was, "That's something you don't forget." I think she's forgiven me, though, because she hugs me now when I visit.

I also got into some fistfights during junior high and high school. I think there were four of them. I'm not proud of that. But, once again, it doesn't seem like that was such an uncommon thing for boys to do when I was a kid.

Two of the fights started because someone was picking on me. Both guys were a year or two older than me, but they were also smaller than me. I think there was some Little Man Syndrome going on. Anyway, during the fights, I punched both guys several times in the face, which stopped the fights pretty quickly. I beat up the first guy hockey-style, and I beat up the second guy boxing-style (just in case you know the general approach to fighting that goes on in those sports). I came away from both of those fights mostly unscathed and the clear victor.

The other two fights started because *I* was messing with someone. One guy was older than me, and one guy was my age, but both were bigger than me. I don't think Little Man Syndrome applied in this case. I don't know. Maybe it did if LMS is a relative thing. But one thing is for sure: I was just an idiot who made some errors in judgment. Unlike in the previous two fights, the guys in these two fights only hit me in the face once, which stopped the fights immediately. I came away from both of those fights with a much clearer understanding of who *not* to mess with and a much better appreciation for the concept of thinking things through before taking action.

* * *

In the late summer of 1974, I began the sixth grade at East Prairie Middle School. My teacher that year was Ms. Perkins. Ms. Perkins was probably in her early 20s and right out of college. In Ms. Perkin's class, I discovered that I could make people laugh by mimicking certain adult behaviors, like lighting cigarettes and smoking them. Because my last name started with a B, I always had to sit in or near the front row of the classroom. Thus, everyone in the room could see me. In class, I usually did my impressions while Ms. Perkins had her back to the class writing on the board. Of course, she sometimes heard the snickering and would turn around to see who was causing the commotion.

The thing about Ms. Perkins was that, when she looked at me, she didn't look directly into my eyes. Instead, she kind of looked at my forehead. I'm not sure if her eyes were off or if she just liked looking at my hair. (If the former is true, please forgive me Lord for tormenting this person. I'm sure was a lovely young woman. If the latter is true, maybe I just had good hair. It *was* the 70's.) One time, she either caught me doing something disruptive, or she just knew it was me. So, she came up to me and looked me directly in the forehead. In response, I turned around and looked behind me to see who she might be looking at. Of course, the class thought it was pretty funny. But in hindsight, it was smart-alecky and unkind.

Yeah, the phrase "class clown" would be a recurring theme on my report card—especially during middle school and junior high school. But at least I wasn't a dud and had a personality. And for the record, my less-than-ideal behavior in school was never criminal. I was just trying to be funny.

* * *

In the sixth grade, I got much more serious about the trombone. I got more serious about it because my friend, Bobby, was serious about it, and that seemed to provide all the motivation I needed to improve. Bobby became a really good friend, and I would sometimes go over to his house to practice. He and I were always battling it out for first chair in the school band. Together, Bobby and I participated in several state-sanctioned band competitions around the area, and we usually came home with a medal or two in events like solo and duet trombone and brass quartet with our friends Steve and Tim who played the coronet.

* * *

In November of 1974, I began playing *organized* basketball for the first time in Tuscola's Biddy Basketball league. Although I had watched a good amount of college and professional basketball on TV, and I had played a whole lot of pickup basketball, it wasn't until I was in the sixth grade that I finally got to suit up and be part of a real team. I loved my red, league-issued uniform. I would set it out on Friday night and, on

Saturday morning, I would put it on and wear it proudly for the game on Saturday morning at East Prairie.

* * *

During the school year, we had to move again because the daughter and son-in-law of the woman who owned our house wanted to move into it. This time, we moved to a subdivision called Meadowview. The move turned out good for me because we were able to put a basketball hoop on the garage of our new house, and it was much closer to my school, which I either walked or rode my bike to. Another bonus was that my friend Mark, a kid from church, lived just a few houses down. Mark was a great friend of mine for many years, but I pretty much lost touch with him when I graduated from high school. I always loved the way Mark's dad, Cecil, interacted with him and his brother and sisters. Although he was a large and powerful man with a booming voice, he was very kind and tenderhearted toward his children. That really made an impression in my mind and would be a huge influence on me later in life.

* * *

In the summer of 1975, I began playing Little League baseball in Tuscola. Since my first season of Little League baseball had been cut short because of our move from Creve Coeur to Tuscola, this was my first full season of organized baseball. The coach that drafted me was Mr. Brookins, and our team was ABC, which I think is an acronym for the American Business Club. I believe the American Business Club was similar to the Lion's Club, Elk's Club, and Rotary Club. I loved playing baseball, and I played Little League baseball all the way through the eighth grade—mostly first base.

Sometimes after one of my Little League games, I'd ride my bike to my grandma Sadie and grandpa Jack's house to have dinner and spend the night. Grandma always made me two hamburgers and a chocolate milkshake with crème de menthe in it. If you don't know what crème de menthe is, it's this very green, very sweet, mint-flavored alcoholic syrup that people use to make flavored coffees, ice cream desserts, and cocktails. Anyway, she would always put a bunch of crème de menthe in my milkshake, which made it take on this beautiful, mint-green tint.

Sometimes I'd get tipsy and could hardly walk. Just kidding. She only put in a little.

Grandma would also make me a bed on the couch using sheets she had washed using Downy Fabric Softener. The smell was sublime! To this day, I love that fragrance, and when I smell it, it takes me back to my childhood at my grandma and grandpa's house. After dinner, my grandparents would sit in their chairs, and I would sit on my bed, and we would all watch *Hee Haw* and *The Lawrence Welk Show* together. Both shows were super dorky (trust me), but I enjoyed them, because I was watching them with my grandparents.

* * *

In the late summer of 1975, I began the seventh grade, where my homeroom teacher was Mr. Russell. In the seventh grade, we started having a homeroom teacher and different teachers for things like math and language arts. One time, I kept annoying Mr. Russell by calling him "Mibber Rubble" in front of the class. After warning me to stop calling him that, I said, "Okay, Mibber Rubble!" At this, he pointed his finger at the door of the classroom and said, "Beasley! Out in the hall!" So, I left the classroom and stood in the hall while Mr. Russell went next door to get Mrs. Hance to witness the beating that would soon take place. A witness for such an event was standard protocol back in the day. When they came back, he took his two-foot-long wooden paddle and gave me three swats across the rear end. Of course, I pretended to take it like a man. And when I walked back into the classroom, I had this smart-alecky look on my face like I enjoyed it. Unfortunately, I would receive more spankings than that during my junior high school days. Always trying to entertain—even at the expense of pain.

My friend Steve would often get spanked in school as well. Like all his brothers, Steve was an excellent athlete. Besides that, he was very tough. Not in the sense that he was a "tough guy." No. He was a nice kid who was just very tough. He was also well built and very strong. In high school, Steve was the quarterback of the varsity football team. And as such, he probably seemed to the opposing teams like an easy target for getting smeared. Well, this one time, right after Steve handed the ball off to his running back, this defensive end from the other team thought he'd come in and drive Steve into the ground. Unfortunately for that guy, Steve saw him coming, aimed his helmet right at the guy's face, and completely flattened him. It was so satisfying to see.

Anyway, back to corporal punishment. This one time, Mr. Russell got really mad at Steve, pointed to the door, and told him to get out in the hall. I don't remember what Steve said, but he was in for a beating. Like me, Steve could be a real smart aleck sometimes. After Mr. Russell and Steve were out in the hall, and the door was closed, those of us left behind in the classroom heard some muffled talk and then this big *Bang!* followed by "Thank you, sir! May I have another!?" After some more muffled talk, we heard it again. *Bang!* followed by "Thank you, sir! May I have another!?" Once again, after some more muffled talk, we heard it a third time. *Bang!* followed by "Thank you, sir! May I have another!?" It seems like this cycle repeated itself a few more times until Steve finally repented and stopped asking for more.

* * *

I made the seventh-grade basketball team that year, so I was a proud member of the Tuscola Hornets. My basketball coach was Mr. Nichols. Mr. Nichols was a good guy, and I liked him. He was a young guy who was probably in his low to middle 20s at the time. In the middle of the season, however, I became ineligible to play in the games for six weeks because I had gotten into trouble again with Mr. Russell. He had flunked me in language arts for some reason. I think it was because I had refused to do something that I didn't want to do. Fortunately, I was still able to practice with the team, and when the six-week grading period was over, I was able to play in the games again.

I was also on the track and field team that year. My coach was Mr. Little. I'd say Mr. Little was around 30 years old. In one sense, I liked Mr. Little, but he was kind of scary. He was a very no-nonsense kind of guy. Like a lot of teachers, he probably went into the profession with high hopes that he would just teach, and all his students would sit there, absorb his knowledge and wisdom, and behave themselves. But when he found out that some students misbehave and can, thus, ruin it for everyone else, he probably decided that he needed to get tough. So, by the time I had him as a coach (and a classroom teacher), he had a reputation for toughness. You knew not to mess with him.

Anyway, for track and field practice, we would always run a couple of miles just to warm up. I *totally* hated that. I was never very good at running long distances. I did try, but I just wasn't born with the lungs, I guess. However, there were a couple of events that I liked and was decent at—the high jump and the pole vault.

In the seventh grade, I earned letters in both basketball and track and field.

* * *

Two memorable things happened during my seventh-grade year. One thing happened when we were playing kickball in P.E. class. It was toward the end of the class period, and the game was close. All my team needed was another out to win. After the kid who was up to bat kicked the ball, one of my teammates fielded the ball and smashed the batter with it as he ran down the first base line, which meant he was out. So, in my competitive excitement, I swung around throwing my fist into the air in a "Yeah, baby!" kind of gesture.

Unfortunately, at the end of that swing was the unmistakable sound of my knuckles hitting someone's face. I had punched my friend Jeff right in the yapper. As soon as he was hit, he doubled over with both hands covering his bleeding mouth. Although Mr. Nichols didn't see it happen, he *did* see the aftermath, and I was about to get into huge trouble. However, after I explained to him and Jeff that it was just an accident—no malice aforethought—Mr. Nichols let me off the hook, and Jeff didn't press charges.

The other memorable thing that happened occurred during recess. We were out behind the school flying kites, so it was probably in March or April when kite-flying was on everyone's radar. The wind that day was blowing perfectly from west to east, from our school toward the interstate highway, which was probably three or four hundred yards away—although it seemed much farther than that at the time. My kite was incredible. I didn't make it or anything. In fact, it was just your plain old cheap kite—the kind you had to make your own tail for, usually out of old, knotted-up bed sheets. I probably bought it at the Ben Franklin Five and Dime store in downtown Tuscola. But for some reason, it was an amazing kite.

While I was flying my kite, after I had let out all my string, someone else gave me their string, which I quickly attached to mine. After I had let out all that string, someone else gave me their string to attach. By this time, the situation had become a thing, and several people were giving me their string. I don't think I'm exaggerating when I say that my kite had reached all the way to the interstate highway and possibly beyond. It was amazing. Of course, eventually the string broke, and my kite faded into the sky and disappeared beyond the highway. Good thing too because who would want to reel that thing in?

* * *

In 1976, my mom and dad were finally able to buy their own home, so we moved one last time during my childhood. Not long afterward, my dad and I put up a basketball hoop in the driveway and attached a floodlight to the house, so we could play basketball at night. My friend Greg and I played a lot of basketball on that court. (Greg lived around the corner from me.) Not only did we play basketball together, but we also played stuff like Nerf basketball (in my room), Frisbee golf (before Frisbee golf was a thing), football, and baseball.

Although Greg was pretty athletic, he was somewhat lacking in eye-hand coordination. One of the baseball games Greg and I sometimes played together was called "five dollars," and one time we were playing it with my dad. Five dollars is a game where the batter hits baseballs to the other players who compete for the catch. If a guy catches the ball before it hits the ground, he gets a dollar. If he catches the ball on one bounce, he gets 75 cents. If he catches the ball on two bounces, he gets 50 cents. And, if he catches the ball on three bounces, he gets 25 cents. After that, no points are awarded. It can get pretty competitive.

This one time, I hit the ball really high, and my dad and Greg were both going for it. When Greg called for it, my dad backed off. For a couple more seconds, Greg stood there with his glove directly over his head waiting for the ball to come down. Then, *knock!* The ball hit Greg right in the middle of the forehead, and he immediately dropped to his knees. It sounded exactly like a golf ball sounds when it hits the trunk of a tree. It was very funny. Well…maybe not to Greg. But luckily, he was okay.

* * *

One of the nice things about our house was that it was just a couple doors down from my cousins Jim, Todd, and Angi—my aunt Barb and uncle Dale's kids. Jim and Tood were some of my best friends, and we spent a lot of time together roller skating in their basement, listening to music, and riding bikes.

Soon after moving into our new house, my mom and dad bought me an orange Kmart 10-speed bicycle. I had outgrown my dark green stingray-style bicycle while we still lived in Creve Coeur, so my parents replaced it with a red, white, and blue bike that looked like a 10-speed but only had one gear. I liked that bike a lot, but I think it got backed over by a car. So, my mom and dad bought me the orange bicycle as a replacement.

One day, shortly before my family left for a trip to St. Louis to visit friends, my cousin Todd asked me if he could borrow my orange bike while we were gone. I told him he could, but because I was afraid it might get stolen, I told him *not* to leave it in his front yard overnight— like he was in the habit of doing with his own bike. Well, he *did* leave it in his front yard overnight, and it *did* get stolen. Lucky for me, my uncle Dale's homeowner's insurance covered the theft. So, Uncle Dale and my dad took me to Durst Cycle City in Champaign, where I picked out the bike I wanted. I chose an amazing cobalt blue Peugeot UO-8 10-speed, which cost like four times what the Kmart bike was worth.

I took really good care of my Peugeot. Every night, I hung it from the floor joists in our basement using two dark brown plastic-covered wire cables. With the bike suspended like that, I was able to polish it easily and spin the wheels freely as I oiled the chain, adjusted the gears, calibrated the center-pull brakes, and tweaked the spokes to get the wheels perfectly true. I was *so* into my bicycle and bicycling at that time that I bought a subscription to *Bicycling* magazine and joined the Prairie Cycle Club in Champaign.

Each year, the Prairie Cycle Club organized what they called a "Fall Century Ride" and a "Spring Century Ride." Both were 100-mile tours through the flat farmland of Central Illinois. My friend Danny and I participated in a couple of them, but we didn't finish. We were pretty young. I also participated in a Prairie Cycle Club *race* once. I think it was a five miler. But I found out very quickly that a young kid like me was no match for those adult guys who took bike racing *very* seriously. During that race, I got my bike up to something like 40 miles per hour going down a long hill. That's just an estimate, but it was easily the fastest I've ever gone on a bike. It was terrifying.

* * *

In the early summer of 1976, I took another big step in my spiritual journey. Although I had put my faith in Christ when I was eight years old, I hadn't yet become a "baptized believer." I guess I just hadn't felt God's prompting to do so up to that point. As I look back at it now, it was probably better that I waited until I was 13—when I more fully understood the implications of living my life as a Christian. So, on that early summer day in 1976, I was baptized in Lake Shelbyville at Sullivan Beach near Sullivan, Illinois. It was Sullivan Beach that I made a public profession of my faith in Christ. Although this event didn't magically change me overnight, I think it did mark the beginning of taking my walk with God more seriously. However, it wouldn't be until college that I really started to get serious about my faith.

* * *

Around this time of my life, my family began traveling to Sarasota, Florida for our summer vacations. Since my dad always insisted on making the 1,100-mile trek in two days, the trip could be grueling. It could get pretty uncomfortable cramped up in the back seat of our gray Honda Accord for that long. But it was bearable, and I don't remember complaining. After all, we were on our way to the tropical paradise of Florida. On the way down there, my dad usually wanted to make it all the way to Perry, Georgia before we stopped for the night. Perry was about 700 miles from Tuscola, so the first day was usually pretty rough. On the other hand, Sarasota was only about 400 miles from Perry, so the second day was relatively easy.

The very first time we traveled to Florida, we stopped for lunch in Henderson, Kentucky, where I saw the word "grits" for the first time. It was on the menu. I had no idea what grits were, but I gave them a try after learning that they were a staple in the South. So, to me, they were kind of exotic. I thought they were delicious too. Even today, I'll sometimes have them when I travel through the South.

Another thing I noticed when we stopped in Kentucky was that a lot of the people there had southern accents. For me, this was always a sure sign that we were making progress on our long trip. And as we got closer and closer to our final destination, the southern accents got stronger and stronger—at least until we made it past northern Florida. It was a great feeling.

Whenever we stopped for gasoline, my mom and sister and I would often see my dad talking and laughing with the other people inside the gas station as he stood in line to pay the bill. The people were complete strangers, but it didn't matter to him. He interacted with them like they were good friends. As we watched him, my mom would sometimes say something sarcastic like, "There goes your dad making best friends with everybody." We would all laugh, but that made a pretty strong impression on me.

At the time, I thought my dad's proactive sociability with strangers was a little odd and unnecessary. I mean, he'd never see those people again. Why didn't he just stare straight ahead and bide his time until it was his turn to pay? That's what I'd do. But eventually, when I grew up, I realized that being friendly to people, even with the ones you don't know, like the boy at your door selling candy bars for his baseball team or the waitress taking care of you at the restaurant, is a way that God uses us to show others they are valued. So, because of my dad's example in that area, I usually try to be deliberate about smiling and being kind and friendly to people—even when I don't know them on a personal level.

When we finally got to Sarasota, I saw the Gulf of Mexico for the first time. I had never seen a body of water that huge. Being from the Midwest, I had only seen smaller accumulations of water, like ponds and lakes. As we drove south on U.S. Highway 41, I could see the gray-blue Gulf behind the hotels and motels, the doctors and palm readers offices, and the banks and souvenir shops. It really sparkled brightly in the late afternoon sun. It not only looked enormous, but it also looked like it was above street level. The horizon looked way higher than what I expected. It was odd. When we reached our final destination, Poor Bill's Motel, just a hundred feet off Crescent Beach on Siesta Key, we were finally in our tropical paradise. Poor Bill's was comfortable, and the beach was beautiful with its pure white powdery sand. We always had a great time there.

* * *

In the late summer of 1976, I began the eighth grade, where my homeroom teacher was Mrs. Hance. I liked Mrs. Hance, and I don't remember causing her much trouble. In the fall and winter of that year, I played basketball again for the Hornets, and in the spring, I was on the track and field team. Once again, my best events in track and field were the high jump and pole vault.

In the East Prairie gymnasium, there was a record board way up high on the west wall that displayed all the school records in track and field. At the beginning of the school year, the record for the pole vault was 8'9". That was pretty pathetic—no offense to the record holder. However, I eventually broke that record with a vault of 9'9", which wasn't quite as pathetic, I guess. Unfortunately, my name never got put up on the record board because my friend Steve, the guy who was the best athlete in my class, took up pole vaulting toward the end of the season and vaulted 10'6". So, I never got the glory. Thanks, Steve. I could have been somebody.

Although I wasn't immortalized on the record board that year, I *did* earn letters in both basketball and track and field in the eighth grade.

* * *

I think it was about this time in my life that I got the dumb idea of using gasoline to burn my initials into the grass of my back yard. After I had taken the gasoline can and spelled out REB in the grass, I realized I had forgotten the matches. So, I ran into the house to get some. By the time I got back, the gasoline had had a chance to evaporate into the air about a foot or so above the ground and migrate south toward the garage. Of course, I didn't see this happen because gasoline fumes are invisible.

When I lit the match and threw it on the ground, this great big blue fire cloud just lit up the entire back yard. I was scared to death because the blue flame was moving rapidly from where I was standing toward our garage. I totally thought the garage was going to go up in flames— and probably our house too. I could just see it. It was *not* a good feeling. Luckily, it didn't happen. I now ask myself questions like "Why would

I start a fire in someone's yard?" and "Why would I incriminate myself by burning my own initials in the grass?" Wow.

I'm so glad I didn't burn that garage down because my cousins and friends and I got a lot of use out of it over the years. On many a crystal-clear night, Todd (or a friend) and I would climb up on the roof, lie flat on our backs, stare at the stars, and ponder the size of the universe and our own insignificant existence. The feelings that were invoked in me as I gazed at all the sparkling celestial bodies set against the pitch-black backdrop of space are hard to define, but I'll give it a try. I would say I felt a combination of awe, wonder, peace, tranquility, mystery, fascination, coldness, and reverence. I just knew there was something out there that was much bigger than me. Or maybe I just thought how cool it would be to be Captain Kirk.

* * *

On the last day of my eighth-grade year, our class had an awards ceremony, where we received awards in various categories based on the number of votes we got from our classmates. Of course, I was hoping to win "most athletic" or "best looking" or "most likely to succeed" or "most likely to invade your dreams", but I won "best hair." I was so disappointed. And to make things worse, I received a cheap (and silly) pink mirror-hairbrush-comb set as an award. At least I won something.

* * *

In the late summer of 1977, I began the ninth grade, my freshman year, at Tuscola Community High School. By that time, I had started to mature some, so I wouldn't be getting into as much trouble with my teachers. I think the last time I actually got into trouble with a teacher was in Mrs. Kleiss's science class. I don't remember the circumstances exactly, but I do know that it culminated in her threatening to kick me out of her class and me letting her know that that would be fine with me. Unfortunately, she called my bluff. It was about halfway through the school year, and she had had enough. So, we went down to the principal's office and had me transferred to Mr. Marx's science class.

As I look back at that now and think about that wonderful woman, I can't believe I was such a nitwit. I'm ashamed of myself. However, something good came from my transfer to Mr. Marx's class. Since Mr.

Marx was significantly behind where Mrs. Kleiss was in the course, and since I had already learned a lot of the material in Mrs. Kleiss's class, I was able to breeze through most of the remainder of Mr. Marx's class.

Now that I think about it, I remember being a headache for Mr. Marx too. But after that, I was pretty good. I think. I was still getting a lot of laughs doing impressions of celebrities and teachers though. But I was beginning to tone that down some. I was learning to do that kind of stuff when and where it wasn't so disruptive.

* * *

As a freshman in high school, I was now eligible to play in the high school marching band. I was excited to do this because I had seen the band perform when I was in junior high school, and I was impressed by the awesome-looking uniforms everyone wore. The uniforms of the Tuscola Community High School marching band back then included a black and gold hat with gold plume, a black jacket over a white dress shirt, a gold cummerbund, white gloves, black pants, black shoes, and white spats. Nice.

All of these items were provided by the school, except for the pants and shoes. However, when the day came for us to perform for the first time, I had neither a black pair of pants nor a black pair of shoes to wear with my marching band uniform. So, my mom or dad asked Cecil, my friend Mark's husky dad, if I could borrow some pants and shoes. I have no idea why they asked that particular guy, but that's what they did. Surely, they had asked around some before landing on Cecil.

Compared to me, Cecil was pretty huge. He probably weighed 250 pounds, and I probably weighed 120. I think I could have fit my whole body into one of his pant legs. He also had huge feet. I'd say he wore a size 13 or 14 shoe. I probably wore a size 7 or 8. My parents should *not* have borrowed clothing from that guy! When it came time for me to suit up for the evening's varsity football game, I looked ridiculous. Not only were the hat and jacket of the uniform ill-fitting, but I was swimming in Cecil's pants. Plus, I looked like I had clown feet. I had to march like I was wearing scuba fins. It was humiliating. Luckily, I got some better fitting pants and shoes soon after that. Not sure about the hat and jacket.

* * *

I had a lot of good friends through high school. I got along with pretty much everyone—the heads, the nerds, the athletes. Some of my friends were heads—you know potheads, burnouts, stoners. And while I didn't hang out with them outside of school for obvious reasons, I did enjoy joking around with them. They could be pretty funny. As for the nerds, they were kind of dorky, but I still liked them for the most part. Most of my friends, however, were athletes. We were the Tuscola Warriors. And since our high school only had four hundred students or so, there was a core group of us that played on most of the sports teams together. It wasn't like it is now, where an athlete concentrates year-round on one sport. No. Most of us played multiple sports, and any weight training we did was done during P.E., not in the off-season.

* * *

Since my high school was only about two or three blocks from my grandma Virginia's house, I would sometimes skip the lunch provided by the school and walk to her house to have lunch with her. It seems like we always had the same thing—Oscar Meyer hot dogs, the Kraft Longhorn Style Colby cheese that came in the wax packaging, and chocolate sheet cake that she made from scratch. She always seemed to have one of those sheet cakes sitting uncovered on the top of her stove. Of course, since it was Grandma, I could have as much cake as I wanted. So, I'd put a bunch of it in a big cereal bowl and drown it in ice cold milk. Uh-huh.

One time, when Grandma was standing at her kitchen sink doing dishes (by hand), I asked her if she liked doing dishes. She told me that she did. I think her response that day triggered something in my mind that suggested that doing dishes didn't have to be a task to be dreaded but could, instead, be an activity that one can actually enjoy. Words can really affect a child's outlook on things, and this perspective would eventually become a blessing to my future wife.

* * *

In 1978, when I was 15 years old, my sister sold me her yellow 1971 Chevrolet Vega for $200. To buy the car, fix it up, and keep gasoline and oil in it, I mowed lawns, detasseled corn, and did a few other things here and there. The car was pretty rusty and blew out blue smoke when I pressed the accelerator, but it had a really nice sporty look. I spent a lot of time fixing that car up. I cut out the rust around the wheel wells, used Bondo to replace the cut-out sections, sanded it down and primed it, and then had it painted its original canary yellow. I also put in gold shag carpeting, installed an 8-track stereo system, and tuned up the car's engine by replacing the spark plugs, adjusting the timing, and so on. So, before I turned 16 years old, the car looked great.

But since I didn't have my driver's license yet, I could only drive the car up and down our driveway, which I did—a lot. I wonder what the neighbors thought. Probably something like, "Look at that Beasley boy wasting gasoline. Does he know that gasoline costs a whole 60 cents a gallon these days?" As I drove my car up and down the driveway using only two gears (first gear and reverse), I dreamed of getting my driver's license so I could take my awesome car out on the road and use the other three gears. The wait was agonizing. Unfortunately, when the day finally arrived for me to get my driver's license, I had the flu and had to wait even longer—like three more days. But the day *did* arrive, and I finally got my driver's license. Yeah. That day pretty much marked the end of my love affair with bicycling.

One night, when I was out in the garage working on my car, I had my head underneath the dashboard on the driver's side. I think I was changing a fuse or something, and the music coming from my 8-track stereo system was pretty loud. While working under the dashboard, my cousin Todd came into the garage. When he saw that I didn't notice his arrival, he snuck around to the passenger side of the car, stuck the entire top half of his body through the open window, and put his face right above the gear shift next to my shoulder. When I pulled my head up from below the dashboard, there was this big face, eyes wide open, one foot away, staring at me. He scared the living daylights out of me! He got me good! But I got him back many times after that. In fact, I honed my skills in scaring people pretty well, which would come in handy in my life.

* * *

My sister sold me her Vega because she had purchased a white 1974 Ford Pinto—the kind that would explode when it got rear-ended. One time, when she was going to be away for a couple of days, she told me *not* to drive her car while she was gone. But of course, I couldn't help myself. On a really wet and soggy day, my friend Mark and I got into her car and drove out to the country looking for a place to do donuts. We eventually found this grassy patch of land that surrounded one of those rural power relay stations. It was probably a mile or two outside of town. I'm almost certain it was out east of town past the interstate highway. After we had been doing donuts for a few minutes or so (I was driving), the passenger-side wheels of the car dropped down into the surrounding ditch. The car had bottomed out. We were stuck.

Despite spinning the wheels forward and backward and rocking the car back and forth, we couldn't get the car unstuck. We were terrified because we had totally destroyed the lawn in front of the relay station, and we knew we'd get into huge trouble with the law if we got caught. As we were frantically brainstorming ways to get out of the mess, one of my sister's friends drove by in his red beat up 1960s pickup truck, so we flagged him down. After explaining our predicament, which was probably obvious to him, he pulled us out of the ditch with the chains he just happened to have in the bed of his truck. Of course, we were super grateful and relieved, and we begged him not to tell my sister. When we got back to town, Mark and I drove straight to the car wash and used the power washer to hose the car down. It took a while, but we eventually got all the clumps of grass and mud off. Good as new really.

Another time when my sister was gone, my friend Greg and I found a brand-new, unsmoked pack of cigarettes under the front seat of her car. So, we thought it would be fun to take them inside the house and smoke. We didn't just smoke a couple of them though. We smoked *all* of them—in one sitting. We smoked those cigs using all the popular cigarette-handling methods of the day—the V, the two-fingered pinch, the palmer, and so on. We also did the Clint Eastwood squint and the James Dean lip-hang. We were giddy with laughter. We also blew a *lot* of smoke rings. In fact, I got so much practice blowing smoke rings that day that, despite the fact that I have never (really) smoked, I can still blow a good smoke ring.

As I write this, I can't help but think about the fact that we smoked that pack of cigarettes in the living room of my mom and dad's home. My sister must have been allowed to smoke in the house or something because, surely, we would have thought it was a stupid idea to smoke cigarettes inside a home where smoking wasn't allowed. It would have been obvious what we had done. But my parents never said anything, so I guess we were good. Also, I don't think my sister ever noticed the missing pack of cigarettes—either that or she was just being generous with her stuff—like usual.

* * *

One night, when I was playing basketball in our driveway under the floodlight that my dad and I had put up, I saw my aunt Brinda inside the house standing by the kitchen window. Her family had come over for dinner that evening, and she was doing dishes at the kitchen sink. Since there was a bright light directly above the kitchen sink, and since it was dark outside, I knew she couldn't see out the window very well. She seemed oblivious to anything that was going on outdoors.

So, I took this thick tree stump we had in our yard, and I placed it right under the window where my aunt Brinda was standing. The tree stump was about a foot or so tall and a foot or so in diameter. We used it to cut firewood for the little cast-iron stove we had that my dad liked to use in the wintertime. After placing the stump under the window, I stood on top of it with my face squarely in my aunt Brinda's line of sight. I stood there for a minute staring at her with my eyes wide open, trying to put on my best Charles Manson face, but she didn't look up from her task. So, I began scratching on the screen to get her attention. Since that didn't get her attention either, I began tapping lightly on the window above the screen. Within a few seconds, she looked up at me, and with complete horror in her eyes, she screamed and put her hand on her chest like she was going to have a heart attack. I laughed so hard that I could hardly breathe. Lucky for me, she was a good sport about it and just laughed it off with me. I love people with a good sense of humor.

* * *

In the 10th grade, I sold my yellow 1971 Chevrolet Vega for a profit and bought a burnt orange 1974 Ford Mustang II. As with the Vega, I spent a lot of time fixing up my new car, including putting in gold shag carpeting, installing an 8-track stereo system, and having it painted. The car looked great.

The thing to know about the Mustang II is that it wasn't the same as the Mustang. Whereas the Mustang was an actual sports car, the Mustang II was not. It was basically a Pinto-based subcompact car. Although the Mustang II that year was available with a few different engine options, mine had an inline four-cylinder engine that produced an unimpressive 88 horsepower. Nevertheless, I was proud of the car after it was all fixed up.

Soon after I had it looking good, I invited my friend Mark to take it for a test drive. After he drove it around for a few minutes, I asked him what he thought. He told me that he wasn't used to driving a car that didn't perform and that you *know* a car doesn't perform when it has a shift light. Although it wasn't the response I was hoping for, it *was* pretty funny. We put each other down like that all the time.

* * *

Since I was 16 and could drive now, I was able to drive to my Uncle Dwight's farm during the summers to work with him and my cousin Darrell. My cousin Todd worked with us as well. My uncle Dwight was actually my mom's uncle, so that makes Darrel my first cousin once removed. During those summers, we braved some sweltering days to walk beans and mow.

Walking beans entailed walking down the middle of eight rows of thigh-high soybeans and cutting out anything that didn't belong. We used a hoe to cut out buttonweed, ragweed, foxtail, lamb's quarter, and rogue stalks of corn. Walking beans was necessary because the plants that didn't belong would compete for the moisture and nutrients in the soil that the soybeans needed to flourish. These days, farmers don't walk beans as far as I know. Instead, they plant genetically modified soybeans that are resistant to the herbicides they spray on their fields. So, the herbicides kill *everything* in the fields, except for the soybeans.

Since Darrell and Todd and I were really good at distinguishing between the leaves of the soybean plant and the leaves of broadleaf and grassy weeds, we could make a soybean field look very clean. To this day, I appreciate the beauty of a healthy, weedless, and uniformly green soybean field during the spring and summer. Some people love mountains, and some people love water. And while I definitely see the beauty in those, the beauty of healthy corn or bean fields is probably my favorite.

Despite the hard work and the sometimes-blistering heat, walking beans was a pretty fun job—but only because of the guys I worked with. As Darrel and Todd and I walked through the soybean fields, we talked about everything—the previous night's David Letterman Show, philosophy, religion, food, the music we had been listening to lately. The list could go on.

We laughed a lot too. Since all three of us were pretty familiar with the music of the last decade or two, we were quick at recognizing when someone uttered a word or phrase during our normal conversation that appeared in the lyrics of a song. For example, if one of us said, "I've got to hit the road," someone else would start singing, "Hit the road, Jack, and don't you come back, no more no more no more no more" from *Hit the Road Jack* by Ray Charles. Or, if one of us said, "You can drive my car," someone else would start singing, "Baby, you can drive my car" from *Drive my Car* by The Beatles. It happened all the time.

When we weren't walking beans, we were often tasked with mowing Uncle Dwight's massive farmhouse property and the ditches around his fields. My favorite part about mowing was using his lime green Grasshopper zero-turning-radius mower. ZTRs were a new thing back then, and they were a blast to ride. Using the string trimmer, however, could be brutal.

* * *

Sometime during my sophomore year, I had an interesting spiritual experience. I was reading my Bible in my bedroom one morning when I came across an interesting passage. I was a regular Bible reader by then, and I had felt God speaking to me about things before, but this was different. It was more pronounced. The verse was Psalm 128:3-4, which says, "Your wife will be like a fruitful vine within your house; your children will be like olive shoots around your table. Yes, this will be the blessing for the man who fears the Lord." The thing about it was that I was only 16 or 17 years old, and I had never thought much about getting married and having children. I don't think such thoughts occur to most boys at that age. A wife and children certainly weren't on *my* radar. That's what made it a little strange. It kind of felt like God was speaking to *me* about that specific thing. It was odd.

* * *

In the summer of 1979, my dad built a wooden deck off the back of our house and had a swimming pool put in. So, you could walk out the sliding glass door of our house, walk another ten or so feet across the deck, and hop into the water. It was nice! My dad even designed and constructed a way to heat the pool with solar energy. He bought some black plastic pipe, hooked the pipe up to the pool pump, ran the pipe from the pool pump to the roof of the garage, spread out several yards of the pipe across it, and then ran the end of the pipe down to the pool, where the solar-heated water emptied into the cooler pool water. When the sun was shining, his contraption could heat the pool up pretty quickly.

We used that pool a lot during those hot Central Illinois summers. One of the things about the pool was that it was situated parallel to the garage. So naturally, my cousins and friends and I used the roof of the garage as a launchpad into the water. We would often climb up on the roof of the garage, find a spot in the water where no one was, and then jump in using our best "cannonball," "preacher's seat," or "slider" to create the biggest, most percussive splash possible. *Kaboom!*

Believe it or not, we would also climb onto the roof of our house and jump into the water from there. Doing that, though, was not for the less than agile or faint of heart. First of all, it was several feet higher than the roof of the garage. And second, it was a good eight or more feet to the water. So, you had to jump really hard to clear the deck. If you didn't clear it, you'd bust your feet (or something else) on it. The good news is none of us ever got hurt doing that stunt. At least that I can remember.

* * *

In the 11th grade, I was 6'2" and had developed the ability to dunk a basketball. I was a relatively good jumper by then, having participated in the high jump in track and field and having played a lot of basketball. These days, it seems like a lot of athletic 17- and 18-year-old boys can dunk a basketball—even guys who are like 5'10". But back then, not a lot of guys my height could dunk. In fact, there was only one other guy in my high school who could dunk. His name was Tom. Tom was like 6'5", and he was the starting center on our varsity basketball team. He was a good basketball player, but I wouldn't say he was particularly springy. But because he was so tall, he could dunk well enough.

On most days, before the school day started, a pretty good number of students would hang out in the gymnasium waiting for the bell to ring for first period. On occasion, Tom and I would be persuaded to engage in a slam dunk contest. Although Tom was tall, his slam dunk repertoire was somewhat limited. Mine, on the other hand, was a little less limited. I was no Julius Erving, of course, but I could dunk with one hand, I could dunk with two hands, and I could dunk behind my back. The kids at school loved it because it just wasn't something you'd see very often, except on television.

* * *

Sometime during my junior year, I traded my burnt orange 1974 Ford Mustang II for a forest green 1970 Chevrolet Monte Carlo. This was a first-year Monte Carlo—not the Monte Carlo that had the long doors. This was the one that looked like the Chevelle and Nova of the same year—but with different frontend and backend styles. Unlike my previous two cars, this one didn't need fixing up. The guy I traded with was a professional mechanic, and he had already done all the fixing up that needed to be done. The only thing I needed to do was install a stereo system. Since the technology had evolved from the 8-track tape player to the cassette tape player, I installed the latter this time. I also installed a standalone amplifier and a graphic equalizer. Those made a huge difference in the power and quality of the sound.

I traded cars with a guy named Don. Don was my friend Mark's stepdad. (Mark was the friend who wasn't impressed with my Mustang II.) Don and his family went to our church, and he would often drive the Monte Carlo to church on Sunday mornings. After church on those mornings, I would frequently admire the car as it sat in the parking lot. Don knew I loved the car, so one day he offered to trade his Monte Carlo for my Mustang II—straight up. The car was awesome, and I was very grateful for the deal. To be honest, I'm not sure what he saw in the Mustang II. Maybe his wife, Marsha, thought it was cute or something. It certainly wasn't the kind of car Don liked. He was totally into classic muscle cars.

Anyway, my Monte Carlo had a relatively powerful 350-cubic-inch V8 engine that could produce 300 horsepower. Back then, that was a pretty strong performer that reflected the muscle car spirit of the day. It also had Firestone raised white letter tires on Cragar SS mag wheels and a dual exhaust system with Orange Peeler mufflers. So, it not only performed, but it looked sharp, and it sounded great. My Monte Carlo actually came with two sets of wheels and tires—the set of mag wheels with raised white letter tires and a set of stock wheels with whitewall tires. Since the mag wheels could corrode from the salt that they put down on the roads in the winter, I took them off before winter and put on the stock wheels. I would then store the mag wheels in my bedroom until spring.

* * *

It was also in the 11th grade that I finally got contact lenses. I had been wearing glasses since the second grade, and I was blind as a bat without them. I was very nearsighted. Without my glasses, everything was completely fuzzy. When I was in my bed, I couldn't even see the red LED numbers on my clock radio. I had to get really close just to know what time it was. And if you were to walk into my bedroom, I wouldn't be able to make out your face. I might be able to tell who you were by your overall appearance, but I certainly wouldn't be able to see any facial details. I had like 20/800 vision. Luckily, that was correctable to 20/20 with glasses or contacts. Anyway, I got the contact lenses so I could be more aggressive on the basketball court. They were great because I no longer needed to worry about my glasses getting beat up playing basketball. They might have improved my looks as well. I don't know. Wire-rimmed aviator-style glasses with thick prescription lenses or contact lenses? You tell me.

One morning when I woke up, I looked over at my clock radio, which was probably three or four feet away, and I could read the time. Then, I looked over at the mag wheels I had stacked up in the corner of my room. They were about nine or ten feet away, and I could clearly see the white letters on the tires. For about 60 seconds, I looked around my room marveling at the utter clarity of everything. At first, I thought

I was dreaming. But, when I realized it wasn't a dream, I thought I had experienced a miracle. I thought I had been completely healed of my nearsightedness! However, I soon realized that I had just forgotten to take my contacts off before going to bed the night before. It was a *huge* disappointment.

The 1980s

54 68 65 20 31 39 38 30 73

In 1980, toward the end of my junior year of high school, I got so sick and tired of people talking and messing around during band practice that I quit. My band teacher had no control over the class, and it really frustrated me. So, I went to my teacher's office and told him that I felt like I was wasting my time in band and that I had better things to do than trying to improve my trombone skills in an environment that just wasn't conducive to that.

Although he tried to talk me out of it, I just couldn't be convinced to stay. I was just done with it. Almost immediately, however, I began to regret my decision to quit. There was something in me that still had the urge to play music. It was a very strong feeling, but I had no idea how that urge could be satisfied, or if it would ever be satisfied again. I remember being moved musically when I listened to the song Grease on my sister's record player. I just couldn't be done with music forever. Somehow, I needed to play music. Something was missing.

* * *

Sometime in the summer of 1980, my friend Mark and I stopped by a small grocery store in town called the Corner Grocery to pick up something to drink. Mark was one of the athletes in my class, and he and I played on the high school basketball and baseball teams together. (In case you haven't noticed, this is the *fourth* Mark I've mentioned in this book so far. There will be more. Evidently, I've had a lot of friends named Mark.) After Mark and I made our selections, we stood in line at the front of the store as we waited for our turn to be checked out. As we stood there, this little kid, who was probably five or six years old, walked over and slid right up next to me. Almost invading my space, he looked up at me like he wanted to be just like us big kids.

In an effort to make Mark laugh, I looked down at the kid, put on my best psycho-kidnapper's face (eyes wide open and creepy smile) and said, "Want some candy?" You should've seen the look on that kid's face! It looked like he had just come face to face with his worst nightmare. At that moment, it seemed like he went into autopilot recalling in his mind what his parents had told him a thousand times, "Never take candy from a stranger." As the kid looked up at me with a terrified look on his face, he began moving slowly and nervously backward away from me, keeping one eye on me while looking for the quickest escape route out of there. Mark and I thought it was hilarious.

Of course, I know now that it wasn't so funny. Well, it was, but it wasn't—if you know what I mean. That poor kid probably ran home and told his parents, and they probably called the police or went out looking for me. That "kid" is probably someone's grandpa now who remembers the experience like it was yesterday and still doesn't know it was a joke. In fact, I'm probably the subject of an object lesson he's told his kids and grandkids many times over the years.

* * *

In the late summer of 1980, I began the 12th grade—my senior year of high school. I absolutely loved my senior year. I was on top of the world. I honestly thought that being a senior in high school was the apex of life and that anyone who had already graduated lived a boring existence and was completely out of touch and irrelevant. Wow. Was that a limited view of life or what?

That school year, I worked at a gasoline station called Bob's Super Service. Bob, my dad's friend, gave me a job pumping gas, checking oil, cleaning windshields, and selling cigarettes. We did a lot of things at Bob's. I mean, "Super Service" *was* in the name. Although I pumped a lot of gas, we did have *one* self-service pump. That was a pretty new thing back then—but hardly anyone used it. I don't know if you can even find a place that pumps the gas for you these days.

Working at Bob's was okay, I guess. One of the things I liked about the job was that, when things got slow, I could put my Monte Carlo up on the lift in the garage, change the oil, and work on other things underneath the car. I didn't like it, however, when middle-aged women pulled up to the pumps when it was pouring down rain just to have me get them cigarettes. They would make it look like they needed gas, so I would run out there in the rain and say, "Can I help you?" But, instead of hearing "Fill 'er up," I heard "A carton of Virginia Slims, please." Couldn't that have waited?

The most important thing I learned working at Bob's was that I *didn't* want to do that kind of work my entire life. Of course, there's absolutely nothing wrong with working at a gas station—or digging ditches or anything like that. But that kind of work wasn't for me. I needed to do something more interesting. I needed to go to college.

* * *

During my senior year, there were two girls that I was aware of that liked me. Both were freshmen. One was a friend of the family, and the other was the younger sister of someone I already knew from school. Both of the girls were very nice, but I just wasn't interested in them in that way.

On Sweetest Day, which is a "Hallmark holiday" in October that is only tolerated in the Midwest and a few other parts of the country, a crowd of students had gathered in the high school gymnasium waiting for the bell to ring for first period. Although most of the students were sitting on the bleachers at the *south* end of the gym, my friends and I were sitting on the bleachers at the *north* end of the gym—right outside the entrance to the boy's locker room. As we sat there on the bleachers talking and joking around, one of the girls that liked me walked across the basketball court to where my friends and I were sitting and handed me a single pink rose—right in front of everyone. I'm sure it took a *lot* of courage on her part to do that, and I hope I was gracious to her and accepted the flower with a smile on my face, but I was mortified—and my friends made sure I stayed that way.

When the bell rang, I put the rose in my locker and went about the day. After school, I took the rose out of my locker and headed home. I'm not sure why I didn't just (discreetly) toss the flower into the trash before going home, but I didn't. When I got home, I walked into the house through the back sliding glass door that led into our dining room and kitchen. Absolutely oblivious to the fact that someone might see me carrying a rose into the house, I carried it right in front of me like I was about to present it to the Queen of England. Unfortunately for me, my mom was standing just a few feet inside the sliding glass door looking straight at me as I held that big pink rose in my hand. I froze for a moment as I desperately tried to think of a way to avoid a second bout of embarrassment in a single day. Finally, I announced, "For you! Happy Sweetest Day, Mom!" She thought I was the most thoughtful son a mother could ever ask for. Don't hate.

* * *

A couple of weeks or so after the basketball season started that year, I was playing volleyball with some girls in the gymnasium before first period. After one of the girls served the ball to our side of the court, I thought it would be funny to nonchalantly *slap* the ball back to the other side of the court—instead of bumping the ball or just hitting the ball back over the net like a normal person. Unfortunately, my goofing around didn't end well. Instead of the ball hitting the palm of my hand and flying over the net, it hit the tip of my right pinky finger and broke the second knuckle from the end. It hurt something fierce. At first, I thought it might just be jammed. But the next day, my entire pinky finger was black and blue, I couldn't straighten it out, and the pain was excruciating.

My injury couldn't have occurred at a worse time. Basketball season was in full swing, and I couldn't dribble with my right hand or catch a basketball with it without experiencing acute pain. I still practiced with the team, but I could only use my left hand. Fortunately, it only took a few weeks before I could use my right hand normally again. To speed up the healing process, I used my left hand to bend my injured pinky finger under and then straighten it out again. It was painful, but after a while my finger turned from black and blue to purple and green and then back to normal. I call it physical therapy—homemade style.

* * *

One night, our basketball team had a game at Decatur St. Teresa High School in Decatur, Illinois. I don't remember if we were winning or losing, but one of the teams was down like 30 points with maybe a minute to go. So, our coach, Mr. Murray, pulled all our players off the court and put in the guys who didn't usually get a lot of playing time.

My friend Rick was one of those guys. Rick was a very good athlete. He was the starting catcher on our varsity baseball team, and he was a starting defender on the varsity football team. He was a pretty good basketball player as well, but he wasn't as tall as some of us. When he *was* in a game, he usually played point guard.

Since Rick didn't get a ton of playing time, he was probably nervous about going into the game. A short time after the game had resumed, and after the other team had made a basket, Rick took the inbound pass and began dribbling down the court. As he dribbled the ball, the St. Teresa side of the gymnasium began shouting *in unison,* "Five! Four! Three! Two! One!" Upon hearing their chant, Rick coiled up and, with two hands in the form of a massive chest pass, heaved the ball from beyond half court in a last-ditch effort to score an awesome last-second goal. Unfortunately, 30 seconds still remained on the clock. The crowd laughed wildly—at least their side did. I'm sure Rick was humiliated. I must admit, though, it *was* funny.

* * *

In 1981, during my last semester of high school, I had to start thinking about what I was going to do next. My dad told me that his cousin Marty was in the field of computing and that Marty had told him that computers were the wave of the future. So, my dad and I set up a time to drive up to Champaign and talk with Marty. Marty worked for a company called Beranek and Associates. Beranek and Associates wrote software that tracked mobile phone usage and billed customers for that usage. The mobile phone was a new technology back then, and Marty had gotten in on the ground floor of the industry and was, thus, doing pretty well financially.

After speaking with Marty in his office that day, it sounded to me like computing would be a fantastic field to get into—especially since so many things were getting computerized. So, I decided that I wanted to be a computer programmer—whatever that meant. Today, I see that meeting with Marty as a "guidepost" in my life that God placed in my path to direct me toward the *field* I was designed for. There would be more guideposts like that in my life—guideposts that God would use to direct me toward the *career* he had in store for me and guideposts he would use to direct me toward the *place* he ultimately wanted me to be.

At the time, I knew absolutely *nothing* about computers. We didn't have computers in schools back then—at least not in mine. I was so profoundly clueless about computers and computer programming that I had to ask my cousin Jim, who had taken a computer programming course in college, what a computer program was. And even after he explained it to me, I still didn't get it. I was just more confused.

I like that story because I often speak with high school students and their parents who come to my office to explore the idea of majoring in software engineering or computer science in college. When a student tells me that he or she has never written a computer program before, I sometimes tell them *my* story to let them know that I was once in their shoes. I tell them not to worry. They can learn to program too.

* * *

For me, high school was all about playing sports. That's what I cared about, and that's what I did. I didn't join any clubs (unless you consider band a "club"). I didn't go on any dates. I didn't go to prom or any other organized social events. And I *certainly* didn't study much. In fact, I don't remember ever studying in high school. Maybe I did, but I *know* that that wasn't a thing for me. In my view, the people who carried their books home to study and do homework were dweebs. Oh, the irony. I must have studied *some*, though, because my dad told me that he'd keep me on his car insurance and pay for my part of it— if I kept a B average. And that's exactly what happened. Yep. Saving a few bucks was all the motivation I needed!

So anyway, I played four years of high school baseball, where my primary positions were first base (early on) and second base (later). I also pitched some, but I was pretty mediocre at it—in my opinion. I must have been adequate, though, or I don't think my coach would have continued to have me pitch. Although I could throw a decent curveball, screwball, and knuckleball, and I could throw the ball pretty hard, I didn't always have the best control over where the ball ended up. So, I occasionally threw the ball away or hit the batter. During one game, I hit the same batter twice—in two consecutive at bats. I thought he was going to kill me.

I also played four years of high school basketball. In basketball, I usually played forward—at least until my senior year. That year, my coach moved me to guard to take advantage of my acceptable ball-handling skills and 6'2" stature in an effort to overmatch me against the usually smaller guards on the opposing teams. I think I was a pretty good basketball player. Sometimes I wonder if I could've played at a small, NCAA Division III college. I mean, I hadn't peaked yet in terms of my skills, and I continued to improve for the next several years.

But such colleges were not on my radar at that point in my life. In fact, I don't think I knew what a small college was. As I look back on it now, though, there *was* this one guy I knew who played basketball for a small college in Illinois called Monmouth College. But for some reason, that didn't seem to register in my mind. The only colleges on my radar in high school were the big universities, like the University of Illinois, Illinois State University, and Eastern Illinois University, and there was no way I could've made the roster on those teams. Most of the guys on those rosters were recruited from Chicago or some other place in the country and were superstars on their respective high school basketball teams.

My freshmen year was the only year I played high school football. During that season, I played offensive end, defensive end, and punter. Although I loved playing football, I really wasn't cut out to play full-contact, organized football. I was just too scrawny at the time, and my glasses kept getting busted up inside my helmet. So, after one season of that, I was done with it. One of the things I remember vividly about that season was how unbelievably thirsty I would get during practice. I had never been so thirsty in my life. To this day, when I drink water to get relief from an extreme thirst, I have visions of drinking water during freshman football practice.

During my junior year, I ran high school track and field after taking a two-year hiatus from the sport. Since I had enjoyed track and field so much during my junior high school days, I wanted to do it again. Two of my usual events were the 120-yard high hurdles and the 330-yard low hurdles. I was *okay* at those events, but my performance was never anything to write home about. My other usual event was the high jump, which I was *much* better at. My best jump was 6'2" (my height), but I *think* my best jump in an official meet was only 5'11". I hope I'm not selling myself short on that. But either way, those were pretty good jumps in those days, so I often earned first, second, or third place in the high jump competition.

I really loved track and field, but it was virtually impossible to play baseball *and* run track and field because their seasons ran concurrently during the spring semester. Since I *had* to make my baseball practices and games (it was more of a team sport), I was never able to get into shape for the hurdles, and I was never able to get much practice for the high jump. So, I decided to forgo track and field the following year and concentrate on baseball.

I also played tennis all through high school. Since tennis wasn't an officially sanctioned high school sport in those days, at least not in my high school, I mostly played during the summers. I played tennis with a lot of different guys, including my dad, but I mostly played with my friends Greg (a different Greg than my neighbor) and Rick. On some days, my friends and I played tennis for hours. One time, one of those guys and I played a hundred games of tennis in a single day. I think we thought we were breaking some kind of record. It even sprinkled some that day, but we kept right on playing.

In addition to playing casual tennis with my friends and my dad, I almost always played in our local (city and county) singles tournaments, which I sometimes did well in. My dad and I also played tennis together in Tuscola's annual junior-senior doubles tournament. I know we won that tournament (at least once) because I have a newspaper clipping that shows my dad and me holding our first-place trophies.

By the end of my high school career, I had earned varsity letters in three high school sports: baseball, basketball, and track and field. I had also earned a number of tennis trophies—enough to fill a small box. There were no participation trophies in those days! I loved high school, especially my senior year. But all good things must come to an end as they say. My narrow focus on athletics would soon begin to wane as I was about to embark on a new phase of life—college.

* * *

In the late summer of 1981, I started college at Parkland College in Champaign. Parkland was a two-year community college. At Parkland, I majored in data processing. The data processing program at Parkland included courses in computer programming, data structures, operating systems, database, and several other courses all focused on teaching you how to design and develop software systems for businesses.

The first computer programming course I took at Parkland College was called *Assembly Language Programming*. Assembly is a very low-level programming language that is made up of highly detailed, mnemonic instructions that require a pretty intimate knowledge of the computer's central processing unit and other related components. So, for someone who had never programmed before, the language was very difficult to learn. In fact, it was only one step easier than writing code in machine language, which consists of numeric instructions written in binary or hexadecimal.

As a professional educator in the field of computing today, I'd like to know who had the lamebrain idea of teaching absolute beginners programing using the Assembly language. What was that!? No wonder half the students who started the course quit. It would have been much better to start students off with Basic or Pascal or Cobol or some other higher-level programming language that didn't require such an intimate understanding of the computer's hardware architecture. Dumb. Not that I have an opinion about it or anything.

I really struggled with Assembly. Before walking into that class for the first time, I didn't even know what a computer program was. So, I eventually went to talk to my professor, Mr. Fisk, about the fact that I just wasn't getting it. Mr. Fisk was very nice and told me to stick with it. He told me that "the light bulb would eventually go on," just like it did for him many years ago. So, I took his advice, and I stuck it out. Soon I began to pick it up a little bit, and I ended up doing well in the course—at least in terms of the grade I received. The truth is, I still didn't fully understand Assembly Language programming. And I still couldn't program my way out of a paper bag. No. That takes the ability to think algorithmically, and I hadn't yet developed that ability.

Even though I struggled with Assembly Language programming, it was while I was studying that topic that I felt significantly stimulated intellectually for the very first time. I remember the moment vividly. I was sitting at the kitchen table at my mom and dad's house in Tuscola reading my Assembly Language programming textbook. As I worked hard to follow a very detailed coding example, it began to make sense to me. At that moment, I thought to myself, "Oh my! This feels good!" Before then, I was much more stimulated by playing sports. But now, something had changed inside. I was becoming much more stimulated by studying.

* * *

At the end of that first semester of college, I was relieved to be done with Assembly Language programming and was ready to move on to a different programming language—Cobol. Cobol was a higher-level programming language than Assembly language, so it was much easier to understand—mostly because of its English-like syntax. During my second semester, I was enrolled in a course called *Cobol Programming 1*. About halfway through that course, the light bulb finally went on! Just like Mr. Fisk said it would. It was all beginning to make sense. I was beginning to understand what it was we were trying to accomplish and how to think algorithmically to accomplish it.

I can't tell you how many times over the years I've told this story to college freshmen who have come to my office to express their own struggles with computer programming. I hope it has been encouraging for them to know that someone like me also struggled with it at first. So, just like Mr. Fisk, I always try to be friendly and tell them to stick with it. I tell them that "the light bulb will eventually go on," just like it did for me many years ago.

* * *

A few weeks before my first semester at Parkland College, I moved from my parents' house into a house in Champaign called the Hebron House. The Hebron House was sort of like a sister church to the house church I attended in Tuscola. Both were part of the network of house churches in The Assembly.

Living in the Hebron House required strict adherence to a certain set of rules, most of which were reasonable, like taking turns cooking, mowing, and going grocery shopping as well as paying your rent on time, keeping your room clean, and so on. A few of the rules might have been a little overboard, though, like the requirement to attend the "devotional time" every morning at 7 am and going to the three weekly church services. At the time, I was *not* a morning person, so the 7 am devotional times were brutal.

My first job in Champaign was at Kraft Foods, Inc. I worked in the Margarine Department two graveyard-shifts a week from 12 am to 7 am. On Wednesday nights (technically Thursday mornings), I packed round tubs of margarine into cardboard boxes as they came down the production line. After doing that for a while, I switched to taking the boxes off the line and stacking them onto palettes to be whisked away by a forklift. The work wasn't bad, but it wasn't fun either. To entertain myself, I pretty much just sang all night. Of course, no one could hear me over the noisy equipment in the production facility, so I could just sing out without having to worry about someone criticizing my skills or telling me to shut up.

Thankfully, Friday nights (technically Saturday mornings) at Kraft were completely different. On those nights, I worked with a crew of guys to clean the place from top to bottom. Sometimes, I would clean the insides and outsides of the long stainless-steel pipes that ran from the huge margarine vats to the tub fillers, and sometimes I would mop floors. Friday nights were great because the guys I worked with were mostly college students. While we all worked hard, we also had a great time telling jokes and stories and just making it fun.

There are two reasons I tell that story. First, whenever I tell people that I used to work in the Margarine Department at Kraft, they usually laugh like it's funny or something. Margarine Department? Why is that funny? I don't get it. And second, working with the older guys on that production line made it very clear to me that doing that particular kind of work, at least long term, wasn't for me. When I tried to carry on a conversation with some of those guys, they just seemed bored with life and uninterested. I'm sure they were very nice, hardworking men, but they just seemed like they wanted to put in their eight hours and get out of there. They were in no way unkind, but the years of that kind of repetitive work had taken its toll on their personalities.

* * *

Part way through my freshman year at Parkland College, I sold my Monte Carlo. I only got rid of it because I wanted a car that got better gas mileage. I sold the car to a guy in Tuscola who *promised* me he would take good care of it if I sold it to him. It may seem strange that I would care about who I sold it to, but I did. It was kind of like wanting to find a good home for a cherished pet that you can no longer care for. Unfortunately, not even a year later, I heard through the grapevine that the guy did the opposite of what he said he would do. I heard that he hot-rodded it and really tore it up. I was pretty disappointed.

Man, I wish I hadn't gotten rid of that car. But at the time, it seemed like the right thing to do. It was a special car—one that I've dreamed about dozens of times in my life. As a matter of fact, I *still* dream about it on occasion. Sometimes, I even google "forest green 1970 Chevrolet Monte Carlo" just to reminisce. Feel free to take a look. There are still some beautiful specimens out there.

So, after I sold my Monte Carlo, I bought a maroon 1982 Honda Prelude that got great gas mileage. It wasn't anything super special, but it *was* a very nice car, and it would serve me well all through college.

* * *

Living in the Hebron House wasn't too bad. I really liked the people who lived there. The first room I had I shared with three guys. One of my roommates was a guy named Verne. Verne was several years older than me and was a graduate student in Chemistry at the University of Illinois. He was also a talented bass guitar player, and since he was from the US Virgin Islands, he had quite the sophisticated-sounding English accent. I really liked Verne, and we had some great laughs together.

I also had a roommate named Kevin. Kevin was very studious, and he drank a *lot* of coffee while he studied. I don't remember ever seeing him study at his desk in our room without having a pot of coffee next to him. That couldn't have been good for him.

When I moved into the Hebron House and was getting ready to start classes at Parkland College, Kevin advised me to study *five* hours outside the classroom for every *one* hour I was in class. So, from that point forward, through five years of college and five years of graduate school, that was my standard. So, when I was enrolled in 12 to 15 hours of courses, that meant I should study 60 to 75 hours each week. In hindsight, I think that was overkill—at least as an undergraduate. I think I could have enjoyed my post-secondary education more if I had relaxed just a little. Oh well, I got good grades! Thanks, Kevin. Now I tell my students that, at a minimum, they should study *two* to *three* hours outside the classroom for every *one* hour they're in class. That seems a little more reasonable.

Mark was another roommate I had at the Hebron House. Mark was from Norridge, Illinois—a small suburb just outside of Chicago. He was probably five or six years older than me, and we got along great. We joked around a lot, listened to a lot of the same music, and always tried to scare each other. One time, I hid under his bunk, and when he got out of the shower and walked into the room and over to his bed, I grabbed him by the ankles and screamed. I got him so good! Mark was a carpenter by trade, and I would occasionally work for him to make a few bucks.

One weekend, Mark and I went to Norridge in his baby blue work van because he had to appear in court for a traffic ticket or something. While we were there, we went to Nancy's Pizza for a slice of authentic Chicago-style stuffed pizza. Since Nancy's husband, Rocco, invented the Chicago-style stuffed pizza in 1971, the restaurant had historical significance. It was the first time I had had Chicago-style stuffed pizza. Of course, it was amazing.

Mark also took me to see where John Wayne Gacy had lived when that all went down. Since Gacy's house was completely demolished in 1979, it was an empty lot when we drove by it that day. It's pretty weird, but somebody bought that lot and built a house on it in 1986. Can you imagine living in a house on that lot knowing what went on there? The owners must have gotten the lot pretty cheap.

* * *

Sometime in the late fall of my freshman year, we did some room shuffling at the Hebron House. I moved out of the room I shared with Vern, Kevin, and Mark and into a different room with just Kevin. It was in this room that I first sensed an interest in playing the drums.

I didn't have a drum set when I lived in the Hebron House, but the comforter on my bed had these big colored squares that were arranged in such a way that it made it easy for me to imagine some of the squares as drums and some of the squares as cymbals. So, I would put a cassette tape into my cassette player, put my headphones on my head, crank it up, and jam to my favorite albums of the time using the squares on my comforter as my drum set. While some kids start out on pots and pans,

I started out on my bed—which, of course, was much less annoying to other people. The only album I distinctly remember playing along with was Journey's *Escape* album. But I'm sure there were others.

During this time, I met a guy named Tom. Tom was maybe a decade older than me and was the younger brother of a friend of mine who I went to church with. Tom played the guitar, and when he found out that I wanted to play the drums, he invited me to his house to jam. He had a really nice set up in his bedroom—complete with a drum set and guitar amplifiers. Tom was a good guitar player, and he could also write songs. In addition to playing some of his original Christian music, we played a bunch of secular cover tunes. We really cranked it up in there.

Playing music at Tom's house was magical because it was the first time I had played an instrument that I really felt in my soul. It was like I didn't have to think so hard as I played. It was natural. I could just sit in the music and contribute to it as it was being played. Although I had played in the concert band, stage band, and marching band in school, Tom's band was the first rock band I had ever played in. It was also the first band I had ever played in as a drummer. There would be *many* more of those over the years.

* * *

In the early spring of my freshman year, after about seven months of working the graveyard shift at Kraft, one of the guys in the Hebron House, Kurt, offered me a job with his construction business. When I worked for Kurt, I learned how to install drop ceilings, hang drywall, build privacy fences, shingle roofs, and paint houses. Although I made less money per hour working for Kurt, I enjoyed the work and daytime hours much more. I learned a lot of skills working for Kurt—skills that I would be able to use later in life as a homeowner.

* * *

In the early summer of 1982, I moved back to my parents' house in Tuscola. I was glad to be back because I had gotten a little homesick living in Champaign. After I moved back to Tuscola, I stopped playing music with Tom and started jamming with two guys I knew from high school—Doug and Danny. Danny was the guy I rode bikes with as a kid before I got my driver's license. Since my house had a three-car garage, Doug and Danny and I had the perfect rehearsal space for a garage band. Doug played the guitar, Danny played the synthesizer, and I played my dad's three-piece, grey-pearl-wrap Pearl drum set with Zildjian cymbals that he had bought in the early 1960s.[2] The band was nothing serious. I mean, we didn't even have a singer. We just met up in my garage periodically and jammed to some of the great rock songs of the day.

* * *

When the fall semester began at Parkland College, my commute to classes took me 30 minutes. The trip wasn't too bad because my cousin Todd and I took turns driving. Todd was now a freshman at Parkland, and every weekday on the way up to school and back, we had a good time talking and listening to the radio. Our go-to radio stations were WLS 890 AM in Chicago and WLRW 94.5 FM in Champaign. Back then, both of those stations played great rock music.

Todd and I were always able to connect through music. When we were in high school, he had this awesome, high-powered stereo system in his room that included an amplifier, graphic equalizer, radio receiver, and turntable. He also had two large floor speakers that could produce fantastic sound—from deep lows to shimmering highs. In addition, he had built a great collection of rock albums by bands like Van Halen, Foghat, Montrose, AC/DC, Molly Hatchet, and Rush. Rush was his favorite. On many afternoons, I'd go over to his house, and we'd crank it up and be blown away by the rock music of the day. It was pretty cool. The musical styles of those bands (and many others like them) greatly influenced my taste in music. Ah. The 70s and 80s. Great music.

* * *

At Parkland College that semester, I met a couple of other guys who were musicians, so I invited them down to my house in Tuscola to jam. I don't remember their names, but I *do* remember having a lot of fun playing music with them—despite the fact that we didn't have a singer. After jamming at my house a couple of times, the whole thing just kind of disappeared. Nobody said anything. We just stopped jamming. I'm guessing everyone just got too busy with their classes. Or maybe I was horrible, and they didn't want to play with me anymore.

---

[2] Technically, the drums belonged to my cousin Jim. My dad had given them to him several years before. So, I was borrowing the drums from Jim.

Practicing in my parents' garage was great. It was a nice space with good lighting, and we had a space heater for when it got cold. It was also convenient for me, since I didn't have to lug my drums around. The only problem with the garage was that its walls were paper thin. Thus, there was very little to keep the noise in. On several occasions, when we were cranking it up at night, our next-door neighbor, Dale, had to come over and quiet us down. He would come to the window of the garage, tap on it with his knuckle, and ask us if we could pull the plug on the music because it was bedtime for his two daughters. It was probably like 9 pm. Of course, we always respected that and called it a night. What I appreciated about Dale was that he never seemed angry. And if he was, he didn't let it show. He was very gracious.

* * *

It was around this time that I had another one of those out-of-the-blue realizations. It was similar to the epiphany-like experiences I had had as a kid when, all of a sudden, I knew I could ride a two-wheeler or catch a baseball with ease. It occurred after one of the band practices in my garage after everyone had left for the evening. As I stood at my dad's workbench under the bright four-foot fluorescent lights, I had this sense that I could play the guitar. The thing about it is, I had tried to play the guitar before, but it just didn't click. But after sensing that I could do it, I grabbed my dad's Yamaha classical guitar and began learning the three or four chords from the sheet music sitting on the workbench in front of me. The light bulb just went on. I'm not sure if that kind of thing happens to everyone, but I *do* know that it happened to me. It was a remarkable moment. Later in life, the ability to play the guitar would be very important for me.

* * *

The third garage band I played in consisted of some different guys from Tuscola—Jim, who played the guitar, and Mark, who played the bass. Once again, we didn't have a singer. Back in those days, you could only be a singer in a band if you could actually sing. So, singers were pretty tough to come by. Anyway, this band practiced in Jim's barn out in the country, so we could play as loudly as we wanted without fear of disturbing the neighbors. I actually got dumped by this band. After playing together for a while, they just stopped calling me to jam. It was kind of weird, but I found out later that Jim's brother, John, wanted to play the drums for them, so he got the gig. That's okay, I guess. I can't blame them.

* * *

In 1983, while I was still attending Parkland College, someone told me that a Christian rock band called Petra was going to be performing at Centennial High School in Champaign and that I should go. I didn't know very much about Christian rock music back then, but I had heard of Petra, so I decided to go. Man, I'm glad I went. I was blown away. Petra was loud, colorful, and very professional. Not only that, but their message really spoke to me and stirred something in my spirit.

One of the things that really encouraged me was seeing probably a thousand other Christians at the concert singing along to their music. That experience opened up my eyes to the fact that Christianity wasn't limited to the people in my little church and its associated network of churches. No. God was much bigger than that. To this day, Petra is one of my favorite Christian rock bands. The skill of their songwriting, the profoundness of their lyrics, and the musicianship of the band is truly exceptional. That Petra concert marks the point in my life that I really began to get serious about my Christian faith.

* * *

Not too long after the Petra concert, I met a guy named Tim from Parkland Christian Fellowship.[3] Tim was the lead singer of a Christian rock band called Judah. Tim was very friendly, and he was very serious about music ministry. One day, Tim invited me to a Judah concert in Mohamet, Illinois, so I went. At the concert, Judah played all original Christian rock music. They were *very* good and sounded a lot like Petra. After the concert, I went up to the guys in the band and introduced myself. I told them that I played the drums and to give me a call if they ever needed a drummer.

Just a few weeks later, I got a call from Tim. Their drummer had left the band for some reason, and they were looking for someone to take his place. So, after talking about the band's vision for a while, we made plans for an audition in Galton, Illinois, which is a tiny little town

---

[3] PCF was the InterVarsity Christian Fellowship chapter at Parkland College.

about four or five miles south of Tuscola. At the audition, we jammed to some of their songs, and it soon became clear that I was a good fit. So, Tim, Paul, and Cliff asked me to join—which I promptly did.

Judah was a very serious band with some pretty ambitious dreams. We played whenever and wherever we could. We played at churches, high schools, colleges, parks, shopping malls, and community centers all over Central Illinois.

By that point, I owned a solid black Rogers drum set with two bass drums and Zildjian cymbals. In addition, I had a set of drum risers that my dad and I designed and built out of plywood and heavy-duty door hinges. My dad has always been good at designing and building things that need to be easily assembled and disassembled, and my drum risers were no exception. The risers were 18 inches high, and all I had to do to put them together was insert the hinge pins into the hinge knuckles that were attached to the various panels of plywood. Very nice. After the risers were assembled, all I needed to do was put my big piece of shag carpeting on the top to keep my drums from sliding around while I played.

It wasn't too long after I joined Judah that a guy named Dick joined the band. Dick was a very talented piano player and vocalist. He had a very high vocal range, so that permitted us to play a few cover songs by artists like Petra and Keith Green. Later, a guy named Robert joined the band as well. Robert was an exceptional guitar player and had some excellent songwriting skills. His guitar playing and songwriting added another dimension to the band's sound.

Over the years, we also had some good soundmen in Libero, Kent, and Dick. In case you didn't know, a band only sounds as good as its soundmen, so they played an important role in the group. Libero was one of my best friends in high school, and he was our first soundman. After a while, my cousin Kent became our soundman. Kent lived in Sydney, Illinois, sort of out in the country, so we eventually made the basement of his house our practice location. That way, we didn't have to worry about disturbing the neighbors. Before that, we had practiced in my garage. And Dick, our keyboard player, helped with sound later after he stopped playing with the band as a musician.

Along the way, Judah experienced a few more personnel changes as well. When Paul and Cliff left the band, we were forced to change the name of the band to something else. After some heavy brainstorming, we settled on the Skylight Band. After Dick left the band, a guy named Carlos joined the group. Carlos was a great keyboardist and became a core member of the band, which at this point was Tim, Robert, Carlos, and me. As the Skylight Band, we had a couple of different guys play bass for us—Randy and Rod. They were both very good, and it was always a pleasure playing with them. Now that I think about it, Judah and the Skylight Band were always blessed with good musicians and songwriters.

The Skylight Band continued to play the same kinds of venues we did as Judah, but our geographical reach expanded some with a gig at a high school in Indiana. As I look back on it now, it seems like the apex of our popularity was when we opened for a couple of national acts (Rick Cua and Rob Castles) in Champaign at the Laborer's Union Hall Theatre.

* * *

In the spring of 1984, I graduated from Parkland College with an Associate of Science degree in data processing. Soon after graduating, I moved back to Champaign, where I lived in an apartment with Libero and Dick—two friends from Judah. I didn't get a job as a computer programmer for some reason, so I took a part-time job at a place called Kuhn's Too in the Marketplace Shopping Center. Kuhn's was a men's clothing store that sold sport and dress shirts, casual and dress slacks, and fine suits. I learned a lot about men's clothing at Kuhn's—the kind of stuff about clothes that would be good to know later in life. I learned about clothing materials. I learned about suits. And I learned how to properly mark clothing for tailoring. I enjoyed working at Kuhn's. Most of the other people who worked there were around my age and still in college, so we had some great discussions and laughed a lot. The only person who wasn't around my age was the manager, Bob.

Bob was in his middle 30s, was married, and had a couple of boys in middle school. Bob and I had some great conversations about life— some philosophical and some not so much. One evening, when we were working together and things were slow, we got onto the topic of evening meals. I told him that I would sometimes make Hamburger Helper for dinner. And when I told him that I would usually eat the whole thing in one sitting, he looked at me and said, "Beas! I feed my whole family on that!" I had no idea I was such a pig. At that point in my life, I could eat all I wanted and never gain a pound. In fact, I would sometimes eat three Quarter Pounders with Cheese, fries, and a Coke at McDonalds, and I would still stay skinny as a rail. Man, those were the days. Of course, I can't do that anymore. Well maybe I could, but I'd get huge.

In addition to working at Kuhn's Too, I occasionally "worked" as a hair model at Chicago Hair Cutting Company in Champaign. I didn't get paid for this job, but I did get free haircuts by young women who were learning to cut hair. I was asked to be a model because I had a long, wavy, chestnut-colored mullet. (It was in style at the time.) Now that I think about it, maybe winning that award in the eighth grade for "best hair" made sense.

It was around that time that I also took a part-time job selling club memberships that provided merchandise to people at wholesale prices. For some people, it was a great deal. I guess the modern-day equivalent would be something like Costco or Sams Club, except instead of going into a physical store, you looked through a paper catalog, filled out a paper order form, and mailed the order form to get stuff directly from the wholesale supplier. Anyway, I did *not* like that job, so I only did it for a brief time. I know some people love sales jobs, but that kind of work was not for me.

In addition to the various part-time jobs that I had after graduating from Parkland College, I continued to play in the Skylight Band. All the other guys in the band had part-time jobs too, and some were still in school at either Parkland or the University of Illinois. We were all young and single, and no one owned a home or had a career job yet. So, we were relatively free. At the time, all of us wanted to be full-time musicians. We wanted to go on tour—just like all the popular Christian bands we loved. But that was not to be.

* * *

In the fall of 1984, my dad fell from a loading dock at the fitness center he owned and broke his leg at the knee. While I was visiting him in the hospital, I experienced a strong sense in my spirit that I wasn't finished with my education and that I should return to college to get a bachelor's degree in computing. The odd thing was, I hadn't thought about furthering my education before visiting my dad in the hospital that day. The minimal post-secondary education that I already had (an associate degree) seemed just fine to me. But the desire to continue my education that welled up inside me that day didn't go away.

The decision to continue on with college was life-changing for me because I would ultimately go on to further my education well beyond the bachelor's degree. At the time, I had no idea what was in store for me academically. All I knew was that I wanted to complete a bachelor's degree before starting my career as a computer programmer. Today, I recognize the experience I had while visiting my dad in the hospital as a guidepost in my life that God used to direct me onto the path toward the *career* he had in store for me. At that point in my life, I could *never* have imagined where that path was leading.

So, in the spring of 1985, I visited both the University of Illinois in Urbana and Illinois State University in Normal. At both schools, I sat down with someone in their respective admissions offices to discuss the possibilities of transferring from Parkland College. The admissions officers at both universities told me that I would more than likely be accepted because of my grades at Parkland. However, the admissions officer at the U of I told me that they would only be able to transfer in a little over half the credit hours I earned at Parkland. The admissions officer at ISU, on the other hand, told me that they would be able to transfer in almost all of the credit hours I earned at Parkland. At the time, I didn't know that the U of I was a world-class institution. And even if I did, I don't think that would've mattered to me. I just liked that ISU was more transfer friendly. So, for me, it was a no-brainer. I was heading to ISU.

Soon after making my decision, I told the guys in the Skylight Band that I would be quitting at the end of August and moving to Normal to attend Illinois State University. Although it was tough to do, they completely understood when I explained that I had felt God directing me in that direction. We had something very good together, so it was difficult for me to let go of it. But in the end, it was the right thing to do.

* * *

In late August, I loaded up my Honda Prelude with everything I owned (except for my drum set) and drove to Illinois State University in Normal. When I got there, they didn't have a dorm room for me, so they put me in a lounge with a bunch of other guys who were dealing with the exact same issue. The problem with the lounge was that it was located in Wilkins Hall, which was located way out in the westernmost part of campus—three quarters of a mile from Stevenson Hall, where virtually all of my classes would be. That distance would make getting back and forth between my room and my classes very inconvenient, and the walk would certainly be brutal when it got cold.

Fortunately, right before classes started, someone introduced me to a guy named Todd who lived on the first floor of Barton Hall. Barton Hall was a coed dorm, so it housed both men and women—in different areas of the building. Todd was a senior, and he needed a roommate. He seemed like a nice guy, so I moved in with him. Todd was an Eagle Scout, and he was *always* prepared—just like the Boy Scout motto says. I kid you not. If I needed a knife, he had one. If I needed a packet of black pepper, he had one. If I needed a slingshot, he had one. Okay, slingshot is an exaggeration, but it was still kind of amazing. Todd was a good guy, and we got along great that year. As for Barton Hall, it was located just a block west of the quad—only four tenths of a mile from Stevenson Hall. So, walking back and forth between my room and my classes was relatively easy.

Shortly after arriving at Illinois State University, I got involved with InterVarsity Christian Fellowship. I had learned that being involved in a Christian fellowship was essential in college because a lack of such involvement can be devastating to one's faith. As a Chinese friend of mine once said, "We are all like pickles in a pickle jar." What he meant by that was we take on the values of the people we hang around with. Of course, the Bible says the same thing. In 1 Corinthians 15:33 it says, "Bad company corrupts good morals." So today, I encourage Christian students to get involved with a Christian group on campus as soon as they can.

* * *

At Illinois State University, I majored in applied computer science and minored in economics. I was a very serious student, so I studied a *lot*. My dad had encouraged me to treat college like a full-time job, and that's exactly what I did. Plus, I still adhered to my first roommate's overkill advice to study *five* hours outside the classroom for every *one* hour I was in class. It seems like I was always reading a textbook and highlighting key concepts, doing homework, writing papers on my Commodore 64 microcomputer, or studying my notes.

In terms of note taking, I developed an approach that worked really well for me. After taking very fast and sloppy notes in the classroom on looseleaf paper, I would go somewhere and copy those notes into the spiral binder I had for the class. Once my messy notes had been translated into much more complete and well-organized notes, I would crumple up the looseleaf paper and slam dunk it into a garbage can. Translating my classroom notes like that required me to really think through what I was learning and to make sense out of it. If I was unable to translate a concept because I couldn't clearly articulate it on paper, I knew that I needed to get clarification on it—from the book, a friend, or my professor. There was no Google, YouTube, or ChatGPT back then!

One of the benefits of the way I studied was that I learned course concepts as we progressed through them in class—not just right before I had to regurgitate them on a test. So, when an exam was approaching, all I had to do was bone up on the concepts a little a day or two before the exam, and I was good to go. I never crammed for an exam that I can remember. I always tried to learn things in lockstep with the course lectures. So, when some of my friends were all stressed out and pulling all-nighters during final exams, I was usually relaxed and sleeping like a baby. Another benefit was that I actually remembered some of the stuff I had learned in my classes after the semester was over. Imagine that. This would come in quite handy later in life when I actually had to know something.

By the way, I've shared my approach to studying and learning with many struggling college students over the years. I hope it has helped.

* * *

Because I was such a determined student, I only came up for air on occasion—usually in the late evenings and on weekends. My social life consisted mostly of attending InterVarsity Large Group meetings and leading a Bible study that met weekly in Barton Hall. I invited people to the Bible study regularly, so we sometimes had as many as 20 people there. I also attempted to stay in shape by running and playing pickup basketball on occasion. I'm sure I did a *few* other things as well. I wasn't a complete recluse. But, for the most part, I went to class and studied.

Despite my serious study habits, my first semester at Illinois State University was very difficult. Although *every* student experiences stress in college, that semester was particularly stressful for me. I think it was because ISU was a new academic environment, and I just didn't know my way around and how things ran. The newness of it all seemed to add this extra layer of confusion to my life. Because of this, my grades suffered some. That semester, I got the only C in my college career. It was in a course called Microcomputer Application and Design I—a course I could teach now with half my brain tied behind my back.

Things got so stressful that semester that I called my mom and told her I was thinking about dropping out of college. As I stood by the butterscotch-colored telephone next to the door of my room with its six-foot spiral cord dangling beside me, I told her that maybe I wasn't cut out to be a computer programmer after all. Although she was very understanding, she encouraged me to "stick it out" saying that it was likely just a difficult season in my life that would eventually pass. Had I not listened to that small piece of advice from my mom that day, the entire course of my professional life might have been altered forever.

* * *

In May of 1986, after the successful completion of my first year at Illinois State University, I moved back to Champaign for the summer. I couldn't have moved back to my mom and dad's house in Tuscola if I wanted to because they were just about to move to Sarasota, Florida. In Champaign, I got my old job back at Kuhns Too, and I moved into an apartment with a guy named Bohdar. I knew Bohdar from Parkland Christian Fellowship, and we got along great. Since I had just finished calculus at ISU, we had some good conversations about it. Man, we were nerds. We also talked a lot about Christian music because we were both big fans.

The interesting thing about my bedroom in Bohdar's apartment was that it had no windows. It was called a "blind" room, and it was pitch black in there no matter the time of day. So, if I didn't set my alarm, I might sleep until two in the afternoon and not even know it. That *did* happen a couple of times. It was an interesting feeling. And it was also a complete waste of a good part of the day.

Since I was back in town for a few months, the Skylight Band did a one-off gig in the Country Fair Shopping Center in Champaign. The lead guitarist for that gig was a guy named Bill. It was the only gig he played with us.

* * *

At the end of that summer, I returned to Illinois State University. When I got there, I moved back into Barton Hall—but this time into a room on the second floor. Since my previous roommate, Todd, had graduated the previous spring, I had a new roommate named Mark. Mark was a graduate student who was working on his master's degree in mathematics. I knew him from InterVarsity, so we decided to room together. At the beginning of the school year, Mark and I committed to praying together every night at 10 pm. So virtually every night at 10 pm, we dropped everything and prayed together. It was a real blessing.

Mark and I spent hours in our dorm room studying. The problem for Mark, though, was that he had this little black and white TV by his desk that he always had on when his beloved St. Louis Cardinals had a baseball game. Although the TV was muted, Mark was very distracted by the game. He just couldn't seem to keep his mind on his studying. One minute, he'd be looking down at his desk, and the next minute his head and eyes would slowly drift toward his TV. He tried to resist, but he just couldn't.

* * *

Sometime during that first semester, an underage friend of mine named Gerry asked to borrow my driver's license so he could perform in an air band competition at a local bar in Normal. Gerry and I kind of looked alike as we both had long, dark hair and a closely cropped beard. However, he was significantly heavier than me, so I was pretty sure he wouldn't get away with it—even if I *did* let him borrow my ID. Although I told him no initially, he begged me and promised me that he wouldn't drink or get into any other kind of trouble. He'd just go, perform, and leave. Unfortunately, I finally acquiesced. I knew it was a stupid idea, but I let him borrow my ID anyway.

On the night of the air band competition, Gerry showed my driver's license to the bouncer who took one look at Gerry and one look at my ID and knew it wasn't him in the picture. Not only did the bouncer turn Gerry away, but he also confiscated my ID and called the cops. I don't remember what happened to Gerry, but I was called down to the police station the next day, where I received a tongue lashing from a police officer and got my driver's license back—after promising that I'd never do that again, of course. I was mad at myself and embarrassed for doing something so obviously stupid. The worst part was that I let someone talk me into something that I knew was irresponsible and foolish after I had already said no.

* * *

On Friday night, October 31ˢᵗ, I saw a girl at InterVarsity's annual Halloween party. She was wearing a green Southside Irish jacket and a green paddy cap and was playing a game by the bonfire, where you had to pick up a piece of paper off the ground with your teeth. I didn't think *anything* about it beyond the fact that I hadn't seen her before. I didn't think she was attractive or unattractive. I didn't think she was short or tall. I didn't think anything other than she must have been invited to the party by someone in InterVarsity.

The next time I saw the girl was just a few days later in the common area that connected Dunn and Barton Halls. I think I was playing pool. Again, I thought nothing of it. Besides, I had a girlfriend at the time.

A few days after that, I got a phone call from a girl named Elizabeth who had heard that I was going to the Michael W. Smith concert the following week at the University of Illinois Assembly Hall, which was in Champaign. She wanted to know if she could catch a ride with me to the concert, where she would be meeting up with her boyfriend who attended the U of I and who had won tickets to the concert on a radio show. Unfortunately, I was taking my girlfriend to the concert. She had bought us tickets for my birthday in September, and I really didn't want a "third wheel" tagging along. So, I basically told Elizabeth that I would find a ride for her, which I did.

On the night of the concert, November 10th, 1986, I met Elizabeth in person. For some reason, she had sought me out at the concert—probably to say thanks for finding her a ride. One of our mutual friends told her that I should be easy to spot because I looked like Jesus. At that point, I was still sporting my dark-brown shoulder-length mullet and dark-brown closely-trimmed beard. So yes, I looked a lot like the Jesus you sometimes see in pictures.

Now keep in mind that the Assembly Hall seats like 15,000 people, and there were at least half that many people in attendance that night. That's a pretty big crowd. So, it's kind of amazing that she spotted me in the audience before the concert began. She saw me standing beside a railing 50 or so feet below, where she was sitting with her boyfriend. What are the odds? Anyway, she came down to where my girlfriend and I were standing and introduced herself. I'm not sure what was said beside the brief introduction, but we parted ways a minute or two later not to see each other again for a couple of months.

* * *

In January of 1987, during the spring semester of my senior year at Illinois State University, my roommate Mark and I were sitting at our desks studying when we heard someone knock on our door. After one of us said to come in, the door opened, and there was Elizabeth. She said she was looking for Bob Beasley, so I told her that that was me. She didn't recognize me at first because, during Christmas break, I had gotten my hair cut off, and I had shaved off my beard in preparation for job interviews. I was also wearing reading glasses. She was inquiring about the Bible study I led in Barton Hall because she had just moved in after living in Hewett Hall previously. After I gave her the time and location of the Bible study, she left the room. She soon became a regular attender of the Bible study, so I got to know her a little bit. She seemed like a nice girl.

Despite the fact that I had a girlfriend at the time, I started to notice Elizabeth some, and I began enjoying some of the conversations we were having. I found out that she was a junior applied mathematics major, and she was from Des Plaines, Illinois (a suburb of Chicago). I also found out that she was Catholic. Although she hadn't really read the Bible much growing up, she had started reading the Bible in college and had a lot of questions.

One evening, after one of our Bible studies, Elizabeth said she had some more questions about one of the topics we had discussed at the study. So, Mark and I invited her and her friend to our room to extend the conversation. After her friend left, Mark and I invited her to stay a bit longer and pray with us at 10 pm. When 10 pm rolled around, Mark asked Elizabeth to go ahead and start, but she was reluctant to do so. When Mark asked her why, she said she wasn't used to praying out loud in front of people—except for rote prayers, like the *Our Father*. Mark and I attempted to allay her fears by suggesting that she "just talk to God." That seemed to help, so she prayed. Part of her prayer that evening was asking God to deliver her dead relatives from purgatory. Since purgatory isn't a concept that Protestants and Catholics usually agree on, we both thought we'd speak with her about it later.

A couple of days later, when I finally got around to speaking with Elizabeth about purgatory, she told me that Mark had already spoken to her about it. She told me later that she wasn't at all embarrassed or upset by the conversation she had had with us because she was just so open to what the Bible had to say about things. She also said that Mark and I were both very kind when we spoke with her. Later that semester, through reading the Bible, Elizabeth came to a full understanding that salvation (being saved from the negative consequences of our sins) was by God's grace through faith in Christ and that it wasn't something that could be earned.

Before the spring semester ended, I had broken up with my current girlfriend. She was the fourth real girlfriend I had in college up to that point, and all of those relationships only lasted a few months or so. I had a few other romantic relationships as well, but because they were so brief, I usually don't call the girls in those relationships "girlfriends."

* * *

When the spring semester ended, Mark and I and a friend named Jim moved into a nice three-bedroom, off-campus townhouse for the summer. The place had an upstairs, a downstairs, and a basement. Jim had first dibs, so he took the upstairs bedroom. That left the basement bedrooms for Mark and me. Unfortunately for Jim, he didn't know how hot it could get upstairs in the middle of the summer. Nor did he know how delightfully cool it could be in the basement after a blazing hot summer day. The rent for the apartment was $150 per month, split between three guys, so it was dirt cheap—even then.

That summer, I worked full time designing and developing software systems for the Office of Residential Life Facilities at the University. I wrote brand-new microcomputer applications using FoxPro Plus (in case that means anything to you), and I loved it. The only negative part about the job was that I only made minimum wage, which was $3.35 per hour—the standard wage for a student worker.

Not too long into the summer break, Elizabeth and her most recent college roommate, Christine, drove down to Illinois State University for the weekend and stopped by our apartment for a visit. Since I was the only one there, they asked me if I wanted to go out to dinner with them at Bennigan's, which was an Irish pub-themed restaurant chain—kind of like Applebee's. As soon as they asked the question, I got that "deer in the headlights" look on my face because I didn't know how to answer them. I was torn between wanting to go and not wanting to spend money. I was, after all, still a poor college student. After thinking about it for several seconds, I patted the front pockets of my jeans as if to say, "Sorry, but I don't have any money." The truth is, I probably had *some* money. I just didn't want to spend it. So, without having to say anything more, Elizabeth said, "Our treat!" Yeah, baby!

Unlike me, Elizabeth had a lot of money. She had moved home for the summer, and she had taken a job with a benefits firm in downtown Chicago making $7.50 per hour—well over twice the amount of money I was making per hour. Since she lived at home and had virtually no expenses, she was swimming in money. At least that's the way it looked from my perspective.

* * *

Two or three weeks later, I heard from Elizabeth again. This time, she called to find out if I was going to the Cornerstone festival in early July. Cornerstone was an annual Christian music festival that was held at the Lake County Fairgrounds in Grayslake, Illinois, which was only about 30 miles north of where she lived in Des Plaines. She had heard about the festival from some of her InterVarsity friends and had asked them if they knew anyone who was going, since she wanted to go and needed a ride. Someone told her that they thought I was going, so she should give me a call.

As it turned out, I *was* planning to go. I had been to the festival at least a couple of times before, and I always liked it, so I had decided to go again. This year, the event was to be held from July 1st through July 4th. I was excited for the festival because, not only would a lot of great Christian rock bands be playing throughout the four-day event, but a lot of interesting seminars and workshops would be held on topics like Christian apologetics (which I was very into at the time), songwriting, and music ministry.

When July 1st arrived, I drove up to Des Plaines, picked Elizabeth up at her house, drove north to Grayslake, and set up camp near my friend Bohdar. After I set up my tent, I helped Elizabeth set up hers. After settling in at our campsite, Elizabeth and I walked around the fairgrounds to scope out the seminars and workshops that would be available throughout the event. I don't remember which ones she went to, but I mostly went to the ones on Christian apologetics and the ones where certain Christian artists were speaking or being interviewed.

One of the things I noticed about Elizabeth was that, when she was finished with one of her sessions, she would find me and sit with me for the rest of my session. (I was starting to think that maybe she liked me or something.) The two of us also went to hear some of my favorite bands play. I say "my favorite bands" because she didn't really know much about Contemporary Christian Music at the time. So, she would just come along with me wherever I went. Throughout the festival, we ran into a bunch of my friends from the Christian band scene in the Champaign-Urbana area, so I introduced Elizabeth as my friend from college. As I think about it now, some of them were probably thinking, "Yeah, right."

On the way back to Elizabeth's house after the festival, we stopped at a Wendy's for dinner. When I asked her what she thought about the experience, she told me that she enjoyed the sessions and the music, but camping wasn't really her cup of tea. She probably wouldn't want to go camping again. While we were on the topic of camping, I said something like, "I've heard that before you marry someone, you should go camping with them." I really *had* heard that somewhere, and I didn't mean anything by it. I was just sayin'. In hindsight, though, that was a pretty weird thing to say. But, in a joking tone, she just said, "Is this a proposal?" Fortunately for me, it didn't go any further than that, and we just laughed it off.

Shortly after attending the Cornerstone festival together, I called up Elizabeth and asked her if she wanted to go to Champaign with me to attend my friend's wedding. She said she did, so on the weekend of the wedding, she drove down to Normal from Chicagoland, and I drove us down to Champaign for the big event. While we were in Champaign, my friend's mom, whom I had known since I was a kid, took me aside and told me that she could tell that "that girl" liked me—to which I responded, "We're just friends." Uh oh.

* * *

Toward the end of the summer, I invited Elizabeth to go on a trip with me to Sarasota, Florida to visit my parents. I didn't want to drive by myself, so I thought I'd invite her along. Later, I found out that her parents weren't very happy about her going on such a long trip with a guy she hadn't known for very long. Besides, they had planned a family vacation for that time. Somehow, she convinced her parents to let her go, so I picked her up at her house in suburban Chicago, and we drove the 1,250-mile trip to Sarasota.

Before the trip, Elizabeth had amassed a good number of questions about the Bible that she wanted to ask me, and I did my best to answer the ones I could. We talked about a lot of other things on the trip as well. We never lacked for things to talk about. In fact, there were times when we talked so much that I had to ask her if we could stop talking for a while because I needed some peace and quiet. That didn't mean I wasn't enjoying our conversations. No. I enjoyed them a lot. I just needed a break from all the words.

When we finally got to my parents' condo, I introduced Elizabeth to my mom and dad—making sure they knew that she was just a friend and that we were *not* dating. My mom and dad adored Elizabeth from the start, and she and I had a great time with them playing cards, going out to eat, watching TV, and just hanging out and talking. Every day,

Elizabeth and I would go to the beach or hang out by the pool. We just took in the tropical paradise like we didn't have a care in the world.

We also began having romantic feelings for each other. And as time progressed, we began feeling more and more like a couple.

On our trip back to Illinois, we stopped at a restaurant one morning for breakfast. I think it was a Waffle House. During our conversation at the restaurant, I asked her about the ring she was wearing. It was an Irish Claddagh ring. She told me that, when the heart of the ring faces in one direction, it means your heart isn't taken. But when it faces the other direction, it means your heart *is* taken. (Here comes the mushy part, so if you don't like that kind of thing, please look away.) So, I asked her if she thought she should turn her ring around. In response, she asked *me* if I wanted her to. So, in response to that, I asked *her* if she wanted to. To that, she smiled and said, "Okay." So, I took her hand, removed the ring, and placed it back on her finger so that the heart faced in the opposite direction. We were officially a couple.

* * *

Since I hadn't completed my degree in applied computer science, I had to return to Illinois State University for one more semester. During that semester, I had a new roommate whose name also happened to be Mark. I knew this Mark from InterVarsity as well, and we got along great. I didn't spend a lot of time with him, though, because Elizabeth and I were together so much. Plus, he had a girlfriend too—whom he eventually married. But when Mark and I were together, we had a great time. He had a big smile and a great sense of humor.

Although Elizabeth and I spent a lot of time together that semester, we weren't inseparable—like those couples that can't stand to be apart so much that you never see one without the other. We still had classes to attend and other friends to hang out with. But the one thing we did together almost every time was walk down to the cafeteria for meals. Since she had moved from the third floor of Barton Hall to the second floor that semester, the same floor that I lived on, her room was only about a hundred feet down the hall from mine in the girls' wing of the dorm. In fact, I could see her room from mine. So, when it was time for breakfast, lunch, or dinner, one of us would call the other, and we'd make plans on the phone while looking at each other down the hall.

One of the best things about our relationship that semester was that we liked to study together. So, we would often find a quiet lounge or some other area in our dorm and study. That semester, everyone knew we were a couple. There was no doubt.

At Illinois State University, Barton Hall and Dunn Hall were twin dorms that were connected by a common area, and that common area was connected to the cafeteria of another dorm called Walker Hall by a 200-foot-or-so underground tunnel. So, when you wanted breakfast, for example, you had to walk through the tunnel to get to the cafeteria.

One afternoon, as Elizabeth and I were walking through the tunnel toward the cafeteria, my previous girlfriend was walking back to Dunn Hall in the opposite direction. As we passed, she looked at me and said, "Hi, Bob!" real-happy-like. But she completely avoided any kind of eye contact with Elizabeth. Later, when Elizabeth told me that the girl was *obviously* mad at her, I told her she was just imagining it. But after the scenario repeated itself a few times during the semester, I knew she wasn't. The strange thing was that the girl acted like she was just fine with me. But you could tell she was *not* happy with Elizabeth.

* * *

By the way, the food in that cafeteria was very good. But for some reason, people complained about it a lot. I'm not sure what they were grumbling about. I knew what good food tasted like. I mean, my mom, my aunts, and my grandmothers were all great cooks. So, whenever someone complained to me about the food, I told them that I thought it was great. I bet they weren't expecting that response!

Now let us take a moment to appreciate all the cafeteria workers of the world who never get any respect. I respect you and the great work you do! Seriously.

Although the food was great, it wasn't like it is today, where on any given afternoon or evening you have all these choices, like hamburgers, pizza, mediterranean, vegetarian, and so on. Nope. We had *one* choice, like meatloaf and green beans or fish and potatoes or pizza. And if *we* were having pizza in the Walker Cafeteria, everyone else on campus was having pizza as well.

The one thing you didn't want to do in the cafeteria was drop your light green fiberglass tray. This was because doing so would produce the exceptionally loud and unmistakable sound of shattering porcelain plates, bouncing plastic drinking cups, and clanking metal silverware as they all hit the floor at the same time. And if you *did* drop your tray, the one or two hundred other people in the cafeteria would stop what they were doing, turn and look directly at you, and give you a great big round of applause. Luckily, it never happened to me.

* * *

Since the beginning of my second year at Illinois State University, I had been attending a relatively large and contemporary church called Eastview Christian Church in Normal. Before that, I had attended a smaller church closer to campus. Not too long before starting my last semester at ISU, Eastview made plans for a new ministry called New Community, which was to be an outreach to the "unchurched" in the Bloomington-Normal area. Eastview had recently hired a new Young Adult Pastor named Darrin who had learned about the concept of an outreach to the unchurched from his previous pastoral job at Willow Creek Community Church in South Barrington, Illinois (a suburb of Chicago). If you haven't heard of it, Willow Creek is a megachurch in the Chicagoland area and is one of the largest churches in the world.

On one Sunday morning, very early in the semester, Darrin stopped me in the hallway and asked if he could meet with me on campus later in the week to discuss the new ministry idea. While he was inviting me to meet with him, I did my best to not let it show that I *really* didn't want to get involved in anything new right now. I mean, it was my last semester of college, and I just wanted to graduate and move on. So, with the best that-sounds-so-cool look on my face, I agreed to meet with him.

On the day of our meeting, Darrin and I met in one of the common areas of Dunn-Barton. After explaining the vision for the ministry, he asked me if I would be a part of the worship team. They already had a drummer, and now they needed a bass player. The problem was, I had never played the bass guitar before. However, my understanding was that, if you could play guitar, which I could, you could play bass. So, after some thought, I agreed to be a part of the ministry—not because I really *wanted* to but because I felt that I should be *willing* to serve if I had the ability to do so.

Since it was supposed to be an outreach to the unchurched, we tried to make New Community as "un-churchy" as possible. The pews in the chapel were replaced by chairs, the pastor avoided using Christian lingo in his sermons, and the music was secular. The band included my good friends Steve and Jim on guitar and drums, respectively, and a young married couple on keyboards and vocals. I don't remember their names.

My contribution to the band was pretty lacking in terms of my bass playing ability. I mostly just hit the root note of the chord being played by the rest of the band. At the time, I had no appreciation of the chord inversion that might have made for a much more awesome sound. No. My playing was pretty basic. Nothing fancy. Jim felt a little limited in his drumming ability as well. He wasn't really a drumkit drummer. He was more of a drumline drummer. So, while he could play complex rudiments on the snare drum really well, and he could do a lot of cool sticking tricks, the drum set wasn't his forte. So, we eventually swapped instruments. I was relieved and happy to be playing the drums again—the instrument I was most comfortable playing.

Some of the songs we played in New Community included *Pride (In the Name of Love)* by U2, *The Power of Love* by Huey Lewis and the News, and *Show Me the Way* by Styx. On a typical Sunday morning, we would play a currently popular song and then Darrin would get up, discuss the central idea of the song, and talk about how the philosophy of the song (good or bad) related to having a relationship with God. It was a great way to bridge the gap for people who weren't used to church.

On the first Sunday morning of New Community, there were like seven or eight of us there. But by the time the semester was over, there were probably 30 or more people attending New Community regularly. During the semester, Elizabeth and I attended together, but she also attended the local Catholic church (at least for the first month) because she was concerned that she would disappoint her family, especially her dad, if she totally stopped going to Mass.

* * *

On a cold and sunny day in December, at the end of the semester, I took my last final exam. It was for a course called Operating Systems. Despite my approach to studying, the course was difficult for me, and it stressed me out. I think part of it was because I had "senioritis" and was, thus, *really* ready to be done with college. My professor wrote the book we used in the course, and he had very high expectations. It was rumored that the course was the toughest course in the curriculum. I don't know if that was true or not, but it was tough.

During the final exam, one of my classmates got up from his chair, walked up to the professor's desk at the front of the room, and handed in his exam. After quietly collecting his things and putting on his coat, the guy walked out of the classroom. About 10 or 15 seconds later, we all heard this massive celebratory "Wheeeewwww!" coming from the otherwise completely quite hallway of the gigantic classroom building. Everyone laughed. When I was finished with my exam, I walked out of the building and across the street on my way to my dorm. I couldn't believe I was finally done with college. It was a great feeling.

* * *

Although my original plan was to move to Florida after graduation, the situation was more complicated now that Elizabeth was in my life. I didn't know what to do. Should I stay in Illinois, or should I move to Florida? That was the big question.

After talking with Elizabeth about it for a while, she suggested that I take a piece of paper and make two columns on it. In the left column, I should write down all the *pros* of moving to Florida, and in the right column, I should write down all the *cons* of moving to Florida. Then, I should put stars next to the most important pros and stars next to the most important cons.[4] After seeing all the pros and cons listed side by side, it became clear that I should stick with my original plan. Elizabeth and I would have to continue our relationship long-distance, since she had one more year of college left.

Since I had made my decision, I began packing my things for the move. I didn't have much. I only owned some clothes, some books, a boombox and some cassette tapes, a guitar, and my drum set. Because the drum set was so large and heavy, I had to rent a small trailer to pull behind my Honda Prelude. It was going to be tough being so far away

---

[4] Elizabeth's dad taught her this technique, and I've used it *many* times in my life when I've needed to make a major decision.

from Elizabeth, but I had to do what I had to do, and I wasn't going to second guess the decision-making process.

Thankfully, Elizabeth helped me with the move. So, after she was done with her final exams, we hopped in my car with trailer in tow and headed to Sarasota. Once again, it was a fun trip, and it was a wonderful reunion for her and my parents.

* * *

Because moving to Florida after graduation had been my plan from the beginning, I hadn't really bothered much with trying to get a job in Illinois. Yes, I had gotten my hair cut, and I might have sent out a few resumes, but that was it. And I definitely hadn't applied for any jobs in Florida because someone (I think my mom) told me that no one would consider my resume unless I was already living there. So, after I moved into my mom and dad's condo in Sarasota, and after Elizabeth went back to Illinois, I began looking through the newspapers in search of a computer programming job.

In January of 1988, after about a *week* of sending out resumes, I began feeling a little depressed, like I wasn't going to get a job. I think I had an inferiority complex or something. I mean, a week wasn't very long at all, and my grades in college were good. Plus, I had been trained to design and develop software on the IBM 3090 mainframe computer and the MVS operating system (a very popular computing platform) using Cobol (a very popular programming language). So, why wouldn't I be a good hire?

Fortunately, after a couple more weeks of sending out resumes, I was contacted by three companies who wanted an interview. Two of the companies were in Sarasota, and one was in Clearwater. Clearwater was about an hour and a half north of my mom and dad's place. After interviewing with the three companies and getting three job offers, I decided to accept the job with Software Enterprises, Incorporated in Clearwater.

Before starting my job at Software Enterprises, my mom and dad went to Clearwater with me to help me find an apartment. While we were up there, I found this nice one bedroom apartment about a mile or two from Downtown Clearwater, where Software Enterprises was located. My mom and dad also helped me find some new furniture for the place as I had absolutely no furniture to my name. Because I was completely broke at the time, they loaned me the $1,000 I needed for the stuff. The deal was I would pay them back $200 per month for five months, which is exactly what I did. So, after five months, I was free and clear of my debt to my parents, and I could buy any other stuff I might need debt-free.

One cool thing about my new apartment was that it was Florida-themed. It had matching mauve flamingo-themed couches and beach-themed pictures and lamps. The apartment complex was nice too and came with a swimming pool that I often made use of on the weekends. Another plus was that my apartment was only about three miles from Clearwater Beach.

* * *

Soon after settling into my apartment, I began getting letters from Elizabeth. Almost every day, I would open my mailbox after work, and there would be a letter from her. It made my day every time. I didn't write letters to her quite as often. I probably wrote her once or twice per week, but she was fine with that. I think.

In addition to that mode of communication, we spoke on the phone twice a week—Mondays and Wednesdays. She paid for one of the calls, and I paid for the other. She wasn't too worried about going over the agreed-upon time limit, but I certainly was. So, on the days I was paying for the call, I cut it off pretty quickly when the time was up. In those days, a telephone call between Clearwater, Florida and Normal, Illinois was like $0.40 per minute, so you couldn't talk too long, or you'd have this enormous phone bill. It wasn't like it is now, where you can email or text or video chat as long as you want for free. Man, that would have been nice.

So, even though we were so far apart geographically, we were able to maintain our relationship over the almost 1,200-mile distance.

* * *

At Software Enterprises, I worked with a guy named Paul. Paul was a couple of years older than me, and we became good friends. He and I would frequently go to lunch together in downtown Clearwater, and sometimes we'd go to Pizza Hut to take advantage of their "Get your Personal Pan Pizza in 15 minutes or less, or its free" guarantee, which was valid until 1 pm each day. Unfortunately for Pizza Hut, Paul and I had noticed that they would stop pre-making their Personal Pan Pizzas around 12:30 pm, so they wouldn't have any left over after 1 pm. So, when Paul and I ordered our Personal Pan Pizzas at 12:55 pm, it was pretty much a sure bet that they'd be out of the pre-made ones and, thus, wouldn't have ours ready in time. This translated into free pizzas for both Paul and me. We had no shame. And no. I wouldn't do that anymore.

* * *

After working at Software Enterprises for a couple of weeks or so, I decided to look into replacing the wheels on my 1982 Honda Prelude. The car was still in good shape, but the winters in Illinois, and the salty roads that accompany them, had taken their toll on the alloy wheels. They looked pretty corroded. So, on a sunny Saturday morning in mid-February, I drove over to *Globe Honda* to see what it would cost me to replace them.

As I walked toward the dealership office, I decided to take a quick detour to look at the new 1988 Honda Preludes. One of them was a fully-decked-out Honda Prelude Si 4WS with a fire-engine red exterior and a black interior. It was Honda's top-of-the-line car with 4-wheel steering (not 4-wheel drive), an Alpine stereo system, power doors and windows, and a power sunroof. It was a beautiful car. And it should've been for a sticker price of $21,848, which was a *lot* for a car back then. To put that into perspective, the price was almost one year's salary for me. Although I appreciated how nice it was, I had *no* interest in buying it. And I mean *none.*

As I stood there in the middle of a sea of brand-new cars peeking into the windows of that beautiful Honda Prelude and looking at all its features on the window sticker, this guy walked toward me smoking a cigarette. I immediately knew he was a car salesman. That didn't bother me or anything. I kind of figured someone might come out if they saw me snooping around. The guy was nice, but I assured him that I wasn't in the market for a new car. I was just interested in seeing how far the Preludes had come in six years.

After we talked about the car's features for a few minutes, he asked me if I wanted to take it for a drive. I assured him, again, that I wasn't interested in buying a car today. But when he persisted, I said, "Sure." When I got in and started it up, the first thing I noticed was that it only had seven miles on it. It was brand-spanking new. I was probably the first potential customer to drive it. So, I took the car out solo and drove it around the immediate area for five or ten minutes. It was super nice, but I still wasn't interested. And even if I were, I wouldn't have bought something like that on impulse. That just wasn't me.

When I got back to the dealership, I thanked the guy and handed him the keys. Of course, he wasn't going to let me off the hook so easily. The next words out of his mouth were, "So…what would it take to put you in that car today?" I think he also said something about how good I would look in it. I told him that there was *really* nothing he could say that would make me want to buy the car. I just wasn't in the market for one right now. I was quite content with the car I had. So, in a last-ditch effort to get me to bite, he asked, "What would you give me for the car?" After thinking about how I could *politely* tell the guy, once again, that I wasn't interested, I said, "Okay. I'll give you $10,000 for the car right now." Keep in mind that the sticker price for the car was over twice that. Without flinching, he said he'd go talk to his manager, which is a pretty standard car salesman thing to say.

A short time later, the guy came back outside and said his manager might be able to do something close to that. So, we went inside the dealership, where I sat down with the guy and his manager. After some negotiations, the manager said he would sell me the car for $12,300, which was $100 over what the dealership paid for it, plus my trade in.

The offer put me in a huge conundrum. On the one hand, it seemed like a deal that I couldn't pass up. But on the other hand, I didn't want to be impulsive and buy a car I didn't need and hadn't even thought about until an hour or so earlier. My indecision was intense, so I called my mom and dad and asked them for their input. I don't remember what they said exactly, but it boiled down to the idea that I had spent a lot of time in college, I had worked very hard studying, I had a good-paying job, and I could now afford to have some nice things. I also called Elizabeth to get her input on the situation, but she didn't answer the phone in her dorm room. She was at a friend's farm snowmobiling in good-old-freezing-cold Illinois.

So, after some intense thought, I decided to go for it. I traded in my old Prelude and bought the new one. It was a beautiful car. I waxed it every weekend for months. I kept that car in pristine condition inside and out for as long as I owned it. Not a scratch.

After making that deal, I thought I was the master of negotiations. The truth is, though, I was just in the right place at the right time. Since it was February, the dealership needed to get their 1988 models off the lot to avoid paying inventory taxes on them. Also, since my salesman had worked at the dealership for well over a month and hadn't sold a single car yet, the sales manager was willing to take a hit on the car so the salesman could make some money. That's what the sales manager told me anyway. Unfortunately, when I tried that same low-balling approach at another car dealership a few years later, the sales manager told me to take a hike.

* * *

While I lived in Clearwater, I attended Countryside Christian Center in Safety Harbor, Florida. Countryside was a large church of probably a thousand or so people, and it was very contemporary. The music was very modern, the pastor always gave a relevant and edifying message, and there was a nice mix of children, young adults, middle-aged people, and older folks. After being there for a while, I thought about joining the worship band, but I decided against it. For some reason, I felt like I should put my drumsticks down for a while. I'm not sure why I felt that way. Even today, it doesn't seem like that made any difference in my life. But at the time, that's what I was feeling in my spirit. So, in the two years I attended that church, I never played in that worship band.

One of the drummers in the worship band at Countryside was a guy named Jim. Jim was probably in his middle 50s, and he was an *excellent* drummer. He wasn't fancy, but he was very solid—always playing to the song in a tasteful and undistracting way. During church, I would sometimes watch Jim play, and I would sometimes see *myself* as a man his age playing the drums in a similar worship band. It was like I was seeing him as me in the future. Those "visions" elicited a strange and vaguely depressing feeling in me—like I was getting a small glimpse of the future after a significant part of my life had already passed. The weird thing is, I'm now older than Jim was then.

Because Countryside was such a large church, it was easy to get lost in the crowd on Sunday mornings. Thankfully, there were a lot of other activities you could get involved with. You know, the regular stuff, like Bible studies and fellowship groups. Since I was into staying active, I joined the church's basketball and softball teams.

Clearwater had a big church-league that included churches from all over the area. I loved playing on those teams and really enjoyed getting to know the guys on them. On the softball team, I played shortstop, and on the basketball team, I played wherever I was needed. Since it was a church league, you didn't expect foul language. And 99 percent of the time, that held true. But there was this one basketball team that was very different. It was the team from the Greek Orthodox church. Nice guys, I'm sure, but their language was really bad. It seemed so out of place. Just sayin'.

One night, when we were playing against those guys, I was coming down with a rebound at the same time one of their players was going up. The guy was right under me. When the bottom of my right ribcage connected with the top of his left shoulder, *bam!* Broken ribs. I had never been in so much pain, and I could hardly breathe. Needless to say, I was out of commission for the rest of the game.

The following weekend, I went on a pontoon boat with my parents and some family who were visiting from out of state. I could breathe a little bit better by then, but it still hurt every time I took a deep breath. To survive, I had to take short little breaths. While on the boat, I took this huge swig of Pepsi that immediately gave me a really bad case of hiccups. With every hiccup, I had this excruciating pain in my ribs, and no matter what I tried, I couldn't stop them. It was brutal.

* * *

On many evenings after work, I sat at my hexagonal kitchen table designing and developing software applications. I really enjoyed doing that. Software design and development was not only my profession, but it was my hobby as well. It still is. Since I had money, I bought a brand-new IBM PC XT compatible desktop computer with a 12MHz Intel 80286 microprocessor, a 20-megabyte hard drive, and an orange phosphorus CRT monitor. If you're familiar with today's processing speeds and data storage capacities, you know that that was nothing. But at the time, it was awesome.

I really loved the electromechanical sounds that my computer made while it was booting up—the power supply fan getting up to speed, the beep after a successful power on self-test, and the hard drive spinning as the bootloader loaded the operating system into main memory. And it smelled so good too. I loved the smell of its new plastic, metal, and electronic components. I still love the smell of a brand-new computer. Even today, when I get a new computer, the first thing I do is wave it around under my nose and breathe it in. Don't judge.

* * *

In September of 1988, Mark (my roommate from college who liked to watch Cardinals baseball when he studied) was getting married, and I had made plans to travel back to Illinois to participate in his wedding as a groomsman. By this time, my relationship with Elizabeth had progressed—despite the geographical distance. As the date for the trip drew closer, thoughts of proposing to Elizabeth kept popping into my head. When the thoughts surfaced, I would always say to myself, "No. I'm not going to ask her to marry me." I don't know why I had such strong feelings about that. I mean, I was crazy about her. Maybe it was because we hadn't been dating all that long. It had only been a year or so.

Anyway, a few days before the wedding, I flew up to Bloomington. At the airport, I was picked up by Elizabeth and our college friend Dan in Dan's big yellow car we called "The Banana Boat." That evening, the three of us spent the night at Dan's parents' farmhouse in Bethany, Illinois. The next morning, we all got ready and drove over to Decatur, where Mark's fiancé, Karen, was from and where the wedding was to be held. That afternoon, we attended the wedding. It was Labor Day weekend.

After the wedding reception, Dan drove us up to Elizabeth's house in Chicagoland. A couple weeks earlier, Elizabeth had made plans for us to go on a dinner cruise on Lake Michigan with two other couples— Joanne and her boyfriend, Ken, and Zohreh and Dan. Joanne and Zohreh were Elizabeth's friends from high school, and since Elizabeth wanted Zohreh to meet Dan, she had paired them up for the evening. It was a triple date.

On the evening of the cruise, Zohreh and Dan and Elizabeth and I traveled to downtown Chicago in Dan's car and boarded the ship. Just in case you didn't know, Chicago is called the Windy City. And on the night of the cruise, it was more than a little windy. It was *very* windy. I'm not sure why I didn't see it coming, but high winds and boats don't usually make for a good time. Anyway, shortly after we got on the boat, dinner was served. As expected, the food was fantastic! They had these awesome Greek sandwiches with meat, feta cheese, onions, oregano, vinegar and oil—all that stuff. Delicious! I had two great big ones.

During the cruise, the ship was being tossed around like a toy boat in a bathtub. After a while, I started feeling extremely nauseous, so I told Elizabeth that I needed some fresh air. After excusing myself from our table, I rushed outside to the wooden deck and stood next to the steel railing overlooking the dark, choppy water. Within seconds, I was vomiting over the side of the boat. Those delicious sandwiches were gone forever. It was a huge disappointment.

Now before you think I was a huge wimp, you should know that at least half the people on that boat got seasick as well. In fact, the waters were so rough, and so many people were throwing up, that the captain was forced to take the ship back to land.

Anyway, soon after my bout with reverse peristalsis, Elizabeth came outside to see how I was doing. I was feeling a little better by then, and I was trying to keep it that way by focusing my attention on the bright and colorful lights of the Chicago skyline. Unfortunately, as Elizabeth stood next to me on the deck with her back against the ship's railing, a huge wave of cold, murky water splashed up over the side of the boat and soaked her from head to toe.

Since I was feeling a little better, I asked Elizabeth to go up to the upper deck of the boat with me for a few minutes because I wanted to ask her something. But because she was so wet and cold, she didn't want to go up there. However, when I told her it would only take a minute, she acquiesced. Unfortunately, it was *really* too cold and windy for her, so we went back downstairs and into the boat's dining room.

I had missed my chance to ask her a life-changing question. Once we got off the boat, I began feeling a lot better. What a relief!

* * *

When we got back to Elizabeth's house, Dan went upstairs to bed, but Elizabeth and I stayed downstairs talking. After talking for a while, I knew the time was right. I knew I loved her and wanted to marry her, so I got down on one knee and asked her to marry me. As we looked into each other's eyes, she said, "Yes." I can't fully express the joy and happiness her response brought me at that moment, but I was on top of the world. That night, we agreed that I would ask her dad for her hand in marriage in the morning.

When the next morning arrived, we all had breakfast together—Elizabeth's mom and dad, Dan, and Elizabeth and me. After breakfast, I told her mom and dad that I wanted to speak with them for a minute, so Dan went back upstairs, where he and I had slept the night before. I'm pretty sure Elizabeth's dad knew what was happening because he *slowly* made himself a cup of tea and then he *slowly* sat down in his chair at the kitchen table. I think he was torturing me on purpose. Whatever it was, he wasn't in a hurry. He was definitely moving slower than usual.

I don't remember my exact words, but they were something along the lines of, "I love Elizabeth, and I'd like to marry her. May I have her hand in marriage?" Sounds kind of mushy to me now, but that's basically what I said. Lucky for me, her dad immediately said, "Yes," stood up, and shook my hand, and her mom gave me a big hug. They both seemed genuinely good with it. We were officially engaged. The date was September 4th, 1988.

* * *

In mid-December, after Elizabeth had graduated from college, her dad, her brothers, and one of her sisters helped her pack up her things and move to Florida to be with me. We found her an apartment very close to mine that we could live in together after we got married. It was a nice two-bedroom two-bath place, so we could have company over for the night if we wanted to.

When the lease on *my* apartment was up, I moved in with Helen—the woman who was my next-door neighbor when I was in the fourth grader in Creve Coeur, Missouri. By this time, Helen was probably in her 80s and had been widowed for a second time. I never knew her second husband. In fact, I had completely lost touch with her until I had moved to Clearwater. My mom and dad, on the other hand, *had* kept in contact with Helen over the years, and when they told her that I had moved Clearwater, she said she'd love to see me. So, I contacted her and would often visit with her in her home, where she lived all by herself.

Helen seemed genuinely happy to have me at her house. I think she felt less lonely having someone else around. Of course, I was equally happy to have a place to stay for five months until the wedding. I really enjoyed my time with Helen. She made me some wonderful dinners, and we often watched television together in the evenings when I wasn't with Elizabeth.

* * *

In April of 1989, about three weeks before the wedding, Elizabeth traveled back to her parents' house in Des Plaines to finalize her plans for the big event. While there, she was in frequent communication with my aunts, Barb and Brinda, who were helping her take care of things in Champaign, which was about two hours or so south of Des Plaines. Elizabeth and I had decided to get married in Champaign because most of my family and friends lived in the Champaign-Urbana area, and most of our college friends lived not too far away in the Bloomington-Normal area.

My aunts were such a blessing to Elizabeth. They found someone to bake the wedding cake, they ordered the flowers, they found a hotel for the reception, and they decorated the church sanctuary on the day of the ceremony. They took care of many other details as well. While Elizabeth was in Illinois getting things ready for the wedding, I moved out of Helen's house and into her (soon to be our) apartment. It was an exciting time.

* * *

On the day of our wedding, May 6th, 1989, it snowed in Champaign, which is a rare occurrence in Illinois at that time of year. It was fine for me, though, because tuxedos can get very hot. I was just glad it wasn't 85 degrees and 90 percent humidity. Otherwise, I would have been miserable in that thing. The wedding took place at St. Peter's United

Church of Christ in Champaign—a beautiful and historic church. The ceremony was beautiful as well with many family members and friends in attendance. (I think it's noteworthy that I married a woman whose favorite number was eight. Remember the significance of that number from the beginning of the first chapter of this book?)

My best man that day was Libero (friend from high school, college apartment mate, and Judah soundman). My other groomsmen were Ron (friend from high school), Mark (college roommate and college apartment mate), Dick (college apartment mate, Judah and Skylight Band bandmate, and Skylight Band soundman), and Kent (first cousin once removed and Judah and Skylight Band soundman). The ushers were John (Elizabeth's youngest sibling) and Darrell (first cousin once removed and farm employer). And the ringbearers were Joshua Robert and Andrew David (nephews).

I participated in some of *their* weddings as well. I was Libero's and Ron's best man, I was a groomsman for Mark, and I was an usher for Kent. I participated in some *other* weddings as well. I was a groomsman for a guy named Tim (friend from my childhood), I was an usher for Nick (ex-brother-in-law), and I was the scripture reader for Todd (first cousin). I was almost a groomsman for Dick, but his wedding day was the same as Ron's. Thus, I had to decline the offer. Yes, sir! There was a whole lotta marrying going on back then, and I was honored to be a part of those special days—except for the tuxedo bills. I had a lot of good friends.

Our wedding reception took place at the Century 21 Hotel (now called the University Inn) in Champaign. The hotel was a beautiful, 21-story high-rise building with a classy reception room in the basement. During the reception, we had music, dancing, a wonderful dinner, and the obligatory cake-cutting and wedding-garter-tossing events.

One of the most beautiful things about that day was how virtually everyone who loved us was there celebrating with and focusing on us. As I looked over the crowd of a hundred family members and friends during the reception, I remember thinking that this must be how God feels when everyone who loves him is focusing on him in worship. The day couldn't have been better. It was the best day of my life.

* * *

After the wedding, Elizabeth and I flew back to Florida, packed up a few things, got into my (now our) 1988 Honda Prelude, and headed north to Hilton Head, South Carolina for our honeymoon. My mom and dad owned a timeshare condo on Siesta Key Beach in Sarasota at the time, so they exchanged two weeks of their condo time for two weeks of condo time at two different resorts in Hilton Head. It was a wonderful wedding gift, and we had a fantastic time there. We went horseback riding, played miniature golf, hung out at the pool, went to the beach, and ate dinner at a different ethic restaurant each evening.

One evening while we were dining out, I told Elizabeth that I was feeling the urge to go to graduate school to get a master's degree. I had been thinking for a while that I should get a master's degree, get a job as a database administrator, and double my salary. I got the idea about database administration from our database administrator at Software Enterprises. I saw the kind of work he was doing, and I knew that guys like him were making a lot more money than I was making.

Anyway, the idea came as a complete surprise to Elizabeth. She had no idea I had been thinking about that. Up to that point, our plan was that she would get a full-time job, we would save all the money she made, and then, after three years, we would use that money to make a healthy down payment on a house in Clearwater. I remembered the plan, but the desire to go to graduate school had only recently become strong for some reason. As I look back on it now, I see that emerging desire to get a master's degree as another guidepost God used to direct me toward the *career* he had in store for me.

* * *

After waking up in our honeymoon condo one morning, I suddenly remembered that my grandpa Jack had given me some money as a wedding gift. During the reception at the hotel, he walked up to me, put his hand in his pocket, pulled out a big wad of cash, and placed it into my hand. And, as if to say, "Do *not* lose this!", he cupped my hand in both of his and squeezed.

Well…I *did* lose it. Evidently, I hadn't taken the roll of bills out of the pocket of my slacks when I returned the tuxedo. It was probably a lot of cash too because my grandparents used to send me two whole dollars every year for my birthday, and this was a *much* bigger occasion.

I bet it was at least 20 bucks. Just kidding. I'm sure my grandpa was being very generous. But I bet I made someone's day when they found all that money in the pants of my tuxedo at the men's clothing store. The lesson I learned that day? Don't be an idiot.

About two or three days before the two weeks of our honeymoon were over, Elizabeth and I got a little bored with living such lives of luxury and were ready to get back to the real world. So, we packed it up, drove down to Orlando to spend some time with my parents who were attending some kind of health conference there, and then drove home to Clearwater, where we began our *real* lives together in our little apartment. Life was good.

* * *

As a married couple, Elizabeth and I began to have married-couple friends. So, sometimes we would have a couple over to our place for dinner, and sometimes a couple would have us over to their place for dinner. The majority of the couples we hung out with back then were from our church, Countryside Christian Center, where we were part of a young married couple's group.

But that didn't mean I neglected my single friends. In particular, I was still good friends with Paul from Software Enterprises. Just like with our married-couple friends, we would sometimes invite Paul to our apartment for dinner, and he would sometimes invite us to his apartment for dinner. The only negative thing about our times with Paul was that the conversation in the room usually gravitated toward computer programming—a subject that Elizabeth had absolutely no interest in. But she sat there with Paul and me, nodded her head, and acted like she was enjoying the conversation. I found out *years* later, however, that she didn't understand a thing we were saying. She was just being a supportive wife.

* * *

After Elizabeth and I talked more and prayed about my graduate school vision, we decided to go for it. She was very supportive. So that summer, I applied for graduate school at Illinois State University—our alma mater. Since I had good grades as an undergraduate student and decent Graduate Record Examination scores, I was accepted into the master's program in applied computer science by my old department.

I also received a teaching assistantship, where I would teach a section of Introduction to Computer Science each semester. In exchange for teaching the course, I would receive free tuition and a monthly stipend for living expenses. It wasn't much money, but it would be enough as long as Elizabeth could find a job as well.

It was all set. At the end of December, I would put in my two-week notice at Software Enterprises and move back to Normal, Illinois to begin graduate school.

Paris Hospital in
Paris, Illinois
where I was
born. The place
is an apartment
building now.

About to go home from
the hospital. Me, Mom,
Grandpa Jack, and Dawn.

My maternal grandparents. Donald
and Virginia McCumber.

A very early family portrait. Dawn, Mom, Dad, and me.

Playing with cars and trucks on the couch. It was one of my favorite things to do.

Riding a two-wheeler. Looks like it was my sister's bike.

At Knott's Berry Farm in California. You can see my mom in the background keeping a close eye on me.

Playing football. A friend (I don't remember his name), me, and Jeff.

Fourth grade school photo. On the back, I wrote, "Beautiful, ain't I?" Horn-rimmed glasses were the style.

Seventh grade school photo. Notice the wire-rimmed, aviator-style glasses. The lenses got darker in the sun.

Eighth-grade graduation photo. Too bad my shoes aren't showing. The heels were probably two inches high. Disco was the style.

My yellow 1971 Chevrolet Vega. My first car.

Tuscola Review newspaper clipping of my dad and me as winners of the Junior-Senior Doubles Tennis Tournament the summer after my sophomore year of high school.

Tuscola Review newspaper clipping of my high school baseball team my junior year. I'm in the back row, third from the left.

Tuscola Review newspaper clipping of me playing basketball on my high school basketball team my senior year. I'm on the right shooting the ball.

My forest green 1970 Chevrolet Monte Carlo. I loved that car.

Official high school graduation photo. I never liked this picture. Although the brown corduroy suit was nice, it wasn't a good hair day.

Judah promotional photo. Paul, Cliff, Tim, Robert, and me.

Judah in concert. Cliff, Robert, me, Tim, and Carlos.

The Skylight Band promotional photo. Tim, Robert, Carlos, and me.

The Skylight Band in concert. Me, Tim, Rod, Carlos, and Robert.

Drumming in the Skylight Band. That's still the look I have on my face when I play the drums.

My and Elizabeth's tickets to the concert where we met in person for the very first time.

Before getting my hair cut off. I got the haircut because I would be graduating from college the following year, and I wanted to look presentable for job interviews.

Cornerstone '87, where I first started thinking Elizabeth might like me.

On the day Elizabeth and I officially started dating.

In my dorm room at Illinois State University on move in day. I was just getting ready for my last semester of college.

Elizabeth and me in the hallway of our dorm at Illinois State University. The shadow on the wall is a painting of me that someone did as part of our dorm's theme.

In front of my first apartment in Clearwater, Florida after graduating from college. Notice my brand-new red 1988 Honda Prelude Si 4WS.

Elizabeth and me at a friend's wedding the day before we got engaged.

Heading out to playing church league softball for Countryside Christian Center in Clearwater, Florida.

Elizabeth and me at our wedding rehearsal.

Elizabeth and me as a newly minted married couple. It was the best day of my life.

Our official family picture. Elizabeth and me with my parents, my sister, and her three children Andy, Katie, and Josh.

My groomsmen and me. Dick, Kent, Mark, Ron, Libero, and me.

Newlyweds.

The 1990s

54 68 65 20 31 39 39 30 73

In January of 1990, Elizabeth and I packed everything we owned into a moving truck and attached our car to it using a car dolly. On the day of the move, she moved in with Helen, and I took off for good old Normal, Illinois in the truck. Elizabeth couldn't move to Normal with me because she still had a job as a mathematics and computing teacher at a private school in Largo called Harvest Temple Christian School, and she didn't want to quit until the semester was over. So, when I got to Normal, I found a nice little apartment for us a couple of miles north of the Illinois State University campus.

When Elizabeth's semester was over, she flew up to Chicago, and her dad drove her down to Normal. Elizabeth says she didn't like that apartment, but I thought it was pretty nice. It was freshly painted and had brand-new carpeting, so what's not to like? Evidently, she thought the kitchen was too small, didn't like the avocado green appliances, and didn't like the fact that both the kitchen and dining areas were carpeted. Oh well. I tried. We didn't have cell phones back then, so it's not like I could just take some pictures or videos of all the apartments I looked at and send them to her before deciding on a place. But in the end, we made the best of it.

Shortly after settling into our apartment, I started graduate school at Illinois State University working toward a master's degree in applied computer science. Elizabeth, on the other hand, got a temp job at State Farm Insurance in Bloomington through Kelly Temporary Services. When her assignment with State Farm Insurance was complete, she began working as the receptionist at Eastview Christian Church—the parent church of New Community. Although I was working part time as a teaching assistant, and she was working full time as a receptionist, we didn't make enough money to make the payments on our Honda Prelude. We were going to have to get rid of it.

It was tough getting rid of that car. It was the last car that I really "cared" about. Of course, there have been vehicles that I've liked since then, but the cars that I owned up to that point in my life were kind of "important" to me—if that makes any sense. I think my priorities in life were just changing. I was more of a family man now. So, from that point forward, I just bought vehicles that were nice yet cost-effective and would get Elizabeth and me from Point A to Point B.

* * *

In the two years we were away from Normal, New Community had exploded in popularity. There were now somewhere between two and three hundred college students, young adults, and families attending each Sunday morning. It had multiplied 10-fold and had moved from the church's little chapel to its large and fully carpeted gymnasium. It was a much bigger production as well—with a setup team, welcome team, sound team, and so on. When we returned, the people who knew us from before were thrilled that we were back. Of course, we were excited to be back as well.

Shortly after our return to New Community, the drummer of the worship band announced that he and his wife were moving, so I was asked to rejoin the band. It was great being involved in that ministry again, especially since many of the same guys and girls were still in the group. It was also good to be drumming again, since I hadn't picked up a set of drumsticks in a couple of years.

One of my bandmates was a guy named Matthew. Matthew was a very calm and thoughtful person, and he was an excellent piano player. But he also wanted to learn how to play the drums, so he asked me to give him some lessons. During the lessons, we worked on the basics of good timekeeping and the fundamentals of using "fills" to signal the transitions that occur between the different parts of a song—like the verses, choruses, and bridges. Since Matthew didn't have his own drum set to practice on, he asked me if he could practice on mine, which I left set up on the stage in the gymnasium of the church. I told him he could, but on one condition: If he broke anything, he had to replace it.

The only reason I made it conditional was because Matthew hit the drums really hard when he played, which was a little odd given his mild disposition. Maybe the physicality of the drums provided some kind of release for his pent-up frustrations or something. Anyway, after our very first drum lesson together, I left Matthew alone with my drum set because he wanted to practice on his own. The next time I went to the church, there sat my drum set—with millions of tiny woodchips all over it. Matthew had hit the edges of my metal alloy cymbals so hard that my wooden drumsticks had been chewed to pieces. And there, right on top of my snare drum, sat a brand-new pair of drumsticks— exactly like the ones he had ruined. He was a man of his word.

* * *

When I lived in Florida by myself, I often came home from work, turned on the TV, and relaxed for the evening. I watched all kinds of shows, but I especially liked the crime shows—like *Cops* and *America's Most Wanted*. I also became a bit of a news junky, so I probably watched two or three news programs every evening. Unfortunately, this habit followed me into marriage.

One evening, while I was watching the news in our new apartment in Normal, Elizabeth was doing something in the kitchen and trying to talk to me. Of course, this annoyed me, so I asked her if she could wait until the news was over. After this happened two or three more times during my news-watching binge, my wife of less than a year said, "You never talk to me anymore!" To that, I intelligently replied, "Yes, I do! During commercials!" Yes. I heard myself say those exact words. Uh, huh. Yeah.

Over the next week or so, I became increasingly convicted of my priorities in those areas, so I put the television in our front room closet. To this day, our television sits in a closet on a rolling cart and is only brought out a few times a week when we want to watch something.

* * *

As part of my teaching assistantship at Illinois State University, I was given a small office on campus, where I could study, prepare for lectures, meet with students, and work on my research. At the time, I knew absolutely *nothing* about teaching. I had never taken a course on how to teach, I was never part of a group of new graduate students who received instruction on how to teach, and the professor I reported to never gave me any ideas or tips on how to teach. Nothing. So, I just wrote out my lectures on a yellow pad of paper and read them off in class. Wow! I cringe when I think about it now. I'm sure it was awful. But I don't remember anyone complaining. Of course, the operative word here is "remember," and my selective memory is pretty good. However, I was able to keep my job until I graduated, so maybe it wasn't as bad as I think it was. No. I'm pretty sure it was.

Although I don't think I was a good teacher at the time, I enjoyed the job quite a bit. I think the part I liked most was studying, learning, and having the opportunity to explain what I had learned to others. I really liked the feeling of being scholarly.

* * *

As I sat in our apartment one day, an idea popped into my head. It was very all of a sudden and out of the blue. But it was more than just an idea because it came with the motivation to act on it right away. This time, I felt stirred to investigate the possibility of earning a Ph.D. in computer science and becoming a college professor.

The strange thing was, I had *never* thought about becoming a college professor until that moment. Never. When I sat in my classes in college and watched my professors teach, I never once thought I wanted to do that. And even as I taught my Introduction to Computer Science course, being a college professor wasn't on my radar. My teaching job was simply a means to an end—to help pay the bills until I could get a high-paying job as a database administrator. Of course, now I see that episode as another guidepost that God placed in my path to direct me toward the *career* he had in store for me.

I will say this, though, when I was a kid, I was almost always drawn to the characters in cartoons, TV shows, movies, and books who were professors. I mean, I never thought about being one someday. They were always dorky nerds, but I liked what they did. They were always building something, conducting an experiment, solving some kind of practical problem, teaching something about the physical world, or explaining how something worked. To me, they were the interesting people in the story.

In cartoons, I liked Mr. Peabody in *The Adventures of Rocky and Bullwinkle*. In TV shows, I liked The Professor (played by Russell Johnson) in *Gilligan's Island*. In movies, I liked Professor Ned Brainard (played by Fred MacMurray) in *The Absent-Minded Professor*, Professor Julius Kelp (played by Jerry Lewis) in *The Nutty Professor*, Dr. Henry "Indiana" Jones (played by Harrison Ford) in *Raiders of the Lost Ark*, and Drs. Egon Spengler (played by Harold Ramis), Ray Stantz (played by Dan Aykroyd), and Peter Venkman (played by Bill Murray) in *Ghostbusters*. And in books, I liked Professor Otto Liedenbrock in *Journey to the Center of the Earth*. Am I right? Aren't all those characters pretty interesting?

* * *

So, sometime in early 1991, I investigated two Ph.D. programs in computer science. One was at Iowa State University, and the other was at the University of Illinois at Urbana-Champaign. Since multimedia design and development was my area of interest, I wanted to continue my research in that area. So, I made an appointment to speak with a professor in the Computer Science Department at the U of I, which was about an hour or so from our apartment in Normal. During our conversation, he kindly explained to me that my research area wasn't a traditional computer science research area and that it was unlikely that a professor in his department would be interested in working with me in that particular area. However, he told me that another department on campus had a Ph.D. program in Computer Assisted Instruction that seemed more along the lines of what I was looking for.

After thanking the professor for meeting with me, I drove across campus and met with a professor in the Department of Curriculum and Instruction who just happened to be in his office that day. He was very supportive of my research interests, thought I would be a great fit in his department, and encouraged me to apply for the fall semester. Needless to say, I felt very good about our conversation.

When I got back home, I completed my application for the Ph.D. program in Computer Assisted Instruction at the University of Illinois and mailed it in. Within a couple of months, I received an acceptance letter. I was in, and I was *very* excited about it.

Since I had been accepted into the Ph.D. program at that University of Illinois, I didn't bother pursuing Iowa State University any further. All I had done with them anyway was request and review the literature about their Ph.D. program in computer science. I didn't need to cancel a trip to Ames or anything. No. I was more than happy to be attending the U of I. That's where I wanted to go.

Since I would be attending the University of Illinois in the fall, and since I had heard Elizabeth talk about getting a master's degree before, I encouraged her to apply for graduate school at the U of I as well. She did and was soon accepted into the Master of Science in the Teaching of Mathematics program.

* * *

Toward the end of the spring semester, I was ready to defend my master's thesis. The title of my thesis was *The Identification of Navigation Patterns in a Multimedia Environment: A Case Study in an Introductory Course in Artificial Intelligence*. The purpose of my thesis was to determine the effects of scholastic aptitude and gender on learner navigation through multimedia/hypermedia systems.[5] A hypermedia system is a collection of interconnected documents that can contain text, audio, images, and video. Wikipedia is a good example of a hypermedia system. But there was no Wikipedia back then! So, I had to design and develop my own little hypermedia system for my research using a software development environment called LinkWay. Hypermedia systems were cutting edge.

The interesting thing about my thesis defense was that probably 20 people showed up to witness it. That was an unusually high number, and it made me a little nervous. Normally, the only people present at a thesis defense are your thesis committee members and maybe one or two other people who have an interest in your topic. But besides the three professors on my committee, several other people showed up, including some of the other professors in my department and a good number of other graduate students. Elizabeth was there as well. I think

---

[5] From this point forward, I'll refer to *multimedia* systems and *hypermedia* systems interchangeably. It probably would have been more accurate to use the term hypermedia in my masters thesis research.

so many people showed up because hypermedia computing was such a hot topic. (Okay, *maybe* my graduate school advisor, Dr. Vila, invited some of his colleagues to the defense, and *maybe* he offered his graduate students some extra credit for showing up or something. But…since I'll never really know, and since I like the "hot topic" story better, I'm going with that.)

I thought I did a pretty good job of answering the questions posed by my committee members. But I had a really hard time understanding a question posed by one particular committee member. His question made *no* sense to me. And since I had *no* idea what he was talking about, I went blank. Eventually, I asked him if he could ask the question in a different way. Although he attempted to restate the question a couple of times, I still *wasn't* getting it. Although my other two committee members attempted to rephrase the question for him, he said that their questions were not really what he was asking. So, I felt vindicated. It wasn't just me. The whole time, Elizabeth knew *exactly* what he was asking and almost couldn't hold it in. But the only ones allowed to ask questions during the defense were the professors on my committee.

When the defense was over, everyone was asked to leave the room so my thesis committee could confer about the quality of my research and defense. In the hallway, Elizabeth told me what the professor was asking. I wish she could have spoken up because I had a good answer for him. A few minutes later, I was called back into the room, where my committee congratulated me on a job well done. I was relieved by their positive response and was thrilled to finally be done!

Two or three weeks after my defense, in May of 1991, I finished up my coursework and graduated from Illinois State University with a Master of Science degree in applied computer science.

* * *

As soon as I was done at Illinois State University, Elizabeth and I drove to Urbana to find a place to live. We found a very nice apartment about two miles east of the University of Illinois campus. A few weeks later, we moved into it with the help of my cousin Kent.

To make the place a little homier, my mom drove up from Tuscola to help us wallpaper the kitchen and dining area using duck-themed wallpaper.[6] Elizabeth liked this place a lot more than the place we had in Normal. She especially liked that the kitchen floor wasn't carpeted, the kitchen and dining areas were larger, and the living room had a big double window that looked out over the large courtyard that separated the buildings of the apartment complex. It was a little more expensive than our previous apartment, but it *was* nicer and more modern.

A huge bonus of our new apartment complex was that it had a nice swimming pool. We made good use of that pool during our summers in Urbana. The complex manager kept it very clean, and it seemed like very few people used it—besides us. We pretty much had the pool to ourselves most of the time.

* * *

Shortly after settling into our apartment in Urbana, I began looking for some kind of assistantship that would pay my tuition and provide a stipend for living expenses. I started the process by speaking with one of the professors in my new department, who connected me with someone else, who connected me with someone else, and so on. I was finally connected with a woman named Deb at the United States Army Construction Engineering Research Laboratory in Champaign. Deb was looking for a research assistant. After being interviewed by her and a couple of other folks in her division at USACERL, I was offered the job, and I promptly accepted.

The agreement was that, during the school year, I would work 10 hours per week, and during the summers, I would work full time—if I wanted to. And if I needed a little time off to study for final exams or something, they would be flexible. It was a great deal because, not only would they let me work as much or as little as I wanted, but they would also cover my tuition and pay me an hourly wage that was significantly higher than the hourly wage I was paid at Illinois State University.

Thankfully, Elizabeth found an assistantship as well. When school started, she would be working 20 hours per week in a place called the Teaching Techniques Lab. Now we were all set. Our tuition would be paid, and we would both have an income to pay our bills.

* * *

---

[6] Although my parents had moved from Tuscola to Florida in 1986, they had moved back in 1989. They moved back to Florida permanently in 1993.

In the late summer of 1991, Elizabeth and I started graduate school at the University of Illinois. The very first class I attended convened on Monday evenings from 6 pm to 9 pm. Although I don't remember the name of the course, part of the course was learning HyperCard. HyperCard was a programming language used to design and develop hypermedia applications for the Apple Macintosh and Apple IIGS computers.

I'll never forget the assignment my professor gave us on that first evening. He assigned the first 400 pages of a 932-page book called *The Complete HyperCard 2.0 Handbook* by Danny Goodman. We were to read it by the following Monday evening. Right then and there, I knew this was on a different level than my bachelor's and master's degrees were. As it turned out, however, reading that particular 400 pages wasn't as bad as I thought it was going to be. Since the book was a programming language manual, and since I had already learned several programming languages, all I had to do was familiarize myself with what was in the book and how the book was organized. HyperCard contained many of the same functions I was already familiar with, so I was able to skim over a lot of it.

* * *

As Deb's research assistant at USACERL, I traveled to a number of academic conferences and research labs to learn all I could about the newest trends in technology and how those trends could be applied to computer-assisted training. It was an honor meeting with some of the leading researchers in the world at Purdue University, Harvard, and the Massachusetts Institute of Technology.

While working for Deb, I also helped design a new user interface for the Geographic Resources Analysis Support System—a geographic information system originally developed at USACERL. Before I got involved with the project, GRASS had a completely command-line-driven user interface. Back then, graphical user interfaces, like the ones you see on computers today, were a relatively new thing, so someone had the idea of creating a GUI for GRASS. It turned out very well and made using GRASS much easier.

* * *

Although Elizabeth and I were very busy with our classes and our assistantships, we *did* have lives outside of school and work. Soon after moving to Urbana, we began attending Stratford Park Bible Chapel in Champaign—mostly because I knew some people from my childhood who went there. The people at SPBC were very welcoming and mature in their faith, and Pastor Lee gave excellent sermons. (Lee and his wife, Carol Lee, would soon become life-long friends.)

The vast majority of the people at Stratford Park Bible Chapel were probably in their 50s or older, and probably a quarter were in their 70s or older. There were only a few young couples and young families at the time. And, of the young folks that that *did* attend SPBS, most were graduate students who would almost certainly attend the Church while at the University and then move away after graduating. SPBC was the polar opposite of New Community in terms of demographics.

Stratford Park Bible Chapel was also very different in terms of the music. The music at SPBC was exclusively old hymns accompanied by an organ and a piano. There were no guitars or horns or bongos or anything like that. Just organ and piano. So, after we had attended there for a while, I offered to play the drums on Sunday mornings. The ladies who played the organ and piano on Sundays *loved* the idea, so I brought my drums in, set them up on the stage, and played along with the organ and piano on Sunday mornings. I didn't use drumsticks. That would have been entirely too loud. Instead, I used brushes to keep the volume down. Of course, playing the drums at SPBC wasn't nearly as fun as playing the drums in some of the other bands I had played with up to that point. But I still enjoyed contributing to the worship service in that way.

Not too long after that, I was made aware of a musical opportunity at another church in Champaign. Meadowbrook Community Church was a much larger and much younger church than Stratford Park Bible Chapel, and their worship music was contemporary. Since my cousin Kent was a soundman there, and since he knew I was back in town, he contacted me and told me that Elizabeth and I should visit MCC and that I should consider joining their worship band.

So, a week or two later, Elizabeth and I attended a worship service at Meadowbrook. After the service, I spoke with several people on the worship team—some of whom I knew from my Judah and Skylight Band days. The urge to join Meadowbrook and be a part of a really good worship team was pretty strong that morning. The people I spoke with were enthusiastic about me joining the team, and it would be a lot more fun for me. But after Elizabeth and I prayed about it for a week or two, we felt God leading us to stay at Stratford Park Bible Chapel to be a young couple there.

* * *

In January of 1992, I met a guy from Taiwan named Mike. Mike wasn't his real name, but since it was much easier for Americans to say Mike than his Chinese name, he just went by Mike. Mike and I met in a statistics class, and we quickly became friends. Mike was also studying for his Ph.D. degree—but in computational linguistics. Since there was some overlap in our respective programs of study, we had a couple of other statistics classes together as well. During the time Mike and I were at the University of Illinois together (he graduated the year before I did), he told me several times that I would go to Taiwan someday to see his beautiful country. Of course, I thought that would be awesome, but I seriously doubted that such a trip would ever materialize.

Because Mike wasn't a native English speaker (his first language was Mandarin Chinese), he would sometimes say things in class that would strike some of us as humorous. One time, on a beautiful sunny day in March or April, the windows of our classroom were wide open to let in some fresh air. When our professor walked in, Mike's hand shot straight up. Seeing Mike's hand, the professor said, "Yes?" With a big smile on his face, Mike announced in his best English, "Spring is here!" The professor chuckled and in agreement said, "Yes, it is!".

A few weeks later, our professor walked into the classroom with a brand-new haircut. He had obviously gotten it cut over the weekend, and it was very short. Once again, Mike's hand shot up. The professor looked at Mike and said, "Yes?" With a big smile on his face, Mike declared, "You look handsome!" The professor reacted like he was a little surprised by the compliment (and maybe a little embarrassed by the attention), but he maintained his composure and said with a smile, "Why, thank you!"

* * *

At the beginning of the summer, after my first year at the University of Illinois, I was assigned to a different team at USACERL. This time, I was assigned to the Utilities Modernization Team, which was part of the Energy and Utility Systems Division. The team included me and about a dozen construction, mechanical, and energy engineers. It was a great team to be a part of. It really jelled. As for my role on the team, I was the software developer. So, I basically spent every day designing and developing engineering software for the team. It was one of the most enjoyable jobs I've ever had.

Although I designed and developed several engineering software systems for the Utilities Modernization Team, the most significant one was the Renewables and Energy Efficiency Planning system. REEP evaluated the impact of current energy- and water-saving technologies (e.g., compact fluorescent lights, window films, waterless urinals) on US military installations in terms of their potential for energy and water reduction, pollution abatement, and cost savings.

The impact of REEP was significant. In the 1990s, REEP played a major role in the Department of Defense's energy planning strategy and was used at the US congressional level to allocate billions of dollars in energy- and water-saving improvements across all the US military installations in the world.

* * *

The first summer we lived in Urbana, Elizabeth and I played on Stratford Park Bible Chapel's church-league softball team. It was a lot of fun, and it was nice to be able to do that together. I played second base, and she played catcher—at least until she broke her toe. I also played for Li'l Porgy's Bar-B-Q—a men's team in the Champaign Park District league. For Li'l Porgy's, I played shortstop. After one season, I decided to stop playing for SPBC and concentrate my efforts on Li'l Porgy's.

I really loved playing softball in the summers when I was in graduate school at the University of Illinois. The great thing about softball was that pretty much everyone hit the ball. So as an infielder, especially as the shortstop, I got a lot of balls hit to me. It wasn't like in high school baseball, where I *might* get a few balls hit to me during a game. No. A *lot* of balls were hit my way, so it was much more fun.

Although I was a slender guy at 6'2" tall and 165 pounds, I could generate a lot of swing speed. Thus, I could hit the ball pretty hard. In fact, during baseball practice in high school, I sometimes hit home runs over the fence, which was like 320 feet. Unfortunately, I never hit one in a real game. Anyway, when I stepped up to the plate in softball, the outfielders would sometimes move in about 20 yards, perhaps thinking that a lanky guy like me couldn't hit the ball all that far. Of course, they were quite surprised when I belted one over their heads (although not over the fence). That usually resulted in at least a triple.

Li'l Porgy's was a very good softball team. Part of the reason was because the coach, who also happened to be the owner of Li'l Porgy's, kept on-base records. Whoever had the highest on-base average batted first, whoever had the second highest on-base average batted second, and so on. This, of course, increased the probability of scoring runs. For the three summers I played on the Li'l Porgy's softball team, we were the Men's Recreation Division Champs.

* * *

In September of 1992, our first son, Zachariah John, was born at Covenant Hospital in Urbana. It was an absolutely beautiful day with clear skies and temperatures in the low 70s. In the afternoon before he was born, Elizabeth had started having regular contractions, and they were getting closer and closer together. As we sat in the living room together, she told me that it wouldn't be long before we could go to the hospital to have the baby. As can be imagined, I was very excited.

As I sat there with Elizabeth, I kept looking at the clock on the wall and asking her how close together her contractions were getting. She told me to calm down and that we would go soon. She wanted to wait another 30 minutes until she was sure it was time because she didn't want to get to the hospital only to be told to go home. So, when the 30 minutes had elapsed, I jumped up and said, "Okay! Let's go!" When she said that she wanted to wait just a little bit longer, I said, "But you said we could go! Your 30 minutes are up!" I had forgotten who was having the baby.

Not too long after that, we went to the hospital and settled into the delivery room. Several hours later, Zach was born. At the moment of Zach's birth, I wept. I had *no* idea I would respond that way. It took me completely by surprise. Although I was a little embarrassed by my response, Zach's birth was a transformative experience for me. I don't want this to sound too weird or anything, but I want to tell it exactly like it was—no holding back and no exaggeration. At the moment of Zach's birth, something changed in me. Something was different in my soul. It was like I had a religious experience or something. On that day, I think God placed in my soul a tenderheartedness of heart for my children—similar to the tenderheartedness I witnessed in Cecil—my friend Mark's dad. Maybe that kind of thing happens to a lot of people. I don't know. But it definitely happened to me.

* * *

In the spring of 1993, I was taking a course in cognitive psychology with a relatively famous professor in the field. I was taking the course because my Ph.D. minor was cognitive psychology. The professor was probably in his middle 60s. He had written a lot of books and articles on the topic and had achieved the status of Distinguished Professor at the University, which is a big deal in academia—especially at a large research university like the University of Illinois. Anyway, the course was a seminar-style course that had several doctoral students in it from a variety of disciplines.

Toward the end of the semester, the professor invited all of us to his house for a cookout. He said we could bring our significant other, if we had one, so Elizabeth went with me. It was very nice. Everyone was friendly. But at one point, someone picked up a magazine that was lying on the coffee table. I'm pretty sure it was *The New Yorker* or *The Atlantic Monthly.* On the cover (or maybe on the inside) was a picture of this pathetic-looking Christian family. They looked like they were inbred and brain dead. The photographer obviously took the picture when everyone was right in the middle of a blink and thought he had hit the negative-portrayal jackpot.

Although I don't remember the title of the article, I *do* remember that it was a "hit piece" on some aspect of Christianity. I think it was about homeschooling, but it could have been about something broader than that, like fundamentalism or evangelicalism. Anyway, a bunch of the people, maybe even the professor, started badmouthing Christians as if they knew no one in the room could possibly be one. The gist of their dialog was that we were all *way* too intelligent for God. And those religious people? They're all *so* unenlightened.

It was a disgusting and shameless display of bigotry. And I let them know it. But I was kind about it. I told them that Elizabeth and I were both Christians who had made conscious decisions to follow Christ. I said a few more things too, but I don't remember the rest. It was pretty brief. Boy, that shut 'em up fast.

* * *

Since I would be done with my coursework for the Ph.D. degree at the end of the semester, I toyed with the idea of applying for full-time professorships for the upcoming fall and working on my dissertation part time. That way, I could start making some real money, and my family could get on with life. However, I decided against it.

When I was still a graduate student at Illinois State University, the chair of the Applied Computer Science Department, who was also my master's thesis committee chair, told me that I might be tempted to take an academic job before graduating and that I should be leery of taking the bait. He encouraged me to stay at the University of Illinois until I was completely done. He told me that most people find it very difficult to finish their dissertation when they also have a full-time job to deal with. So, I took his advice and decided to stay at the U of I for another year and work on my dissertation full time.

* * *

In May of 1993, I finished my coursework for the Ph.D. degree and passed all my qualifying exams. By passing my qualifying exams, I was deemed competent enough in my field of study to continue on to the last phase of my formal education—the dissertation. So, when the fall semester began, I dove headlong into my dissertation research. I also began applying for tenure-track positions in academia that would begin the following fall semester.

* * *

One of the things you have to do for your dissertation is conduct a thorough review of the academic literature that relates to your research. You do this to demonstrate that the research you intend to do has not already been done by someone else. In other words, you have to prove that your research is *original.* Then, once your research is complete, you have to show how the results of your research support or don't support the results of any related research and how the results of your research support or don't support any relevant theories. Back in the day, all of that required a lot of *library* research.

The library at the University of Illinois at Urbana-Champaign is the fourth largest academic library in the US with over 15 million volumes. The library at the U of I is actually a collection of libraries that includes the Main Library, the Undergraduate Library, and several specialized libraries.

I loved going to the Main Library and using the computers there to find the studies in the academic literature that related to my research. I really loved its Beaux-Arts exterior architecture. It looked so stately to me. And its interior architecture, with its grand entrance and soaring ceilings, elicited feelings in me of elegance, dignity, history, tradition, sophistication, and an odd connection to the past. I was really inspired by it all.

In those days, using computers to perform automated keyword and phrase searches (as opposed to using the card catalog) was a relatively new thing. It worked pretty well, but you couldn't just download the pdf of a journal article like you can today. No. Once you identified a journal article you wanted, you had to jot down the call number of the journal, take the elevator up to the correct floor in the "Stacks," locate the journal you were looking for, find the specific article in the journal, and then make a photocopy of it. That was a lot of work just to find one article. Of course, the whole process is significantly more efficient these days. Today, I can sit in my office, do a Google search, download a pdf, and print it off. Done. It's a beautiful thing.

Being up in the Stacks of the Main Library was a pretty interesting experience. It was relatively dimly lit up there, and it smelled like old, dusty books—many of which probably hadn't been cracked open for decades. It was unusually quiet as well. So, whenever I was up there, I felt kind of lonely and isolated. It seemed like I was the only person in the entire place. On more than one occasion, it crossed my mind that, if someone really wanted to, they could burn the whole place down with a single match.

Of all the articles I had to track down in the Stacks, I only remember looking for and finding one of them specifically. The article appeared in the July 1945 issue of the *Atlantic Monthly*, and it was called *As We May Think* by American engineer, inventor, and science administrator Vannevar Bush. Way back in the mid-1940s, Dr. Bush described, for the very first time, the concept of what we now call hypermedia—that collection of interconnected documents (like Wikipedia) that we often use to represent human knowledge.

Of course, his idea was theoretical at that time. In fact, it wouldn't be until the very late 1980s that the technology required to support his idea was mature enough to make hypermedia something most of us take for granted today. I'm glad I still remember looking for that article because its historical connection to my research was pretty important. Nearly half a century prior to my research, Dr. Bush had conceived of a network of interconnected documents, and here I was one of the first researchers in the world to study how people navigate through such a network.

* * *

In February of 1994, our second son, Isaac Benjamin, was born at Covenant Hospital in Urbana. It was icy out with low-hanging clouds and temperatures hovering around freezing. With little warning that late morning, Elizabeth began having contractions regularly and pretty close together. She didn't tell me at first because I was studying, and she wanted to have lunch. But when she finally said something to me, it was *really* time to go.

We began calling the people on our list who said they could watch Zach for us when the time came, but no one was home. Finally, we got ahold of some friends who weren't on our list but were happy to watch Zach for us while we were at the hospital. So, we got in our car, drove very carefully through the sleet and rain, and dropped off Zach at their apartment. Since the conditions were so treacherous that day, I had to take my time driving—despite the urgency to the situation.

When we finally got to the hospital, we went straight to the delivery room, where a nurse checked Elizabeth to determine just how close to having a baby she was. As it turned out, she was dilated ten centimeters and was fully effaced, which basically means she was beginning to give birth. The nurse seemed a little alarmed and told us that she was going to go call the doctor and get him there right away. Fortunately, he was there in about ten minutes or so. Within about 20 minutes of getting to the hospital, Isaac was born. It happened that quickly. I wept again, but not as much this time. I guess I knew what to expect, so I had my guard up. Still, it was another moving experience.

The interesting thing about Isaac's birth was that it occurred while my great grandmother, Florence, was being buried in Tuscola. She was 97 years old when she died. Although I had planned to attend my grandma's funeral that day, I decided against it because it was so close to Elizabeth's due date. Man, that was a good decision.

* * *

In May, I was contacted by East Carolina University in Greenville, North Carolina. Although I had applied to several other universities as well, those universities either sent me a polite letter of rejection, or they sent me more information about their university or the position I was applying for. To those in the latter category, I politely responded that I no longer wanted to be considered for the position—for one reason or another. So, as it turned out, ECU was my only open door. All the others had been closed. It was a guidepost that God placed in my path to direct me toward the *place* he wanted me to be.

I had applied for the position of Assistant Professor of Educational Technology at East Carolina University, and they wanted to interview me. So, they flew me down to Greenville, where I met with some of the professors in the department, the dean of the College, and a couple of other people. I had never heard of Greenville, nor had I ever heard of East Carolina University. ECU sounded like a pretty strange name for a university in North Carolina. But I liked what I saw of Greenville and ECU, and the job looked great from what I could tell. If I got the job at ECU, I would be teaching in the Graduate School, which meant that I would only be teaching masters and doctoral students.

After my interviews, I flew back to Illinois and told Elizabeth all about the trip—who I met with, what my impressions of the University were, what the town was like, and so on. A few days later, I got a call from the dean of the College who offered me the job. I told him that I needed a day or two to speak with my wife about it, and he happily agreed. Elizabeth thought North Carolina sounded great, so I called the dean back and accepted the position. I would start in late August.

* * *

About two-thirds into my last semester at the University of Illinois, I was done with my dissertation, and I was ready to defend it. The title of my dissertation was *The Effects of Three Browsing Devices on Learner Structural Knowledge, Achievement, and Perceived Disorientation in a Hierarchically Organized Hypermedia Environment*. That's a mouthful, but the title says it all. The purpose of my dissertation was to determine how three different navigation methods (hyperlinks, spider maps, and hierarchical maps) affect knowledge organization, achievement, and feelings of disorientation as learners navigate through the related pages of a hypermedia system.

My dissertation defense didn't draw nearly as much attention as my master's thesis defense did. In fact, the only people in the room besides me were the professors on my dissertation committee. The defense went well, but once again, I stumbled over a question posed by one of my professors. His question seemed very philosophical or abstract or something, and I couldn't figure out what he was asking. Luckily, after asking the question a couple different ways for me, he just said, "Never mind. It's not that important." I was *so* relieved. But, of course, I didn't let them see me sweat.

When my defense was over, I was asked to leave the room so my dissertation committee could discuss what they had just witnessed. A few minutes later, I was called back into the room and congratulated on a job well done. I was *finally* done with all the requirements for the Ph.D. degree. After all those years of graduate school and all that hard work, I was finally done. All I had left to do was format my manuscript properly and deliver it to the Graduate School.

Here's the thing to know about my thesis and dissertation studies. The technology that made it possible to move from one document to a related document by clicking on a link or other mechanism was in its infancy. And, although I was *one* of the first researchers in the world to study hypermedia systems, I was *the* first researcher in the world to study how people navigate through such systems and how different navigation mechanisms affect knowledge, learning, and confusion as people move from one document to another. All of that may sound boring to you, but I was really into it at the time. I loved working on my research. It was the best part about being in graduate school.

* * *

A week or two before graduation, I was sitting in the Illini Union—the University's student union. I hadn't spent a lot of time there before, so I wanted to hang out there for a little bit and reflect on my graduate school journey that would be coming to an official end in a matter of days. As I sat there in one of the big brown leather chairs in the main lobby, I saw all kinds of people. Some were in a hurry to get somewhere else, some were studying with friends, and some were just hanging out like I was.

At one point, an older couple, probably in their 70s, walked into the lobby and sauntered up to the main desk. Of course, I had no idea why they were *really* there that day, but I figured they were alumni who had been feeling nostalgic and had come to town to visit their alma mater. Since the Student Union housed the Illini Union Hotel, I figured they were checking in to their hotel room after having been away for many, many years. And finally, I figured he was a retired professor who was already years removed from the career that I was just about to begin.

As I watched the older man at the main desk, I saw *myself* checking in to the Illini Union Hotel at that age. It was another "vision," like the ones I had when I watched Jim play the drums at Countryside Christian Center in Florida. It was like the man was me after a significant part of my life had already passed. It was a strange and depressing feeling.

* * *

On my last day at USACERL, just a few days before the end of the semester, my team in the Energy and Utility Systems Division took me to lunch at the Silvercreek restaurant in Urbana. After sitting down and ordering, our team leader said some very generous things about me and my contributions to the Utilities Modernization Team—especially with regard to the REEP system. He then presented me with an official commendation from the US Department of Defense, Department of the Army, Corps of Engineers, Construction Engineering Research Laboratory, Energy and Utility Systems Division. The other guys said some nice things about me as well and how much they hated to see me leave. The whole thing meant a lot to me.

Although I was done with my research assistantship at USACERL, I was asked to stay on as a software consultant to perform maintenance activities on the REEP system and the other software systems I had designed and developed for them. I would continue in that role for the next decade.

* * *

On May 14th, 1994, I graduated from the University of Illinois with a Ph.D. degree in Computer Assisted Instruction. The weather was perfect that day with lots of sunshine and temperatures in the low-70s. The commencement ceremony took place in the Assembly Hall—the indoor arena where Elizabeth and I had met in person for the first time almost eight years earlier. As I walked across the big stage to accept my diploma in front of thousands of people, I paused to have my dad place my doctoral hood over my head signaling the exact moment that I had *officially* graduated.

Earning a Ph.D. degree was by far the most difficult thing I've ever done. To earn a Ph.D. degree, you've got to have a lot of intellectual energy, you've got to be a very hard worker, and you've got to be okay with very little free time. Over the years, I've spoken to several people considering pursuing a Ph.D. degree, and my advice has always been the same. I basically tell them that they should only attempt it if they're *really* into it. It's tough, but it's manageable—if you treat it like a full-time job that requires overtime on nights and weekends.

I still have some bad dreams about college and graduate school. In one recurring dream, I'm a freshman in college all over again. I haven't really gone through college and graduate school, so I still have all that stuff ahead of me! In another recurring dream, I'm within a week or so of graduating from the University of Illinois when I suddenly realize I haven't been attending a mathematics class all semester that I need to graduate! When I wake up from one of those dreams, I always lie there for a minute thinking, "Where am I? Have I been through college and graduate school already?" Of course, when I finally get my bearings, I'm completely relieved that it was all just a dream.

* * *

Although Elizabeth and I started graduate school at the University of Illinois at the same time, she wasn't able to finish her degree before I graduated, and we moved away. Although she completed her student teaching the summer before Zach was born, she took the fall semester off because Zach was due in September. She then took the following spring semester off because she was having difficulty getting Zach on a uniform nursing schedule. The summer after that, though, she began taking classes again. However, near the end of the summer, we found out that she was pregnant again, so she decided to forgo school for the time being and concentrate on being a mom.

As it turned out, that was a good decision because Elizabeth began having premature contractions during the fall semester, and her doctor put her on bedrest for a while until he could get her contractions under control with medication. Of course, she didn't take classes during the spring semester either because Isaac was due in February.

* * *

A few weeks after graduation, we drove up to Des Plaines, left Zach and Isaac with Elizabeth's mom and dad, and flew down to Greenville, North Carolina, so we could spend a few days looking for a home. We eventually found a house we really liked in a nice area of town just a few miles east of East Carolina University. The house was four years old, and it had three bedrooms, two bathrooms, and a nice bonus room above the garage that I could use as a home office.

When we got back to Des Plaines, we told Elizabeth's parents about our trip and the house we were planning to buy. Although he could tell we were excited about owning our own home, Elizabeth's dad advised us against buying something the first year we lived somewhere. That way, we could make sure we liked the area, and I liked my job. Despite his advice, however, we went ahead and bought the house.

* * *

In July, Elizabeth and I packed everything we owned into a moving truck and then attached our car to a tow dolly. After strapping Zach and Isaac into their car seats, which were secured to the back seats of our extended-cab truck, we took off on our 830-mile trip to Greenville, where I would soon be starting my very first academic job. My title at

East Carolina University would be Assistant Professor of Educational Technology.

In late August of 1994, I started my job at East Carolina University, where I would be teaching three masters- and doctoral-level courses in educational technology. These were:

- EDTC 5020 (Authoring Systems for Instructional Product Development)
- EDTC 5375 (Multimedia Instructional Product Development)
- LIBS 6903 (The Internet: Organization, Design, and Resource Discovery)

The titles of those courses seemed like a pretty good match for my interests in multimedia design and development, so I was very excited about what lay ahead.

* * *

It didn't take long for Elizabeth and me to find a good church in Greenville. One Sunday morning, we visited a church called Greenville Christian Fellowship. GCF was very multigenerational, and they had a lot of young couples about our age who had young kids. The people at GCF were welcoming and serious about their faith, and Pastor Mike was an excellent speaker. The music that morning was very good and contemporary. But there was something conspicuously missing. They didn't have a drummer in their worship band.

Elizabeth and I really liked the church, and we knew right away that we wanted to be a part of it. So, after the service, I introduced myself to the worship leader. I told him that I was a drummer and that I would love to try out for the worship band sometime. A week or so later, the worship leader, a few key people in the band, and I met at the church and played through several songs together. We had a lot of fun that evening, and the music sounded great, so the band invited me to be their drummer. They told me that they had been praying for a drummer for quite a while and believed that God was going to bring one to them soon. They thought I was the answer to their prayers.

The keyboardist in the band at Greenville Christian Fellowship was a guy named Reed. Reed and his wife had a son who was about three years old. The funny thing about the little boy was that he always called his parents by their first names. So, instead of saying, "Daddy, can I have some milk?", he'd say, "Reed, can I have some milk?" Because it was so unusual and grownup-sounding, it was very funny to hear. Of course, his parents didn't think it was funny at all. Although they had tried and tried to break him of it, he just wouldn't change.

Since there were so many women in the church who also had young children, Elizabeth fit right in. I fit in with the ladies as well. Because the courses I taught at East Carolina University met in the evenings, I sometimes went to the park with Elizabeth and the boys during the day to meet up with her friends and their kids. On those days, I just talked away with the ladies and watched the kids as they ran around on the woodchips and climbed on the jungle gym and other playground equipment.

* * *

In November of 1994, I did my first conference paper presentation as a professional academic. The conference was the North Carolina Educational Technology Conference, and it was held at the University of North Carolina Greensboro. The title of my paper was *The Internet: Access Trends and Commercialization*. The timing of my presentation was important because the Internet had recently become commercialized, and no one really knew the impact that commercialization might have on the world.

Before it was commercialized, only people at research and academic institutions could use the Internet. I had been using it since 1990 when I first began graduate school, and some of the applications I made use of included Telnet (an application for logging in to other computers), File Transfer Protocol (an application for transferring files from one computer to another), Email, Gopher (an application for distributing, searching for, and retrieving files), Internet Relay Chat (an application for chatting with others), and the World Wide Web. Back then, using the Internet to advertise and sell stuff was anathema.

I'll spare you the details of my talk, but I'd at least like to summarize the major parts of it before discussing some of my speculation that day and an incredible prediction I made. First, I described the Internet in terms of the number of computers and networks currently connected to it and how rapidly those numbers were increasing. After that, I described the Internet's geographical scope. I then described who the Internet's owners had been in the past and who they were now. Next, I described the most significant events in the Internet's history that shaped people's access to it. And then I discussed the ways that people might be charged to access the Internet. Riveting, huh?

After all that, I discussed the impact commercialization might have on our day-to-day lives. I speculated that we *may* soon have *hundreds* of entertainment websites to choose from. Yes. I said *hundreds*. I also speculated that we *may* soon be able to shop for products and services, purchase software products and have them delivered via download, get customer service, conduct research, and watch product demos—all while sitting at home. And finally, I speculated that we *might* soon be put on marketing email lists and receive junk email. I was correct, sir!

Toward the end of my talk, I made an actual prediction. Although this prediction wasn't in the notes I used during the presentation (the same notes I used to recall this story), I remember hearing myself say it out loud—in front of people. I said that the Internet was probably in a "fad stage" right now and that, after the excitement wears off and the dust settles, it will go the way of the telephone and just be used as a tool. The entertainment aspect of it would probably not last long. Ouch! Hopefully, the people in the audience were so bored with my presentation by that point that they were no longer listening and didn't hear me say that.

* * *

As it turned out, I didn't like my job at East Carolina University that much. I mean, there were some things I liked about it. I got to study and teach, and I was able to work on my research in hypermedia design and development. But there were several things I didn't like about it as well.

First, I was made the director of the departmental computer lab, which looked like it hadn't been used in quite a long time. Since I had three brand-new courses to prepare for and teach, and since I was still deeply immersed in my research, I didn't have the time nor the energy to figure out what was wrong with the lab and get it up and running again. I shouldn't have been given the responsibility of that lab my first year. I think they gave it to me because no one else wanted the job.

Second, all the classes I taught were night classes that met from 6 pm to 9 pm. Because of that, I didn't go into my office until like 3 pm on most days, when most of the other professors in my department had already gone home. Even though I didn't mind teaching in the evenings, the idea of doing that my entire career was depressing.

Third, my department was kind of dysfunctional. There were some people who just couldn't get along for some reason. It was very petty. On several occasions, someone would complain to me about someone else and try to get me to take their side on the issue. Of course, I tried to stay neutral because I was new and didn't know these people from Adam. I wasn't going to let someone taint my view of someone else before I had even had the chance to get to know them. Unfortunately, I think my neutral position was sometimes interpreted to mean that I was on the other person's side.

Fourth, when I got evaluated by my departmental colleagues at the end of my first semester, someone wrote that I wasn't collegial enough. I think that assessment was based on the fact that I wasn't showing up to work until the afternoon on most days, and I wasn't sympathizing with the complaints of some of my colleagues.

And fifth and most importantly, I was teaching courses on how to *select and use* software applications in the classroom instead of teaching courses on how to *design and develop* software applications for use in the classroom. Since I was a computer programmer at heart, I just felt like I wasn't doing what I was designed to do. I was cut out to design and develop software.

So, in May of 1995, at the end of the school year, I was torn. Should I stay or should I go? We had moved to Greenville less than a year ago and had bought a house. We had joined a good church and had made a lot of friends. Since I didn't know what to do, I decided to fast and pray until I felt that I had heard from God on the issue.

After about two days of doing almost nothing but reading my Bible and praying, I finally felt like I had an answer. I was supposed to leave East Carolina University. Without going into any of the details about what I think I heard from God while I fasted and prayed, I'll just say that it mostly related to the strife between my department colleagues. What I sensed God speaking to me about was another guidepost that he placed in my path to direct me toward the *place* he wanted me to be.

* * *

Shortly after that, I began applying for other jobs in academia and was soon contacted by four colleges that wanted to interview me—the University of New England (in Biddeford, Maine), the University of Northern Colorado (in Greeley, Colorado), Bridgewater College (in Bridgewater, Virginia), and Union College (in Barbourville, Kentucky). At UNE, I applied for the position of Assistant Professor of Computer Science. At UNC, I applied for the position of Assistant Professor of Educational Technology (to give the field another try). At Bridgewater College, I applied for the position of Assistant Professor of Computer Science. And at UC, I applied for the position of Assistant Professor of Computer Information Systems.

The first three colleges flew me to their campuses for interviews, but none of them offered me a job. Union College, on the other hand, asked me to *drive* to their campus for my interviews. Since UC was in southeastern Kentucky in the foothills of the Appalachian Mountains, which might not be the most desirable location for some people, they wanted me to bring Elizabeth along as well, so she could see the area.

So, Elizabeth and I left the boys with some friends in Greenville and drove the 460 miles or so to Barbourville for my interviews. The people at Union College were very friendly and welcoming, and after my interviews, I really felt like the professors in the department wanted me to join them on the faculty. I also liked the courses I'd be teaching. They were all right up my alley—all software design and development. I was very impressed with UC. At the end of my interviews, the dean of the College offered me the job. Although the other three doors had been closed for me, this one was wide open. All I had to do was walk through it.

Unfortunately, the town of Barbourville was very small, and it had very few things that were attractive to us in terms of quality of life. It pretty much had a Pizza Hut, a small Walmart, a few shops in a small strip mall, a four-aisle grocery store, a drive-through hot dog and root beer stand, and a bunch of drive-through cigarette shops. In addition,

Barbourville was in a region of the state that was rather economically depressed. Although a thriving coal mining industry was once a major contributor to the economy there, most of the coal mines had long moved out—leaving a lot of people unemployed and on welfare.

On our way home to Greenville, I noticed Elizabeth crying. When I asked her what was wrong, she said she knew I was supposed to take the job at Union College and that we were supposed to move there—despite the fact that she would really miss North Carolina and all her friends there. So, a day or so after we got home, I called the dean of the College at UC and accepted the position of Assistant Professor of Computer Information Systems. I then called the dean of the College at East Carolina University and resigned my position there. I would be starting my new job at UC in late August. Once again, God had placed a guidepost in my path. This time, he used Elizabeth's sensitive spirit to direct me toward the *place* he wanted me to be *and* back to the *field* I was designed for.

* * *

In early August, with the help of our friends at Greenville Christian Fellowship, we packed everything we owned into a moving truck and said our goodbyes. After putting Zach and Isaac into their car seats in the back seat of our car, we took off for Kentucky. I drove the truck, and Elizabeth and the boys followed me in the car. I was very excited about my new job. In just a few short weeks, I would be starting my second professorship. This time, my title would be Assistant Professor of Computer Information Systems.

When we got to Barbourville, we moved into a small motel right off the highway on the outskirts of town. Like it usually is in August in southeastern Kentucky, it was very hot and humid. Luckily, the motel had a swimming pool, which we made frequent use of while we stayed there. The boys loved it.

After about a week of living in the motel, we moved into a one-room campus apartment. (It was more of a motel room if you ask me.) We had to stay in *that* apartment until the *actual* apartment the College had for us became available for us to move in to. Fortunately, we had a nice window air conditioner that kept the place nice and cool.

When the apartment the College had for us was ready, we moved in. The apartment building was pretty old, and our apartment wasn't the nicest thing we had ever lived in, but it would certainly do until we found something nicer in the area. What I liked about it, though, was that it was only a three-minute walk to my office in the main classroom building.

* * *

In late August, I started my job at Union College. At UC, I taught several undergraduate courses in software design and development. These were:

- COMP 121 (Basic Programming)
- COMP 211 (Introduction to Business Information Systems)
- COMP 221 (Cobol Programming I)
- COMP 222 (Cobol Programming II)
- COMP 241 (Advanced Microcomputer Applications)
- COMP 331 (Structured Systems Analysis and Design)
- COMP 441 (Database Design and Implementation)
- COMP 455 (Applied Software Development Project)

I loved teaching those courses. They were very technical, which is what I was the most comfortable with. I felt like I was in my element.

My colleagues at Union College were very friendly and supportive, and everyone got along well. I also had a decent office. Well, it wasn't great, but it was definitely better than the one I had at East Carolina University, which was a lone cubicle in a former classroom—not very cozy. I really liked working at UC. For the most part, I was left alone to study, teach my classes, and work on my research. It was really ideal in that sense. I didn't even have a committee assignment. (I'm not sure why.)

* * *

Finding a church in Barbourville was a bit challenging for us. The church culture in southeastern Kentucky was much different than what we preferred. It seemed much more traditional. Choirs. Hymns. Pews. Suits and ties. Southern Gospel music. All that. Although we visited a couple of the larger, more mainstream churches in town, we weren't really sold on either of those. Of course, the people were very nice, but Sunday mornings were too churchy for us.

We also visited a church that we found downright strange. As usual, the people were very nice, but the sanctuary was a bit creepy with its blood-red shag carpeting and its blood-red stained-glass windows that made the place look really, well, blood-red. There's nothing wrong with that necessarily, but it was kind of strange. Anyway, before the service began, everyone went into the sanctuary and sat down in the pews. I'd say there were no more than 15 people in attendance—four of whom were Elizabeth, the boys, and me. After the pastor got up, welcomed everyone to the church, and made some announcements, he called the choir up to the stage to help him lead the first hymn of the morning. I think we were the only ones who were not in the choir. There we were. The only ones still in the pews. All by ourselves. Talk about awkward.

We found a church eventually. It was a home church, which means that it met in someone's house. One weekend morning, Elizabeth and I were taking groceries out of the trunk of our car when a couple from down the street walked over and introduced themselves. Their names were Steve and Chris. Steve and Chris were from Wisconsin, and they had lived in Barbourville for several years already. Steve was a doctor, and Chris stayed home with their two daughters. They had moved to Barbourville so that Steve could practice medicine in a relatively poor region of the country. It was their ministry.

At the end of our conversation, Steve and Chris invited us to their church, which consisted of three doctors, their wives and children, and a few others. On the morning that we visited the church, we felt very welcome, and we liked everyone. The people who attended the church were from outside of southeastern Kentucky, so we found the church culture much more like what we were used to.

* * *

Shortly after arriving in Barbourville, we drove to the local bank to open a checking account. When we got there, I had this strange feeling that the people in the bank were looking at us funny. I mean, everyone was friendly, but I just couldn't shake the sense that folks were looking us over. When we left the bank, I mentioned it to Elizabeth, and she said that she had sensed the same thing. But after talking about it for a minute, we both dismissed it as being in our imaginations.

But it kept happening. The townspeople weren't rude or anything. In fact, they were very friendly. But when we interacted with them, it just seemed like something was different. It seemed like a "You're not from around here, are you?" kind of vibe. When we were on campus, though, things weren't like that at all.

A few months later, I was talking to a friend of mine named Bill. Like us, Bill was from somewhere else in the country, but he had been practicing optometry in Barbourville for like 20 years. Somehow, the subject of what we thought we were perceiving in the community came up. When I asked him if it was just in our imaginations, he told me flat out that it wasn't—it was quite real. He told me that the people of the community who are not from southeastern Kentucky are viewed by many of the locals as "outsiders" and are generally distrusted. When I asked Bill if *he* was still viewed as an outsider after having lived in Barbourville for so long, he told me that he *was*. I then asked him if he would ever *not* be viewed as an outsider. After thinking about it for a moment, he said, "Maybe my children won't be."

Bill went on to tell me the story of an older woman who had worked at Union College in the Housekeeping Department and had recently retired. At her retirement reception, one of her former coworkers, who happened to be from Barbourville, asked her if she was going to move back home now that she was retired. To that, she replied, "Move back home!? I've lived in Barbourville for 40 years!? I raised my kids here! My grandchildren are here!" After all those years, she was still viewed as an outsider.

One time, I asked a colleague of mine at Union College about what seemed like a lack of participation at the College's sporting events. It seemed like the basketball and football games were sparsely attended. My colleague, who was from southeastern Kentucky herself, told me that most of the people at the games were either college administrators, faculty, staff, or students. Relatively few of the folks were locals. She went on to tell me that most of the townsfolks viewed the College as full of outsiders, and many of them were even resentful of the College because they felt like the people there looked down on them. To be honest, I never got the impression that anyone at the College looked down on the locals. But who knows?

* * *

Before we left North Carolina, we had our realtor put our house on the market. Unfortunately, the house didn't sell very quickly. In fact, it still hadn't sold after we had been in Barbourville for several months. So, I asked our realtor to put renters in the house, so we wouldn't be burning money each month on a mortgage payment without having some rental income to replace the expense. However, he advised us against that. He said that it would be easier to sell the house if no one was living in it, and it was move-in ready. So, we took his advice. But after a year, the house still hadn't sold. This time, I insisted that he rent it out, which he did, but not before we had lost a lot of money. If only we had taken my father-in-law's advice and waited to buy a home until we were sure we were going to be in Greenville for a while. We had learned our lesson.

* * *

While working at Union College, I attended a workshop at Eastern Kentucky University in Richmond. I attended the workshop to learn how to program in the *Object-Oriented* Cobol programming language. Although object-oriented programming had been around for a fairly long time (since 1967 with the Simula programming language), it had only become mainstream recently. By the mid-1990s, everything was moving away from non-object-oriented programming and moving to object-oriented programming. And now, Cobol had an object-oriented version of the language. So, when the chance to learn object-oriented Cobol presented itself, I jumped at the opportunity.

At the workshop, I had a tough time wrapping my head around the concept of object orientation and just as much trouble understanding object-oriented Cobol programming. I wasn't alone. Virtually all of the professors at the workshop were struggling as well. For people like us, moving from the non-object-oriented programming paradigm to the object-oriented programming paradigm was no small feat.

Fortunately for me, I eventually caught on. But it took me a couple of years. Of course, now I love object-oriented programming. In fact, I think it's the best thing since sliced bread—except for some of the dumb terminology used in the paradigm, like using the term "method" instead of "function" or "procedure." Dumb.

* * *

One of the things I liked about working at Union College was that administrators, faculty, and staff could participate with the students in the College pep band. When I arrived on campus, I found out that the pep band needed a drummer. So, I auditioned and got the job. That was a great gig! It was probably the most fun I ever had playing music because all we did was play great songs that everyone knew, like *25 or 6 to 4* by Chicago, *Bad Bad Leroy Brown* by Jim Croce, *Wipeout* by The Surfaris. Just the good stuff. During pregame warmups, halftimes, and other extended breaks, we performed entire songs for the crowd. And during timeouts and other brief interruptions, we played short snippets of songs.

At home basketball games, the band set up in the upper deck of the gymnasium overlooking the basketball court. At home football games we set up way up in the home crowd bleachers. In the football stadium, the College carpenters built me this awesome drum deck that my whole drum set could sit on. It was great sitting up there on a sunny Saturday afternoon looking out over the mountains. It was especially beautiful after the leaves had changed from their summer greens to their autumn yellows, oranges, and reds. It was an awesome view.

* * *

I really enjoyed my students at Union College. Most of them were traditional college students, meaning they were somewhere between 18 and 22 years old and were straight out of high school. One of my non-traditional students was a guy named Dave. Dave was about my age, and he would sometimes stop by my office to chat. Dave was from the area and had served in the Marines. He was now going to college to get his bachelor's degree.

One day, Dave suddenly realized that he was in a class with my wife, so he came to my office to tell me he had met her. Elizabeth was taking classes at Union College that she could transfer back to the University of Illinois to complete her master's degree. When he got to my office, he poked his head in the door and excitedly told me that he had just met my "old lady." I didn't react outwardly to him calling Elizabeth my old lady, but I was definitely taken aback by it. But not in a negative way. I actually thought it was pretty funny. My old lady. It kind of had a ring to it. To this day, I call Elizabeth my old lady sometimes—just to be funny, of course.

Another time, Dave and I started talking about high school. He told me that, when he was a senior in high school, Kentucky had the lowest-scoring high schools in the country, and he went to the lowest-scoring high school in Kentucky. He then told me that he and a friend looked through the student records in his high school office to find out who the lowest-scoring student in his senior class was. According to Dave, he and his friend were able to identify the dumbest high school senior in the entire United States of America. Although I laughed at his story, Dave wanted me to know that he was completely serious. He told me he could show me the guy right now. He knew where he worked. Dave also told me how he and his friend were able to gain access to all those student records, but I forget the details of that part of the story. I think he said something about breaking into the high school office, but that sounds pretty far-fetched to me.

One of the nice things about my chats with Dave was that he loved to share his insights into the culture of southeastern Kentucky. Once, I asked him about all the litter I saw everywhere. It was shocking to see when we first moved to Barbourville. Along the highways, people threw their fast-food plastic cups and wadded up paper bags out the window. Out in the country, people dumped their kitchen trash, old furniture, and dead appliances into the ditches. On the softball field bleachers, people left their hot dog plates, napkins, and pop cans where they had been sitting. In the park bathrooms, people threw their beer bottles, pop cans, and other trash into the toilet. And cigarette butts? Fuggedaboutit!

In the mountains, things were equally bad. Although the mountains of southeastern Kentucky were beautiful, they were also replete with trash in many places. In the spring, summer, and fall, the mountains were covered by a lush canopy of leaves. But in the winter, when the canopy had fallen to the ground, litter, junk cars, and all other kinds of trash were exposed. It was very sad. I had never seen anything like it. When I asked Dave about it, he told me that that was just what he had learned to do as a kid and that he didn't know any better until he went into the Marines and found out that that wasn't acceptable behavior.

Another thing about southeastern Kentucky was that there was a lot of cigarette-smoking. Much more than I was used to seeing anyway. Besides the drive-through cigarette shops, Walmart had an entire wall of cigarettes for sale. Taped to the shelving that held all those cigarettes were policy signs that said you could only purchase so many cartons of cigarettes per day. I thought that was kind of funny—like who smokes that many cigarettes? But I eventually found out that the policy was necessary because people from Tennessee would drive the 35 miles or so up to Barbourville, buy a few dozen cartons of cigarettes, take them back to Tennessee, and sell them to their friends and neighbors at a handsome profit. The scheme was possible because the state sales and cigarette taxes in Tennessee were significantly higher than they were in Kentucky. That's what someone told me anyway.

* * *

In July of 1996, our third son, Nathanael David, was born at Knox County Hospital in Barbourville. It was a sunny day with temperatures in the middle to upper 90s. Since Nathan was at full term, and we were tired of waiting, Elizabeth and I decided to take a walk around the cul-de-sac to get things going. After she and the boys and I walked around the cul-de-sac about ten times, we went back inside and put Zach and Isaac down for a nap. Since Elizabeth's contractions had begun to get stronger and more regular, she said we should probably get going to the hospital soon. So, we called our friends Steve and Chris (who lived just down the street), and they sent their two young daughters, Rebecca and Jessica, over to our apartment to keep an eye on Zach and Isaac while they napped. When the boys woke up, the girls walked them back to their house, where they would stay for a few hours while Elizabeth was having the baby.

After giving the girls a few instructions, Elizabeth and I got into our van and drove to the hospital. When we got there, we settled into the delivery room. After checking on Elizabeth, the doctor left the hospital for a meeting. About 45 minutes or so later, Elizabeth began going into labor. So, the nurse called the doctor and let him know that things were moving very fast. Since his meeting was only a block away, the doctor *ran* back to the hospital. When he got there, he was huffing and puffing and soaking wet from the heat and humidity. Twenty minutes later, Nathan was born. It was another wonderful and moving experience.

* * *

Although I *really* liked my job at Union College, Elizabeth didn't like living in Barbourville. Being from Chicago, Barbourville was too small and remote for her. The closest significant city was Lexington, and that was almost two hours away. She also had difficulty connecting with the women in our home church as their lives and conversations frequently revolved around the medical profession.

So, once again, I was in a dilemma. Should I stay or should I go? I really didn't know what to do. So, I spoke to a couple of people about my situation, and they both said the same thing. They basically told me that life was too short to have an unhappy wife. The decision was clear. I needed to go. For a second time, God had used Elizabeth's sensitive spirit as a guidepost to direct me toward the *place* he wanted me to be.

* * *

In early December, toward the end of my third semester at Union College, I began applying for academic jobs elsewhere. And in January of 1997, I was contacted by Franklin College in Franklin, Indiana. At FC, I had applied for the job of Assistant Professor of Computing. It was kind of strange because I had never heard of Franklin, Indiana—even though we had driven by it on I-65 every time we drove between Barbourville and Chicago.

After a very pleasant phone interview with the search committee at Franklin College, I was invited to the FC campus for several in-person interviews. A week or so later, we left Zach and Isaac with our friends, Steve and Chris, and drove up to Franklin for my interviews. We took Nathan with us because he was still nursing.

When we got to Franklin, the sky was clear and very sunny, but it was very cold, and it had recently snowed leaving a nice white blanket of snow on the ground. To us, Franklin was a charming and attractive town. It had about 23,000 people at the time and was located about 20 miles south of Indianapolis. The first thing we did when we got to the campus was drive around looking for Old Main—the main classroom building, where my interviews were to take place.

The campus was very beautiful, but I wasn't thrilled about the looks of Old Main—at least on the outside. It didn't look bad or anything. It just looked kind of old. But when we went inside, I was impressed with how elegant the place looked. I found out that the interior of Old Main was so classy because the building had been completely gutted by a fire in 1985 and had been restored to its original interior architecture. The beauty of the inside of the building excited me because Old Main was where my office would be if I got the job.

The next day, I had my interviews with the members of the search committee and a few other key people on campus, including the dean and the president of Franklin College. After the interviews, I felt pretty good about everything. I thought the interviews went very well. Great people! The next day, we headed home to Barbourville and waited to hear back from FC.

* * *

Before I heard back from Franklin College, I received a phone call from the University of Indianapolis. At UIndy, I had applied for the position of Assistant Professor of Computer Information Systems. I told the person on the phone that I had just interviewed at FC, so if I was going to interview at UIndy, I needed to do it right away. So, they set up the interviews for a couple of days later. On the day before my interviews, we drove up to Indianapolis. Once again, we left Zach and Isaac with our friends, Steve and Chris, and took Nathan with us.

Although the University of Indianapolis campus was very nice, we were not thrilled with the surrounding neighborhoods. UIndy was an urban university on the south side of Indianapolis, and since we knew almost nothing about the area, we thought that our only choice would be to live on the south side of the city. We didn't know, for example, that we could live in Greenwood, which was a nice suburb just a half dozen or so miles south of UIndy.

The next day, I had my interviews at the University of Indianapolis. And just like at Franklin College, I met with the members of the search committee and some of the other key people on campus, like the dean and the president of the University. When the day was over, I felt like the interviews had gone well. The following day, we headed home to Barbourville and waited to hear back from UIndy.

*　*　*

The next week, I got calls from the deans at Franklin College *and* the University of Indianapolis, both of whom offered me jobs at their respective institutions. While both deans offered me more money than I was currently making at Union College, the dean at UIndy offered me more money than the dean at FC. A big bonus was that both offers came with three years applied toward tenure for my previous teaching experience at East Carolina University and Union College. Someone had advised me to negotiate for that, so I did, and both deans happily agreed.

So, God had opened two doors for me that week—one at Franklin College, and the other at the University of Indianapolis. That meant that Elizabeth and I had a decision to make. Although we liked both colleges, we liked Franklin College better for several reasons.

First, Franklin was really close to Indianapolis, with its professional sports teams, shopping malls, movie and dinner theaters, concerts, and restaurants, but we wouldn't have to live there. If we lived in Franklin, we'd only be 20 to 60 minutes away from pretty much anything special we might want to do.

Second, the Franklin Community School Corporation had excellent schools that we could send our boys to when they were school age. When I asked the dean of the College at the University of Indianapolis about the local school district, she gave me her advice by whispering, "Keep your kids out of IPS." She meant the Indianapolis Public School district. I don't remember if she even mentioned that there were other school districts in the area, but if she did, I was probably so fixated on her comment about IPS that I didn't hear her. Saying that to me really affected Elizabeth's and my general perception of the area.

Third, I liked the office I would be getting at Franklin College much more than the one I would be getting at the University of Indianapolis. The office at FC had carpeted flooring and drywall walls, whereas the office I would be getting at UIndy had linoleum flooring and cinder block walls. The former seemed warm and comfortable, whereas the latter seemed cold and sterile.

And fourth, Franklin College offered free tuition to the children of its employees who had worked there for three or more years. As can be imagined, this was a huge benefit because tuition at a private, liberal arts college was *not* cheap.

Although I would have taken either job if the other one hadn't been offered to me, I chose to accept the position at Franklin College. To us, the choice was obvious. The *negative* feelings we had about the south side of Indianapolis, and the *positive* feelings we had about the City of Franklin and FC turned out to be the final guidepost that God placed in my path to direct me toward the *place* he wanted me to be. He wanted me to be at Franklin College.

* * *

In mid-May, after the spring semester was over at Union College, and I had submitted my final grades, we drove up to Franklin to look for a place to live. Since we had learned our lesson, we decided to rent for a year to make sure I liked my job, and Elizabeth and I liked the area. Renting for a year would also give us some time to get the lay of the land, which would help us make a better decision about where we might want to live longer term if we decided to stay.

After looking around for a while, it appeared that we were going to have to rent a place in Greenwood. Franklin just didn't have anything available. However, before we pulled the trigger on the apartment we had found in Greenwood, a future department colleague of mine, Dan, contacted me about a house-for-rent flyer he had *just* come across. The owner of the house was a Franklin College graduate who was hoping to rent the house to someone associated with the College.

The house was nicer than our apartment in Kentucky, and since it was a house, we liked the idea that we wouldn't have to worry about noisy children disturbing the neighbors. Plus, it had a nice deck and back yard, and it was only a mile north of campus. The only negative thing about the place was that it was small. It only had two bedrooms and a single bathroom. That meant that all three boys would have to sleep in the same room. Although the house would suffice for the time being, we knew it wouldn't do in the long run. It would be far too small as the boys got bigger. But it was very nice, and the price was right, so we took it. Feeling satisfied that we had found a nice place to live, we drove back to Kentucky excited about the next step in our lives.

* * *

In mid-June, with the help of some friends and a couple of students from Union College, we packed everything we owned into a moving truck and said goodbye to everyone. After putting Zach, Isaac, and Nathan into their car seats in the back seat of our van, we took off for Indiana. Once again, I drove the moving truck, and Elizabeth and the boys followed me in the van. It was an exciting time. In less than two months, I would begin my third academic job. This time as Assistant Professor of Computing at Franklin College.

* * *

After unpacking our stuff and settling into our new home, we began looking for a church. Since Franklin (and Johnson County in general) had a lot of good churches, it didn't take us long to find one that we felt was a good fit for us. On one Sunday morning, we visited a church called Franklin Community Church. After the service, a couple about our age invited us to their home for lunch. That afternoon, we met one or two other couples from the church as well as another couple who was looking for a church in the area like we were. After visiting FCC the next few Sundays, we decided to join. The people at FCC were very warm and welcoming, and the church had a really good mixture of age groups, including a number of young couples about our age with young children. We also liked the pastor, Dave, who always delivered practical and encouraging sermons.

As for the music, it was okay. On some Sunday mornings, the music consisted of traditional hymns—led by a singer who was accompanied by a pianist. On other Sunday mornings, the music consisted of more contemporary praise songs—led by a singer who was accompanied by a couple of guitarists. Although the people that led the praise songs did a great job, the music was a little thin. There were no other instruments involved. So, after attending Franklin Community Church for a while, I spoke with one of the guitarists. I told him that I was a drummer and that I'd love to be a part of the worship team. Soon after that, I began playing the drums regularly on Sunday mornings.

* * *

In late August of 1997, began my third academic job—this time at Franklin College. At FC, I was in my element teaching undergraduate courses in computer science and software engineering (software design and development). The work environment at FC was very good, and my department colleagues were very supportive and helpful in getting me up to speed in terms of where things were, who to contact for what, and when things needed to be done. I was thankful to be at FC.

During my first few years at Franklin College, I played basketball at noon three days a week in the Spurlock Center—the College's main indoor sports facility. The guys I played with were all professors at the College, and some of them became life-long friends. Playing basketball during the week kept me in pretty good shape, but it was always tough teaching the first section of my Introduction to Computing class right afterward. I was always hot and sweaty when I got to my classroom—despite having showered and changed back into my work clothes.

Even though it was just pickup basketball with a bunch of grown men, it could be very dangerous. And accidents happened. Sometimes, people twisted ankles or got hit in the face with an elbow. Stuff like that. During one game, a teammate threw me a pass, and for some reason, instead of catching the ball with the palms of my hands, the ball hit the tip of my right ring finger snapping its flexor tendon. This made the last knuckle on that finger point downward when the rest of the finger was pointing straight. To correct that particular injury, you usually have to have surgery—or so they say. But I just taped my finger to a popsicle stick for a few weeks, and it was as good as new.

During another game, another professor and I dove for a loose ball, and as we crashed into each other, his shoulder hit me right under my left ribcage, breaking a couple of my ribs. Sometimes, I wonder if we both just tripped over our own feet or something. I really can't imagine *diving* for a basketball in my middle 30s, as if something were at stake—and he was at least 20 years older than me. Whatever happened, it was incredibly painful, and I could hardly breathe—just like the first time I had broken ribs playing basketball in Florida.

* * *

In January of 1998, our fourth son, Elijah Michael, was born at Johnson Memorial Hospital in Franklin. It was a beautiful, sunny day, but it was very cold with temperatures in the upper 10s or lower 20s. That afternoon, while we were at a small group meeting at our church, Elizabeth began having contractions *very* regularly. So, we called her mom in Des Plaines and asked her to come down to Franklin as soon as she could to watch the boys while we were in the hospital. Shortly after Elizabeth's mom got to our house, we put the boys to bed. A little while later, at around 10 pm, we hopped into our van and drove to the hospital. Almost eight hours later, Elijah was born. It was a very special experience. We now had *four* sons. I couldn't believe it.

The fact that we now had four sons is interesting because, before I even knew her, Elizabeth had been told by a doctor that she probably wouldn't be able to have children because of her endometriosis. (What a thing to say to a young woman.) Anyway, when Elizabeth and I got engaged, she told me what the doctor said and asked me if I still wanted to marry her. She tells me that I responded with something like "If you marry me, you'll have children." I know that sounds presumptuous, so I probably said it in passing. But I *did* believe what I thought God had spoken to me about back when I was a sophomore in high school—that thing about my wife being like a fruitful vine within my house and my children being like olive shoots around my table.

* * *

In June of 1998, we moved out of our rental house and into a home we had built in a much newer neighborhood in town, about a mile and three quarters from campus. During the year that we lived in our rental house, I rode my Peugeot ten-speed bicycle to work almost every day. It was about a mile ride each way. After moving into our new house, I continued the tradition of riding my bicycle to work. I even rode in the winter. As long as it wasn't raining or too cold, I rode.

* * *

Like most colleges and universities, Franklin College has a fall term and a spring term. But we also have a winter term that lasts somewhere between three and four weeks during the month of January. As a full-time faculty member at FC, I've always been required to teach a winter term course every other year (or so).

Winter term courses are supposed to be different from the courses we teach during the regular school year. In fact, we aren't permitted to offer a course that's found in the course catalog. Because of this policy, we might have a mathematics professor teaching a winter term course on marriage and the family, or we might have a journalism professor teaching a winter term course on Alfred Hitchcock films. Basically, we can choose any topic that interests us—as long as the course gets the stamp of approval from the Faculty Curriculum Committee.

So, in January of 1999, I began teaching a winter term course called Inner-City Missions. It was a course that I would end up teaching for the next 20 years. During that time, my Inner-City Missions course was very popular, and it often filled up with students within an hour or two of open registration. The word around campus was that the course was both enjoyable and life changing.

During the course, my students and I traveled to Indianapolis four days a week to work at three Christian-based inner-city missions. The students in my course didn't have to take quizzes or exams. Instead, they were graded on their daily attendance, daily group responsibilities, daily journal entries, group presentations, and final reflective essays. It might sound easy, but it required a *lot* more time than most on-campus courses. Each day, we left campus at 9 am in our big Franklin College vans and didn't return until around 3 pm. Sometimes the days seemed long, but helping others in need was always rewarding.

* * *

Sometime in early 1999, I purchased a brand-new Pearl Export Select drum set with a burgundy lacquer finish. I had made some pretty good extra money working as a software consultant for USACERL, so I decided to treat myself and buy something new to replace the black Rogers drum set I had been playing on since the early 1980s. The only things I didn't replace were the cymbals. I kept my Zildjians, not just because I was a big fan of the brand, but because replacing them would have cost me more than the drum set itself.

Shortly after getting my new drum set, I began playing in a band called Midnight Transit. Midnight Transit was the brainchild of a friend of mine named Duane. Duane was a keyboardist and singer who had a vision for a blues band that would play blues cover songs in the blues clubs of Indianapolis. It would be fun, and we could make some extra money playing a couple of Friday nights a month. Duane had a friend named Pat who played the bass and a friend named Rich who played the guitar. So, we were all set. We began rehearsing regularly, playing songs like *Pride and Joy* by Stevie Ray Vaughan, *The Thrill is Gone* by BB

King, and *Blue on Black* by Kenny Wayne Shepherd. Once we had about 40 songs ready to go, we began playing in the blues clubs in the city. We also played a few gigs in Franklin. When Rich moved away, he was replaced by a guy named Jeff.

Midnight Transit was a decent band. But sometimes things would go wrong during gigs. Since Duane was the frontman of the group, and since he was the one who decided how long to keep a given song going, he was responsible for giving us some kind of musical or vocal cue to indicate that the song would be ending the next time around.

Unfortunately, Duane sometimes forgot the cue, which left the rest of us hanging and the song in an endless loop. The rest of us just stared at Duane and then looked around at each other like, "When is he going to get us out of this thing?" So, with a half-cool half-nervous look on his face, Duane would slowly and discreetly look back at us hoping that someone would give him a clue about how to signal the end the song while simultaneously praying that no one in the audience would notice he was lost. Sometimes this went on for a minute or two, so what was meant to be a five-minute song ended up being significantly longer.

Although I really enjoyed playing in Midnight Transit, there were a couple of negative things about playing in the blues clubs. First, we didn't start playing until 9 pm. That meant that we weren't done playing until 1 am. And since we had to get there a couple of hours early to set up, do a sound check, and all that, it made for a pretty late evening out after having worked all day at Franklin College. And second, the places we played were so filled with cigarette smoke that it was pretty hard to take. After those gigs, I would usually get home around 2:30 or 3:00 in the morning smelling so smoky that Elizabeth made me take a shower before getting into bed.

Unfortunately, Midnight Transit only lasted a year because Duane moved to Florida to start his own business.

* * *

Before Rich left Midnight Transit and moved away, I invited him to the Billy Graham Crusade that would be taking place in Indianapolis a couple of weeks or so later. I felt like I should take advantage of the opportunity to go and invite someone along. After all it wasn't often that you got to see Billy Graham in person. In fact, the last time I saw him speak was way back in 1973 when he spoke in St. Louis at the St. Louis Arena, which later became known as the Checkerdome.

In 1973, on the evening of the event, my parents and I sat so high up in the seats that I was terrified. The upper-level seating was so steep that the heads of the people in the row in front of us were at our feet. Today, I wonder if that experience is where my acrophobia came from. I don't remember being afraid of heights before that. Anyway, I don't think I got much out of Billy Graham's message that evening because I was far too busy trying to figure out how I was going to launch the paper airplane I had made out of the program—without anyone seeing me do it, of course. I'm pretty sure my parents didn't notice what I was trying to do, or I'm sure they would have stopped me. But they didn't, and my little airplane flew for a very long time—almost to the floor of the Dome. What a knucklehead.

On the day I was planning to invite Rich to the Billy Graham event, I was sitting in my office at Franklin College. When I reached for the phone to call him, I felt strongly in my spirit that I wasn't supposed to call him. Instead, I was supposed to go to his house and invite him in person. I wasn't sure what difference it would make, but that was what I was feeling. Since I *really* didn't want to ride my bike home after work, get into my van, and drive to his house, I brushed off my feelings and reached for the phone. However, once again, I felt strongly that I was supposed to go to his house and invite him in person.

So, just in case it really *was* God speaking to me, I went to Rich's house after work. When he came to the door, he invited me in, and we shot the breeze for a little while. Soon, he began sharing with me some of the trials he was going through in life. A little while later, I told him about the Billy Graham Crusade and asked him if he'd like to go with me. He said he would.

On the evening of the big event, Rich and I traveled to Indy, parked in a $3.00 lot, walked into the RCA Dome, and took our seats in the nose-bleed section. Before the event even started, I could tell that Rich was affected by the whole thing. He just kept looking around the place, like he couldn't believe there were so many people at such an overtly religious event.

After Billy finished speaking, he gave his alter call, and hundreds of people began walking forward to give their lives to Christ. It was an amazing thing to witness. Rich, however, sat there quietly watching the whole thing, like he was amazed at what was happening. I could tell he was in deep thought.

After what seemed like ten minutes of just sitting there, I asked Rich if he wanted to go forward to accept Christ. He said that he did, but he wanted to know if I'd go with him. So, we both walked down to the front of the stage in the RCA Dome, and Rich gave his life to Christ. His life has never been the same—and neither have the lives of his kids and some of his other family members.

I like to tell that story because, although I've heard God "speaking to me" many times in my life, that was one of the times I heard Him pretty clearly. I'm glad I listened, and I know Rich is too.

The 2000s

54 68 65 20 32 30 30 30 73

In early 2000, the pastor at our church left, and a new pastor was hired. The new pastor at FCC was a guy named Mike. Mike was a great guy and brought great sermons. Neither Elizabeth nor I disliked him in any way. In fact, we liked him a lot. The only problem was, we no longer played any upbeat music that required the drums. Instead, Mike and his wife led the music on Sunday mornings with a guitar and a piano, and the songs we sang were mostly calm and contemplative—kind of like Michael Card's music, if that's helpful.

Of course, there's nothing wrong with that kind of music, but it was very boring for our children. They had become accustomed to having upbeat music in church, and the style of music they were singing along with now left them yawning and lethargic. Plus, I was completely "out of a job." Since we were no longer using the drums on Sundays, I was no longer using my musical talents to serve the church. So, although I'm an opponent of church hopping, Elizabeth and I decided to begin looking for a church that played music our children wouldn't find dull and one that I could contribute to as a musician.

* * *

Soon, we began attending the Church at Stones Crossing—a young and growing church that met in the auditorium of Center Grove High School in Greenwood. We liked the church pretty much right away. The pastor there was a guy named Scott. Scott was a relatively young guy who was an excellent speaker. Although the church was biblically based, Scott tried to avoid the use of too much church-speak during his sermons. He wanted CSC to be "seeker-sensitive" so that people who were exploring Christianity wouldn't get lost in the jargon. In that sense, CSC was a lot like New Community.

In terms of the music, the Church at Stones Crossing played mostly upbeat contemporary songs. One of the things I liked about it was that the music was played at a volume that was loud enough to move the worshipper—yet not so loud that it was a distraction. Elizabeth and the boys and I loved the music on Sundays. It was fresh, and the lyrics made sense to the modern listener. The worship team was excellent as well. In addition to the main worship leader, the band included several backup singers, a couple of guitar players, a bass player, a keyboardist, a percussionist, and a drummer. The worship team also had a number of soundmen—one of whom was a professional sound engineer. So needless to say, the quality of the music at CSC was very good.

After attending the Church at Stones Crossing for a while, I spoke with the worship leader about filling in on the drums when they needed someone. Shortly thereafter, I was invited to audition at their practice facility, which was in a strip mall storefront in Greenwood. After the audition, I was offered a spot on the worship team. So, on the Sundays that the primary drummer wasn't there, I filled in on the drums. But on the Sundays that he was there, I was the percussionist.

I hadn't been a percussionist in a worship band before, but I really enjoyed it. I played the congas, tambourine, shaker, chimes, triangle, cabasa, and some other interesting percussive instruments. After about a year, the main drummer in the band dropped out for some reason, and I became the primary drummer for the Church at Stones Crossing worship band. I felt quite blessed to be serving in the music ministry with such a great group of people.

* * *

In the summer of 2000, Elizabeth completed the last two courses she needed to finish her master's degree at the University of Illinois. Previous to that, she had taken three courses at Union College, one course at the U of I in the fall of 1999, and one course at Indiana University Purdue University Indianapolis in the spring of 2000. All of the courses were required and were applied toward the master's degree she began all the way back in 1991.

In those days, online courses were a relatively new thing and were virtually unheard of at most traditional colleges and universities. So, when she took her courses at the University of Illinois, she had to drive all the way to Urbana. And, since her classes met during the week that summer, she had to stay with my Auth Barb in Tuscola from Sunday night through Friday morning.

When Elizabeth was gone that summer, the boys and I had a great time together. As a matter of fact, we always had a great time when she was gone. Sometimes, for example, we'd go to Krispy Kreme (donuts) for dinner and then Rally's (hamburgers) for dessert. Then we'd take in a movie at the dollar theater in Greenwood. And sometimes, we'd just watch some TV and eat dinner right out of the can. Think Momma would have let those boys have donuts for dinner or eat dinner out of a can? If yes, think again.

One summer evening, when Elizabeth was on a week-long, out-of-state trip with a friend, all the boys and I had the stomach flu at the same time. When she called to see how we were doing, I let her know that we were all sick, sitting around the "big green bowl," and vomiting into it. Fortunately, we survived.

* * *

Not too long after Midnight Transit broke up, I was contacted by Jeff—the guitar player who replaced Rich in Midnight Transit. He told me that his friend Scott was putting together a "positive new country" band called Reedy's Dream. After telling me a little bit about Reedy's Dream, Jeff got me one of Scott's CDs. He and Scott wanted me to take a listen and let them know if would be interested in joining the band. After listening to the CD, I was very impressed with the music. I also liked Scott's vision for a positive new country band that wouldn't talk about negative things, like betrayal, beer-drinking, and dying dogs. Instead, they'd talk about more positive things, like God's love, healing relationships, and hope.

Shortly after listening to Scott's CD, I got back with Jeff and told him I'd be interested in auditioning for the band. So, a few days later, I auditioned in the Chapel at Franklin College. After the audition, Scott invited me to join the band, and I accepted. The guys in Reedy's Dream (Scott, Jeff, Dave, and another Jeff) were all very good musicians and were generally fun to be around. We played in at least one church, but we usually played at the Sonshine Inn Christian Coffeehouse in the Fountain Square area of Indianapolis.

Scott was an exceptional songwriter who had written and recorded a number of original songs before I joined the band. One time, he told me that he would sometimes wake up in the middle of the night, walk out into the middle of the cornfield behind his house, and write music under the stars. That may sound strange, but there's no doubt Scott's music was inspired. He was a gifted songwriter who had an excellent voice and vocal style that fit the new country musical genre perfectly.

Unfortunately, Reedy's Dream didn't last long. The band just wasn't capturing the sound that Scott was going for. We broke up in less than a year.

* * *

Shortly after Reedy's Dream broke up, a department colleague of mine, Robert, called me into his office, handed me a CD, and asked me to take a listen. He told me that his friend Steve was forming a new Christian band, and he had already joined. They were now looking for a drummer and wanted me to audition. When I got home after work, I put Steve's CD into the CD player and was immediately excited about what I was hearing. I loved the mixture of musical styles from folksy, to rocky, to funkadelic, so I told Robert to set 'er up.

A few days later, I auditioned for the band on my electronic drum set in our living room—a room our family called the "Red Room." After the audition, Steve invited me to join the band, and I accepted. There were only three of us in Once a Child—the band name that we eventually came up with. It was just Steve, Robert, and me, so it was relatively easy to get "tight" musically. We mostly played in Christian coffeeshops, including the Sonshine Inn Christian Coffeehouse, but we also played a couple of times in the morning along the route of the 500 Festival Mini Marathon in downtown Indianapolis.

Like Scott, Steve was an exceptional songwriter who had already written and recorded many original songs before I joined the band. And during my tenure in Once a Child, Steve wrote many more. He was a prolific songwriter whose music was truly inspired.

* * *

In August of 2001, I reached an important milestone in my career. I was granted tenure and promoted to the rank of associate professor. In case you're not familiar with how things work in academia, tenure is the most important professional goal a college professor can achieve. Being a tenured professor means that you have an "indefinite academic appointment" at your college or university. In other words, you have the job as long as you want it. You can't be fired just because someone doesn't like you or because you hold an unpopular opinion. You have "academic freedom." In theory, a tenured professor can only be fired if the academic program he or she teaches in is discontinued, or his or her institution has to eliminate their position for budgetary purposes.

The tenure system is an interesting thing, and I have some mixed feelings about it. In some ways, it's good, and in some ways it's not so good. I think it depends on the side of the system you're on.

On the untenured side of the system, you're not really free to be yourself. There's always this little pressure to make everyone around you happy. Being untenured can make a young professor feel like he or she is walking on eggshells. I know this because, not only did *I* feel it, but I've had untenured professors seek my advice on how to handle issues with colleagues or the current political environment so that it doesn't jeopardize their prospects for tenure.

On the tenured side of the system, you're freer to be yourself— within the bounds of proper decorum, of course. When I was granted tenure, I finally felt like I could say "No" to people, if I really didn't have the time, or if I really didn't want to do something—like serve on an ad hoc committee or participate in a fund raiser.

Of course, some professors abuse tenure and academic freedom. I don't know, maybe you've seen some of those college students on TV who have all kinds of divisive and destructive ideas swimming around in their heads about economics, society, and culture—much of which just defies reality. Well, those ideas don't appear out of nowhere. They usually come from tenured professors (usually in the humanities and social sciences)[7] hiding behind academic freedom.

---

[7] Just sayin'.

I'm shocked by some of the things I sometimes hear my presumably intelligent peers in academia say these days. Well, thanks to tenure, they can say those things. Luckily, I teach in the formal sciences, where logic and reason are the standard.

* * *

On September 18th, 2001, I received a burgundy Fender Jazz Bass guitar from Elizabeth for my 39th birthday. When I received the gift, two things went through my head. First, although I tried to be grateful, such a gift was far too expensive. Elizabeth and I had previously agreed that we would only spend a certain amount of money on each other for birthday gifts, and this gift was close to ten times the agreed-upon amount. And second, I thought, "What in the *world* am I going to do with this?" I barely played the bass guitar, and I certainly had no desire to play one. My interest was drumming.

After my initial attempts at being grateful, I asked Elizabeth why she had bought the guitar for me and why she went so far over budget on it. She basically said that she felt like God wanted her to buy it for me. Of course, I thought that was an excuse to ignore our agreement and to buy me what she wanted to buy me. I mean, if God tells you to do something, who can argue with you? Right? She also told me that, if I really didn't want it, she had 24 hours to return it for a full refund. Anyway, I accepted the gift and tried to be happy about it.

Later that evening, I was noodling around on my new bass guitar in our Red Room. I was playing along with *Blue on Black* by Kenny Wayne Shepherd. It was a song that Midnight Transit had played in the blues clubs, so I knew the song already, and it was pretty easy to pick up on the bass, since it only had four chords.

While I was playing, Zach walked into the room and asked me if he could give it a try. Because the bass was so heavy, he had to sit down with it. He was twelve days short of his tenth birthday. As we sat there together, I showed him where the four notes of the song were on the fretboard and when to play them. Within a few minutes, he had picked up both concepts. So, I grabbed my dad's Yamaha classical guitar (the same classical guitar I had learned to play the guitar on 20 years before) and started playing along with him. Shortly after that, we were playing the entire song together.

A little while later, Isaac came into the room and asked to play with us. Isaac was eight years old and was already a pretty good drummer, since he had been playing the drums since he was four. When he came into the room, he sat down behind my electronic drum set and started playing with us. It happened that fast and that organically. Within a day or two, the three of us were playing several other simple songs as well.

After we started playing music together, it didn't take long for me to get much better at playing the guitar and singing at the same time. Although I had been able to play the guitar and sing simultaneously a little bit before, it did *not* come naturally to me. Now, however, I could do it without looking at my hands to make guitar chords and without reading the words from a sheet of paper. Another thing I could now do was play the *lead* guitar parts to songs. That was something I could *not* do before.

The realizations that I could play the guitar and sing simultaneously as well as play the lead guitar weren't quite on the level of the out-of-the-blue realizations I had had earlier in life when I suddenly knew I could do something, like ride a two-wheeler, catch a baseball, or play the guitar, but they did come to me very quickly. In hindsight, I think those new skills were gifts from God because, before too long, I would be forced into a musical role that I would not have been prepared for otherwise.

* * *

A month or two after my birthday, Elizabeth told me about a talent show that would be taking place in the middle of January at Franklin Community Church—the church we had attended from 1997 to 2000. By that time, Elizabeth was homeschooling all four boys, and FCC was where our homeschool group met once a week for special events and activities. At first, I was reluctant about performing at the talent show. I'm not sure why. But after Elizabeth kept encouraging me to do it, I agreed that we would do it if the boys were okay with it—which they were.

Of course, we had to come up with a band name if we were going to be performing for an audience. So, I suggested the 4th Normal Form Band—a name that I had pitched to Steve and Robert before we finally landed on Once a Child. I liked the name because 4NF was a database concept that would take me an hour to explain to you—if you were a computer science major. Anyway, the boys thought it was good, so we went with it.

When the Franklin Homeschool Group Talent Night event rolled around, we played our very first gig as the 4th Normal Form Band. It was January 17th, 2002. Since I didn't have an amplifiable guitar then, my friend Paul let me borrow his black Takamine acoustic guitar with built-in pickups. After we connected the drums, the bass, and Paul's guitar to the church's sound system, we played our two-song set, which went off without a hitch.

Shortly after our first gig, Nathan wanted to be in the band. He was six years old. Although I didn't know how to play the piano, I knew where the individual notes were, so I taught him which notes to play and when to play them. Since we didn't have a real keyboard at the time, Nathan had to play a little Casio Concertmate keyboard that my grandma Sadie had given me when she was getting rid of stuff.

It didn't take Nathan long to pick up the songs his brothers and I had already learned, so on April 12th, 2002, he played with us at our second gig, which was held at Benjamin's Coffeehouse and Bakeshop in Franklin. That evening, the place was packed, thanks to some simple signs we had put up at Benjamin's a month earlier.

Since three of the four boys were now in the band, and since playing at Benjamin's was so much fun, I really wanted Elijah to be involved. But since he was only four years old, he was pretty nervous about being on stage in front of people. Although I had taught him how to play the shaker and tambourine, he wasn't as enthusiastic about playing music as the other boys were. Maybe it was because he didn't get to choose his role in the band like the other boys did. I tried to tell him how much I loved playing percussion in the Church at Stones Crossing. I also tried to tell him that percussion was the "salt and pepper" of a band, but he didn't buy it.

Fortunately for the rest of us, Elijah finally joined the band, and on July 18th, 2002, he played with us at our fifth gig, which was held at the Johnson County Fairgrounds in Franklin.

* * *

It didn't take long until we were traveling to play gigs. Since I had the summers off, we played the bulk of our shows between late May and late August. Because we were playing so often, I quit Once a Child to focus my attention on the 4th Normal Form Band.

Since we were making some good money, we were able to purchase our own PA system, a better electronic drum set, some electric guitars, two keyboards, some more percussion instruments, and a few other things we needed. We were also able to purchase an equipment trailer (with custom 4NF graphics) to pull behind our van. Everything we bought was new, and we did our best to keep our stuff in good shape. Our band's philosophy was to only buy good equipment, so we used Pearl drums, Fender guitars, Yamaha keyboards, and Latin Percussion percussive instruments.

The boys split half the money the band brought in, so they usually had some pretty decent spending money—at least for kids their age. The other half of the money went to pay for the band's expenses, like gasoline, food, new equipment, equipment upgrades, and so on. When Elizabeth went to gigs with us, she got paid as well. I, however, never got paid. I just never felt the need to take money from the band.

The 4th Normal Form Band played gigs in several different states, including Indiana, Illinois, Iowa, Ohio, Pennsylvania, Georgia, Florida, and South Dakota. We also played dozens of gigs in Taiwan (Republic of China). In terms of venues, we played at churches, family camps, conference centers, colleges, coffee shops, parks, city festivals, county fairs, state fairs, and a convention center. When Elizabeth went with us, she sold CDs and t-shirts, talked with people, answered questions about the band, and ran sound for us when the venue we were playing at didn't provide a professional soundman. Her biggest claim to fame was that she played the keyboards for us on a song once at a conference center in northern Indiana. Well, that and she gave birth to four-fifths of the band.

Depending on the venue, we played Christian music, secular music, or a mixture of both. We also played a mixture of original music and cover songs. As for our original music, we had exactly 30 songs that spanned several different musical genres from folk to soft rock to blues to country to new country to hard rock. In terms of Christian cover songs, we played things like *A New Hallelujah* by Michael W. Smith, *Holy is the Lord* by Chris Tomlin, and *Love the Lord* by Lincoln Brewster. And in terms of secular cover songs, we played things like *Carry on Wayward Son* by Kansas, *Margaritaville* by Jimmy Buffett, and *With Arms Wide Open* by Creed. (See Appendix A for the band's complete musical repertoire.)

From 2002 to 2011, we recorded six full-length CDs: *Seeds of Time*, *Here in America...*, *Mothers of Invention*, *HumaNature*, *Coram Deo*, and *Shen Shen Ai Ni*. (Shen Shen Ai Ni means "Deeper in Love with You" in Chines.) We recorded all six of our CDs in the Red Room—our home rehearsal space and recording studio.

* * *

Back in those days, people would send me emails or write things in our website's guestbook that expressed their appreciation for what we did. Here are a few of the comments we received when the boys were very young:

- "Good morning! ...I saw the band at St. Stephen's Family Fest (Des Plaines, Illinois). It was a blast! When I saw their banner, I knew who they were, and I told my son Andy - woo hoo!! It's the band from Indiana!! These people that were sitting next to us said that they were good. I told them that I knew one of the family members! I bought both CDs and I must say that when we are in the car Andy loves to listen to them." – G

- "Being geeks and occasional academics by avocation who pursue 'most normal' databases in our design process, we enjoyed speculating about your name as well as enjoying your music." – NF

- "My twelve-year-old son, Mathew, and I were amazed at the talent and dedication of the band members. They serve...as a form of 'positive peer pressure' for promoting hard work and dedication during a time when there is so much 'negative peer pressure' on our youth." – FB

- "I had heard that the 'kids' were going to surprise me.... Well...the 'kids' absolutely blew me away! What stage presence they had! Extremely cool characters on stage and very humble for being as talented as they are! I look forward to watching them grow up and surpass the talent of their dad!!!" – MM

- "What you do with your boys is truly remarkable." – JC

When we were playing gigs, people often asked me where the boys got their musical talents from. As I reflect on that question now, I think several factors contributed to their abilities to play music at the level they did—especially when they were so young.

Part of it is probably because I began teaching them at home when they were young and expressed a desire to play. Part of it is probably because they practiced frequently for gigs and performed regularly for live audiences. Part of it is probably because they watched my friends and me play music from the time they were old enough to understand what was going on. And part of it is probably because they come from a relatively long line of musicians. Maybe there's some kind of genetic component to it or something. My grandma Virginia was a pianist, my grandma Sadie was an organist, and my dad was a drummer. But I think the most important factor is that *God* chose to gift them musically, so they could use their skills for his purposes and to bring glory to him.

* * *

The boys and I played together 327 times from 2002 through 2017. Although all five of us played the vast majority of those gigs together, some of the gigs included only four of us. Elijah missed our first several gigs. Nathan missed our very first gig. Isaac missed some gigs when he was in Army Basic Training in 2012. Luckily, Elijah was able to fill in for him on the drums. Zach missed some gigs when he moved away to graduate school in 2015. Fortunately, Elijah was able to replace him on the bass. And I missed a gig after getting injured playing racquetball. Thankfully, Nathan was able to fill in for me on lead vocals and play my guitar parts.

Although we kept the band together as long as we could, I knew it wouldn't last forever. When Zach graduated from college in 2015 and moved away to graduate school, we just led worship at church without him. But when Isaac graduated from college in 2016 and moved away to start his career as an officer in the US Army, it was all over. I wasn't really sad about it or anything. That's just the way life is. Kids grow up and move away.

But not too long after Isaac moved away, we all played together one last time. This time, it was at Zach's church (Cornerstone Community Church) on the University of South Florida campus in Tampa, Florida. The date was Sunday, June 25th, 2017, and we played the song *[Lord] You are Good* by Israel Houghton as special music. It was an appropriate ending song to an amazing era.

* * *

One of the mission organizations we worked with in the early years of my Inner-City Missions course was called the Lighthouse Mission. The Lighthouse mission served the homeless men of Indianapolis by providing food, clothing, spiritual counseling, addiction recovery help, emergency sheltering, and other assistance. Eventually, the Lighthouse mission would become part of Wheeler Mission Ministries, which was founded in 1893.

The first time I took a group of students to the Lighthouse Mission, which would have been in January of 1999, I watched as probably 200 men made their way through the line as they were being served lunch by a group of volunteers that included my students. As I pondered the scene, it struck me that, except for the grace of God, that could be me.

One of the most important things my students and I learned during our work at the Lighthouse Mission was how easily *we* could become homeless too. One wrong decision, and *we* could be out on the street. That lesson was brought home to my students one day when they met a homeless guy who had a master's degree but had also made some bad decisions about drugs. His experimentation with drugs had slowly morphed into abuse, and that abuse had severely damaged his closest relationships and had messed up his life in general. The idea that this highly educated man could be homeless made a very strong impression on my students who were only undergraduates themselves. During our debriefing in the classroom at the end of the week, we all came to the same conclusion—if it could happen to him, it could happen to us. So, the same year that the 4th Normal Form Band began, and the same year I started writing songs, I wrote a song about our experiences at the

Lighthouse Mission. I called it *There Go I*.[8] (See Appendix B for the lyrics to all the band's original music.)

There Go I

Verse 1
He stood in line at the mission. He looked a lot like me.
He ate wilted lettuce and day-old bread. He had no place to sleep.

Chorus
But for the grace of God, there go I.
But for the grace of God, there go I.
I'm blessed to live the life I see.
But for the grace of God, there go I.

Verse 2
He went to school, and he did really well and held a job for a while.
Then the lure set in, like a dear old friend. Now he'd sell his soul for a smile.

Verse 3
He had a family, a wife, and some boys. But he made a few mistakes.
In spite of all the warning signs, what a difference those choices make.

* * *

In the late summer of 2002, I became chair of the Mathematics and Computing Department at Franklin College for the first time. At FC, you're appointed by the dean to a three-year term. So far, I've served as department chair for a total of nine years—from August 2002 to August 2005, from August 2008 to August 2011, and from August 2016 to August 2019. I like to tell people that my claim to fame is that I succeeded as department chair a colleague of mine named Dick who worked at the College from 1958 to 2003—45 years. That's a long time. I wasn't even born when Dick started working at FC.

---

[8] You can listen to the song on SoundClick
(https://www.soundclick.com/4thnormalformband).

Although I've always seen it as an honor and privilege to serve my colleagues in the department, I've never really *liked* being department chair. While I've always tried to serve happily and do a good job, I've just never enjoyed being a full-time faculty member *and* being a part-time administrator at the same time.

Being a department chair at Franklin College isn't too bad, but the thought of being a *full-time* administrator is depressing. I mean, some professors relish the idea of becoming the dean of their faculty. And some even have dreams of becoming a college president. Not me. You couldn't pay me enough to do either of those jobs. I look at it like this: The dean is stuck in the middle between the president and the faculty, and the president is stuck in the middle between the board of trustees and the employees of the institution. No thanks. I'll stick to studying, teaching, and conducting research.

* * *

During the school year in 2003, I felt inspired to write a song about my computing students—specifically the ones who were heavily into video games and chat rooms. (I've had a lot of those over the years. I can promise you that.) As I wrote the song, I began thinking more and more about this one particular guy in my class who really embodied the idea I was trying to capture in the song. So, in a sense, the song is mostly about him. (Please note that I shall *never* reveal the name of this tremendous nerd for fear of embarrassing him.) The song is called *The King of Cyberspace.*[9]

The King of Cyberspace

Verse 1
His best friend is his computer.
It's something that he can adore.
It helps him expand his horizons.
To the world, it's his open door.

Verse 2

---

[9] You can listen to the song on SoundClick (https://www.soundclick.com/4thnormalformband).

He's among the digerati.
Well versed in the knowledge of bytes.
He stays up late to battle
Other nerds who will fight.

Verse 3
His identity is clandestine.
Anonymity is his thing.
He loves to debate in the chatrooms.
In cyberspace, he is king.

* * *

After experiencing life in the Hoosier state for six years, Elizabeth and I were really sold on Indiana. We felt like Franklin was a great place to live and work and raise a family. Plus, we enjoyed the four distinct seasons. My favorite seasons in Franklin are spring and fall. In the spring, most of the trees in the city bud into beautiful displays of white, pink, red, and purple before turning light green and finally transitioning to a much darker green. And in the fall, they transition into awesome shades of yellow, orange, and red. The flowers in Franklin are beautiful as well. Of course, the summers and winters have their colorful virtues too. So, I wrote a song about living in Indiana that I *cleverly* titled *Livin' in Indiana.*[10]

Livin' in Indiana

Verse 1
In the springtime when the daffodils awake to the early morning sun,
Singing birds, the smell of fresh-cut grass. New life has indeed begun.

Chorus
I love livin' in Indiana, where the air I breathe is clean.
And I love all the changing seasons and all the friendly people that I meet.

---

[10] You can listen to the song on SoundClick
(https://www.soundclick.com/4thnormalformband).

Verse 2
In the summer when the fields have almost touched the periwinkle sky,
County fairs and playing basketball 'til the evening dark draws nigh.

Verse 3
In the autumn when the trees have dressed themselves in their colorful
new hues,
Covered bridges and a homecoming queen and a school year that is new.

Verse 4
In the winter when the earth has wrapped herself in a blanket of pure
white,
Shoveling the driveway, frozen fingers, and hot chocolate after a snowball
fight.

Sometimes when I talk to people who live in Central Indiana, they bad-mouth it as if it's just not as beautiful as this place or that place. I don't know what they're talking about. They're always surprised when they hear me say something like, "I think Indiana is great! I've lived in Illinois, Missouri, Florida, North Carolina, and Kentucky, and I can't think of any place I'd rather be. Of course, those places are beautiful too, but I think Indiana has its own beauty." They usually stare at me like they've never heard anyone say something like that before. Like, "Wait. Someone thinks Indiana is beautiful?" Yes.

* * *

In October of 2003, I published an informative article in *Modern Drummer* magazine called "What makes a drummer good?" At the time, I participated in an online drum forum, where people asked all kinds of questions and gave all kinds of answers. When one guy asked the question, "What makes a drummer good?", several folks chimed in to help provide him with an answer. Surprisingly, the responses to the guy's question focused on things like being good at the fundamentals of drumming and possessing good character traits—not on things like fancy chops, rudimental facility, album credits, band affiliations, and status. So based on the wisdom of the folks in my online drum forum, I wrote the article.

The article I wrote was good because the ideas presented in it could be used to help *anyone* become a good drummer—even if they didn't aspire to be a professional musician. Although I had published many *scholarly* articles by this time in my career, I was most elated when this particular article was accepted for publication. I think it was because the readership would be broader, and it kind of made me feel validated as a drummer.

One of the interesting things about my online drum forum was the number of participants who were involved in the field of computing in some way. It seemed like the majority of us were either information technology specialists or software developers. I myself have always felt a strong connection between computer programming and drumming. If you think about it, they're both highly algorithmic.

If you've studied structured computer programming, you already know that any computable problem can be solved using a combination of three programming constructs: iteration (repeating something over and over), sequence (moving through a series of steps), and selection (making decisions). Well, the same thing is true in "solving a drumming problem," that is, playing the drums to accompany a song.

In terms of iteration, we're always repeating what we're doing with our hands and feet to create a rhythm for the song, and we're usually repeating certain sections of the song—like the chorus. In terms of sequence, we're always moving through the song a single beat at a time from the beginning of the song to the end. And, in terms of selection, since the drum set is an improvisatory instrument, we're always making decisions about what to play and when—like what fill to use and when to use it to signal the change from one section of a song to another. And by the way, as bonus content, drum fills are like the methods in a class library (or the procedures and functions in a subroutine library) that we call upon as needed.

If any of that made sense, you're a software developer. If it didn't, your eyes are glazing over.

* * *

You may recall from earlier the interesting spiritual experience I had during my sophomore year of high school when I came across Psalm 128:3-4 that says, "Your wife will be like a fruitful vine within your house; your children will be like olive shoots around your table. Yes, this will be the blessing for the man who fears the Lord." Well, on the evening of January 18th, 2004, as Elizabeth and I and all four of our sons were sitting around our kitchen table, the words of that scripture came to mind again and in an equally unmistakable way—as if I were being blessed with the knowledge that those words had been fulfilled in my life.

Having children truly transformed me as a person. From the very beginning, I think God put a strong desire in my heart to be a good and present father—a father who wouldn't wake up one day when his kids were all grown up and on their own and regret that he hadn't spent more time with them because he was too busy pursuing other things. So, to express my thoughts and feelings about being a father, I wrote a song called *Seeds of Time*.[11]

Seeds of Time

Verse 1
One day when I wake up, my boys will be all grown.
Their memories of me will amount to the seeds that I have sown.
I don't want to be like those who wish they'd spent more time.
They're only children once—and that for a very short while.

Chorus
I'm not gonna be too busy. I'm not gonna be too late.
Gonna sow the seeds of time. My affairs—they can wait.
I'm not gonna be too busy. I'm not gonna be too late.
Gonna sow the seeds of time because the price is just so great.

Verse 2
My sons are a heritage entrusted to my care.

---

[11] You can listen to the song on SoundClick
(https://www.soundclick.com/4thnormalformband).

I'm gonna seize the moments and be a father who is there.
So, I'm gonna guard my time and mitigate the pull.
Because I'm a man who is blessed with a quiver that is full.

* * *

Sometime in 2004, I stopped consulting for USACERL. After ten years, I had just grown tired of it. Besides, I had other things to do. In addition to REEP, I designed and developed three other important software systems while I worked for USACERL.

The first one was the Building Use Categorization and Scale-Up system. The BUCS system extrapolated the impact of current energy- and water-saving technologies on certain categories of buildings (e.g., family housing units, barracks, administrative buildings) at US military installations based on a sample of the buildings within a given category. The second one was the Window Econometric. The WE determined the respective economic feasibilities of *replacing* or *repairing* the windows on federal-government-owned buildings. And the third one was the Project Assistant. The PA helped USACERL researchers format their research proposals so that the chances of their proposals being funded were increased.

* * *

In the summer of 2004, my mom and dad traveled from Florida to Tuscola to visit family and friends. While there, one of my dad's friends gave him a zip-lock baggie full of habanero peppers that he had grown himself, dehydrated, and ground up. The peppers in the baggie were so dry and finely ground that they were more like habanero flakes and fine dust.

On their way back home to Florida, they stopped by Franklin for a few days to visit with us. When they got to our house, my dad asked me if I wanted the peppers as he probably wouldn't eat them. Since I love hot peppers and hot sauces, I was more than happy to take them. When he handed me the baggie, I immediately placed it in the upward-facing palm of my left hand, put it under my nose, and smacked the top of it with my right fingers in the hopes of getting a small whiff of the habanero aroma I love.

Unfortunately, I hit the baggie too hard, and the seal gave out. This caused a huge orange cloud of habanero dust to hit me in the face. And since my eyes were open, a bunch of the pepper dust got into my eyes. Within a few seconds, I was in a tremendous amount of burning pain. In response to the mishap, I ran into the bathroom and began flushing my eyes with water. Although I thought it might take half an hour or so to get rid of the pain, it only took a few minutes. Man, I was lucky.

* * *

During the fall semester of 2004, I was riding home from work at Franklin College when I had a bad crash on my bicycle. It was rather misty that afternoon, but not wet, and I was riding my bike at a decent clip. My plan for the rest of that afternoon and evening was to help my next-door neighbor set up his wireless router and take the boys to their Awana program at church. As I was riding through Blue Herron Park, I took a rather sharp left turn toward the parking lot on my way to the sidewalk that would take me the rest of the way home. As I took that sharp left, my bike slipped out from under me, and I slammed into the asphalt. Hard. The impact knocked the wind out of me and broke my helmet. If I had not had that helmet on, I believe I would have been severely injured.

As I was lying on the asphalt, a woman walked by and acted like she didn't hear me when I told her I had crashed on my bike, and I needed help getting to my feet. She probably thought I was some kind of crazy guy who was going to grab her as soon as she got close, so she kept on going. When I finally stood up, I could hardly breathe, and I could feel my left arm hanging abnormally from my left shoulder. Of course, this was before cell phones were common, so I had no way of calling for help.

After checking myself out and making certain I was going to live, I walked my bike the rest of the way home, which was still a quarter of a mile or so away. Because I was late getting home, Elizabeth and the boys were sitting at the table eating dinner without me. When I told them that I had crashed on my bike, they thought I was joking around. But when I showed them my helmet and the rip that was created over my pants pocket when I landed on my keys, they knew I wasn't joking.

Elizabeth insisted that I go to the Immediate Care Center in town, which I finally did—but only after I protested. The x-rays confirmed my diagnosis. I had broken some ribs on the left side of my body. I had also broken my left collarbone. I couldn't believe it. I had broken my ribs three times now. What are the odds? Was I unlucky or what?

After the crash, I was out of school for a week. When I finally went back to work, I had to wear this ridiculous-looking brace over my shirt that held my shoulders back. I also had to wear an arm sling. To make matters worse, I was completely oblivious to what we had done in my classes before I got injured. Perhaps that was due to hitting my head on the asphalt. My students thought that was really funny. When I got to my lab on the third floor of Old Main, someone in the class had written on the board, "When you mess with The Beas, you get stung. When you mess with pavement, you get broke!"

* * *

In April of 2005, I traveled to Taiwan to deliver a keynote address at the Second International Conference on the Teaching of Language, Linguistics, and Literature at National Kaohsiung Normal University in Kaohsiung. I was invited by my friend Mike from graduate school— the same guy who told me that I would visit his beautiful country one day. My talk for the conference was titled, *The Effects of Web-Based Music Study on Listening Comprehension, Language Acquisition, and Lifestyle Literacy in Taiwanese ESL Learners.* The talk was based on the research that Mike and I had been working on together for a year or two.

When I got off the plane in Tokyo to make my connecting flight to Kaohsiung, I immediately sought out a men's restroom in the airport. In the restroom, I noticed two things right away.

First, they didn't have western toilets like most of us are used to. Instead, they had what looked like urinals embedded horizontally into the floor. I actually said out loud, "What in the *world* am I going to do with *that?*" I found out later that many places in modern Asian cities have western toilets as well, but you have to look for them.

And second, there was a *woman* in the men's restroom just cleaning away while a dozen men were in there using the toilet. No. You weren't warned or anything. There was no "Bathroom Closed for Cleaning" sign, no "Restroom out of Service for Maintenance" sign, no "Baño

Cerrado Por Limpieza" sign. There was absolutely nothing. Of course, as a westerner, that made me pretty uncomfortable.

After arriving at Kaohsiung International Airport and getting off the plane, I was immediately greeted by a great big sign that said, "WARNING: Drug trafficking is punishable by death in the Republic of China." Imagine what it would be like if you saw that sign for the first time and actually had drugs on you!

* * *

When I got to my hotel room, I watched some YouTube videos to learn some Chinese so I could lay it on some people while I was there. I tried my best to learn some basics like, "Good morning," "Hello," "Goodbye," "Thank you," "Delicious," "Bathroom," and so on. The next morning, I got on YouTube again to refresh my memory on how to say, "Good morning." I practiced it over and over until I thought I had it just right. (I was pretty proud of myself.) When I left the room and got on the elevator to go down to the restaurant in the basement of the hotel for breakfast, there was an Asian man in a suit and tie who was also going down. So, I smiled at him and said, "Zow shung how!", which is kind of how it sounds to say "Good morning" in Chinese. The guy smiled back at me and said politely, "I'm from Korea."

At the restaurant, there were a number of Chinese dishes prepared. But there were some American dishes as well. The only thing was, the American dishes weren't dishes we wouldn't normally eat for breakfast. For example, I could have hot dogs and French fries and ketchup for breakfast—if I felt so inclined.

* * *

Although the food in Taiwan was fantastic, I craved some good old American food by the time my trip was drawing to a close. So, when I landed at Chicago's O'Hare International Airport on the trip home, I went straight to McDonald's and got myself a Big Mac, Fries, and a Coke! Normally, I wouldn't do that out of principle because the prices are so high at airports. But this time, I didn't care. It was so delicious.

By the way, the flights to and from Kaohsiung were about 18 hours each. That's a *very* long time to be on an airplane. Since I can't sleep on planes, and since I'm tall, the flights were pretty miserable. And that says nothing about the hideous jetlag. When it was 4 pm in Kaohsiung, my brain thought it was 4 am. So, it wanted me to sleep, and it worked *overtime* to get me into that state. It took me three days just to function, and I was only there for eight days. When I got home, I swore I'd never go to Taiwan again. It *was* a great once-in-a-lifetime experience, but the trip was just too brutal.

* * *

It was also in 2005 that we decided to leave the Church at Stones Crossing in Greenwood and start attending church in Franklin again. It wasn't that we didn't like CSC anymore. On the contrary, we thought it was a wonderful church. But I thought we should be going to church closer to home—for a couple of reasons. First, our boys were getting older, and I knew they would soon want to be involved with a youth group. Since I had band rehearsals on Thursday nights and church on Sunday mornings, I was already driving 20 or 25 minutes to Center Grove and back an awful lot, and I really didn't want to drive up there one more time per week to take my kids to youth group. And second, I wanted us *all* to have church friends in our own community.

I thoroughly enjoyed being part of the worship band at the Church at Stones Crossing, but we really felt led to fellowship in Franklin. So, I met with Pastor Scott over lunch one afternoon and told him why and when we would be leaving CSC—we weren't mad about anything, we hadn't been offended by anyone, we just felt like God was leading us to be involved in a church in Franklin. He was very understanding and gracious—just as I knew he would be.

After visiting a few churches in Franklin, Elizabeth and I decided that we should return to Franklin Community Church—the church we had attended from 1997 to 2000. By the time we returned to FCC, the church had hired a new pastor named Dan and had returned to having a worship band, which I soon rejoined. We had never really lost touch with FCC because many of the people in our homeschool group went to church there. Plus, I had continued to take our boys to the church's Awana program every Wednesday evening during our absence. Those two things made our transition back to FCC pretty easy.

* * *

In 2006, I wrote another song about the inner-city missions that my students and I worked at during my winter term course. Before those experiences, many of us thought that the people who sought help from such ministries were just lazy and just didn't want to get a job. Or we thought that they were just trapped in the cycle of poverty they grew up in. Or we thought that they had just dug themselves into a hole by the horrible decisions they had made in their lives—like abusing drugs and alcohol, dropping out of school, having multiple children out of wedlock, or ruining relationships with loved ones.

To be honest, there *was* a lot of that. But we also learned that some of the people were victims of mental illness or were just down on their luck for some reason. Perhaps they had lost their job. But regardless of the reasons behind a person's plight, I think most of us learned that God wants us to be compassionate toward the people seeking our help and to extend a caring hand when it is within our power to do so.

One of the missions that we always worked at during winter term was the Metro Baptist Center. The Metro Baptist Center is a mission that serves low-income people in the city by providing food, clothing, spiritual counseling, and other assistance. Homeless people can also go to the MBC for help, but after they're given some food, they're directed to the other missions in the city that specialize in serving the homeless.

Whenever we worked at the Metro Baptist Center, I always tried to imagine what it would be like if *I* were the person in need. If *I* were the one standing in line at the mission's door on a frigid January morning waiting to be let in. Somehow, I was able to sense what those people were feeling. Somehow, I was able to see the world through their eyes. Somehow, I was able to picture myself in their situation. That scene inspired me to write a song about the Metro Baptist Center from the perspective of someone who had come to the mission for help. The song is called *Down from the Mountain*.[12]

Down from the Mountain

Verse 1
Out in the cold in the city, it's time to go stand in the line.
There's a serious hunger within me, an ill-feeling that's hard to define.

---

[12] You can listen to the song on SoundClick
(https://www.soundclick.com/4thnormalformband).

As I stand by the doorway, I see all the others in need.
And then I stare as I wonder, how could this happen to me?

Chorus
I've looked down from the mountain. I've looked up from below.
I've known an unshackled spirit. I've known a desperate soul.
Looking back on the broken, picking up all the pieces
Was a hand that was caring and a heart that releases.

Verse 2
In the warmth of the mission, I take my seat in the room.
There are some baskets of clothing and some tables of donated food.
As I sit with the troubled, a woman calls out my name.
And then she shares of a future of hope and a heavenly rain.

One of the many passages from the Bible that we used to prepare ourselves for working at the missions was Matthew 25:31-46. Maybe you're familiar with it. It's the story of the sheep and the goats. One hot and humid summer day, when Elizabeth and the boys and I were in downtown Chicago, that passage came to mind as I watched all the people around us going about their busy days with little to no regard for the homeless people in the area. I'm not being judgmental because I'm almost certain that if I lived and worked in that particular area of the city, it would be easy for me to ignore the homeless people on the streets as well. After a while, I'm sure that kind of stuff just becomes background noise. Anyway, I was inspired that day by the scene, so I wrote a song about it called *The Distance*.[13]

The Distance

Verse 1
At the L station on a muggy summer day,
A blind man plays for tips for those who walk his way.
She walks on by annoyed by his infirmity.

---

[13] You can listen to the song on SoundClick
(https://www.soundclick.com/4thnormalformband).

Thinks that he should get a job just like you and me.

Chorus
I hear the goats out in the distance.
I see a stranger standing near.
What you do to the least of my brothers....
A look around is all you need.
What you do to the least of these others....
You're doin' it to me.

Verse 2
On a Sunday morning on a sidewalk in the city,
A woman begs for change and hopes that someone will take pity.
He pretends he does not hear her plea to lend a hand.
Thinks it's time for folks like him to finally take a stand.

* * *

In September of 2006, we moved into the new home we had built farther back in our subdivision. This house was about two miles from campus, and I continued to ride my bicycle to work on most days. One of the reasons we built the new house was because our homeschooling activities were expanding, and we needed more room for desks. (I *really* wanted to get the desks out of our living room in the old house!) Plus, our boys were getting bigger and wanted to have their own bedrooms, where they could keep their own stuff and could have their own space to do school. So, two of the boys had bedrooms on the second floor, and two of them had bedrooms in the basement.

* * *

It was around this time that I started giving the boys opportunities to make money around the house. Although they made money playing gigs and earned a small allowance for doing their chores, sometimes things came up that I just didn't want to do myself. So, it was either pay someone else to do it or pay them.

For some jobs, I'd pay them per unit of work. For example, when we first moved into our house, the yard was rife with rocks and hunks of concrete because our lot was the last one to be built on. Essentially, the construction workers had used our lot as a dumping ground for their unused pea gravel, concrete rubble, and just about everything else. So, I paid the boys a dollar or two for every bucket of rocks they filled and loaded into our trailer. After a couple of hours or so, the yard was virtually rock free, and the boys had made some good money.

For other jobs, I'd pay them half of what I'd pay someone else. After all, they got to live in the house for free. For example, if someone would charge me 20 dollars per hour to clean my garage, I'd pay one of the boys ten dollars per hour to clean the garage. They'd estimate how long it would take them to do it, and we would arrive at a mutually acceptable deal. If they did a good job and didn't waste time, but the job took longer than expected, I was perfectly fine with paying them more to make it right.

The boys always welcomed the opportunity to make money like that. In fact, I don't remember a single time when I needed something done, and at least one of them wasn't willing to do it for money. For their age, the pay was exceptionally good. They couldn't make that kind of money anywhere else. As for me, I felt really good about paying my kids to do work for me instead of paying someone else.

After the boys were around 10 years old, I no longer just outright bought them stuff—like bicycles and other relatively expensive things. Instead, they had to save half the money. Then, when they were ready to make the purchase, they paid half, and I paid half. My thinking was that they'd be more inclined to take care of their things if they had some skin in the game. Eventually, when they were old enough to mow yards and shovel snow, they made enough of their own money that I no longer needed to subsidize any of their purchases.

* * *

When Zach and Isaac were 14 and 13 years old, respectively, they started their own business called Beasley Quality Lawn Care and Snow Removal. To drum up business, they made refrigerator magnets with their contact information (our home telephone number) on them and went all around the neighborhood handing them out to homeowners. They also made professional-looking invoices that they filled out and delivered after finishing a job.

When Nathan and Elijah became old enough to mow, they joined the business as well. When Zach started college, he passed the business to Isaac. When Isaac started college, he passed the business to Nathan. And when Nathan started college, he passed the business to Elijah who kept it going until he graduated from college.

The lawn care and snow removal business was very lucrative for the boys because they had no competition to speak of from other kids in the neighborhood. Their only competition was from the professional lawn mowing companies around town who charged twice as much, finished the job in ten minutes, and didn't bother with the details. Just sayin'. All that added up to many loyal customers over many years. As a matter of fact, for a year or two after the business finally ended, I still got an occasional phone call from someone in the neighborhood who had a refrigerator magnet and wanted someone to take care of their yard or do a special project—like mulch around their house.

As I look back on it now, I feel good about the "gradual approach to financial independence" that Elizabeth and I employed as parents. For her part, Elizabeth taught the boys things like how to create and maintain a budget and how to complete and submit a tax return. I think the things we did helped make the transition from "little boy who got everything for free and had no financial obligations" to "adult who had to pay his own bills and taxes" pretty seamless.

* * *

In December of 2006, I learned a valuable life lesson. And that was to never say "never." Although I had sworn that I'd never travel to Taiwan again because of the shear brutality of the trip, I found myself there again at the invitation of my good friend Mike. Mike had invited me to deliver another keynote address. This time, the address would occur at the Fourth International Conference on Multimedia Language Education of APAMALL and The Tenth International Conference on Multimedia Language Education of ROCMELIA. The location of the conference would be the National Museum of Science and Technology in Kaohsiung. My talk was titled, *The Effects of Web-Based Music Study on Taiwanese EFL Learners: A Summary of Current Findings.*

On one of the evenings during the conference, dinner was served at a bookstore (for some reason), and the food was laid out buffet-style. There were dozens of dishes to choose from, and I was curious as to what each one was. So, Mike's daughter Alice was kind enough to walk around with me and answer my questions about each beautiful dish. At one table, I sampled the meat of a dish and commented to Alice about how incredibly delicious it was. When I asked her what it was, she said, "Pig intestine." Valuable life lesson number two? Ask first.

After the conference and right before heading back to the US, Mike sat down with me and asked me if I would be interested in designing and developing a software system for his organization—the Republic of China Multimedia English Learning and Instruction Association. The purpose of the system would be to deliver and score Web-based listening, reading, writing, and speaking tests for individuals seeking English language certifications in Taiwan.

The Web-based system ROCMELA was currently using to deliver its online language tests was developed by a team of professors and graduate students at National Taichung University, but since it didn't automatically grade the multiple-choice sections of tens of thousands of tests, the entire process of language certification was very inefficient for ROCMELIA. They needed something significantly better if they were going to survive in the competitive business of foreign language testing.

So, even though I had grown tired of it just a couple of years earlier, I began consulting again at the end of 2006. I designed and developed a software system for ROCMELA that was called the Language Test of Proficiency for All on the Web (LATPAW). Evidently, I just needed a break.

* * *

On June 7th, 2008, the boys and I played a gig in Bradenton, Florida. Although it was a beautiful and sunny day in South Florida, it wasn't so beautiful and sunny back home in Franklin. When the gig was over, we packed up our equipment and went back to my grandma Virginia's house, where we were staying for the week. On the national news that evening, the big story was the weather in the Midwest. As I watched the radar image on the TV, I could tell we were getting a ton of rain in Indiana. The radar showed this long, trainlike line of green, yellow, red, and purple as it traveled in a straight line over Indiana and several other eastern states, from the Gulf of Mexico north-northeastward, while the storm front refused to move off to the east to provide relief.

As we traveled through southern Indiana on our way back home, the water had receded some, but we could still see signs that significant flooding had occurred. At home, our basement had been completely flooded. Although we had two working sump pumps down there, they had been overwhelmed by the water. We didn't live in a floodplain or anything, but we had gotten 7.6 inches of rain in a 24-hour period. The sump pumps just couldn't keep up.

Since we were in Florida when the flooding occurred, my mother-in-law, who now lived in Franklin part time, called on some of our neighbors and friends who helped her clear out our basement and get some fans going so we wouldn't get mold down there. Unfortunately, a lot of the stuff was completely ruined, including the carpeting, the bathroom vanity, and many of our homeschool books. Thankfully, our homeowner's insurance company was very generous, and we were able to get the basement back to normal.

But we were relatively fortunate. In some of the lower lying parts of Franklin, homes were completely ruined by the water and were torn down—never to be rebuilt. The event was eventually declared a 500- to 1,000-year flood. No one had ever seen anything like it in Franklin. A few years later, Nathan and I wrote a song about the flood called *The Rain is Falling.*[14]

The Rain is Falling

Verse 1
In the distance, I can hear the echo roll.
The night is grumbling awakening my soul.
And in the droning of a cloudy melody,
The river is rising, fighting to get free.

---

[14] You can listen to the song on SoundClick (https://www.soundclick.com/4thnormalformband), or you can see a very cool video on YouTube (https://www.youtube.com/watch?v=m29pccX0imA) that will show you the full effect of the storm.

Chorus
The rain is falling. Been pouring for so long.
The rain is falling.
The rain is falling. Been pouring for so long.
The rain is falling.

Verse 2
From the heavens, I can see the train below.
Colored image of a figure we all know.
But in my mind's eye, that vision's turning gray.
'Cause when it gets here, I know it's gonna stay.

* * *

In August of 2008, I was promoted to full professor. The rank of full professor at most academic institutions is the final destination of a "tenure-track" position. Someone with a Ph.D. degree begins his or her academic career as an assistant professor, is promoted to associate professor, and then is promoted to full professor. All promotions are earned. No one is promoted automatically.

To be promoted in academia, you have to go through a thorough review of your accomplishments by a group of your peers who have been elected by the faculty. Obtaining the rank of full professor means that your peers recognize you as one who has done exemplary work in the areas of research, teaching, and service to your department, the institution, and your field as a whole. Once you achieve the rank of full professor, there is nowhere else to go—although some institutions also have the designation of distinguished professor.

* * *

That fall, I stopped riding my 1976 cobalt blue Peugeot UO-8 10-speed bicycle to work. I had ridden it to work for many years and had kept it in pretty good shape, but I had to stop riding it because I began to develop pain in my wrists from putting so much forward-leaning weight on them—like you do when you ride any kind of road-racing bicycle. Earlier, I had complained to a colleague of mine that my wrists were hurting when I rode my 10-speed, so she recommended that I get a mountain bike. So that's what I did, and my wrist pain vanished.

I kept my Peugeot around for a few more years, but since it was just taking up room in my garage, I decided to get rid of it. So, I put it out on the curb with a sign on it that said, "Free." It was gone the next day. Someone got a nice bike that day. I wish I hadn't gotten rid of it. If I still had it, maybe I'd take it out for an occasional afternoon ride, or maybe I'd display it like a museum piece in my home office.

* * *

In the summer of 2009, my friend Mike asked me to collaborate with a professor in Taiwan on a song called *The Song of ROCMELIA*. I agreed to do it, albeit reluctantly, but only because I didn't want to disappoint a good friend. After the professor sent me his lyrics, I put them to music—music I had already written and recorded with the 4th Normal Form Band. When I finished the song, I sent it off to Mike thinking that that would be the end of it.

That October, I traveled to Taiwan for a third time. Once again, my good friend Mike had invited me to deliver a keynote address at one of the several conferences he was involved with. This time, I would be speaking at the 13th International Conference on Multimedia Language Instruction, which would soon be taking place at National Kaohsiung Normal University. My talk was titled, *The Effects of Test Type and Gender on Elapsed Time and Language Placement Testing Outcomes: An Analysis of 3250 Online NETPAW Tests.*[15]

Although I thought I would never hear *The Song for ROCMELIA* again, I was wrong. At the conference, the song played repeatedly over the conference center's PA system during break times and other lulls in the program. Although I tried not to let it show, I was mortified. Not because the song was bad or anything. It was a decent song. But, hearing myself sing it over and over and knowing that everyone at the conference knew it was me singing made me very uncomfortable. In fact, when I tried to talk with people, I couldn't really concentrate on

---

[15] NETPAW stands for National English Test of Proficiency for All on the Web. NETPAW is a *test* and shouldn't be confused with LATPAW, which is the Web-Based software system I designed and developed for ROCMELIA. The LATPAW system administers NETPAW tests and many others.

what they were saying because all I could hear was my voice singing that song in the background.

Dad, Elizabeth, me, and Mom after graduating with my master's degree from Illinois State University.

In our apartment in Urbana, Illinois when I was in graduate school at the University of Illinois. I'm reviewing the proofs of my first published research article.

On my 30th birthday.

Elizabeth right before going into the hospital to have our first son. I was so excited I could hardly contain myself.

Elizabeth, Isaac, me, and Zach in front of the Alma Mater after graduating with my Ph.D. degree from the University of Illinois.

Me, Zach, Isaac, and Elizabeth at my graduation party after graduating from the University of Illinois.

Zach, me, Elizabeth, and Isaac in front of our very first home in Greenville, North Carolina.

Elizabeth in Greenville, North Carolina.

Behind the drum set at a Union College football game in Barbourville, Kentucky.

Elizabeth with Nathan, Zach, Elijah, and Isaac on Christmas Eve in Franklin, Indiana.

My paternal grandparents. Jack and Sadie Beasley.

My burgundy Pearl Export Select drum set with Zildjian cymbals all set up and polished in our living room. I loved that drum set.

The Midnight Transit website that I created for the band. Pat, Duane, Rich, and me.

Reedy's Dream. Jeff, Dave, Scott, me, and Jeff.

Once a Child. Robert, me, and Steve.

The 4NF Band's first gig. Me, Isaac, and Zach.

The 4NF Band's second gig. It was Nathan's first gig with us. Zach, me, Isaac (partially hidden), and Nathan.

The 4NF Band's fifth gig. It was Elijah's first gig with us. Zach, Isaac, Elijah, Nathan, and me.

My first trip to Taiwan. Mike, the president of National Kaohsiung Normal University, and me.

After landing in Kaohsiung, Taiwan for the first time as a family. Isaac, Zach, Elijah, me, and Nathan.

In Mike's mother-in-law's fruit orchard in Kaohsiung, Taiwan. It was a magical moment in my life. Isaac, Zach, me, Elizabeth, Elijah, and Nathan.

Visiting Kun Shan University in Tainan, Taiwan. I was always treated like a king in Taiwan thanks to Mike. Mike and I are in the front row. He is on my right.

Talking to professors and graduate students at Kun Shan University in Tainan, Taiwan.

Playing music at a summer English camp at Bilingual Community Church in Kaohsiung, Taiwan. Zach, Elijah, me, Isaac, and Nathan.

My mom and dad's 50th wedding anniversary photo.

After an indoor soccer game. All the boys and their wives and children were in town for Christmas. Nathan, Isaac, me, Zach, and Elijah.

Elizabeth and our four beautiful daughters-in-law. Abigail, Camille, Elizabeth, Jaycee, and Andrea.

Dad playing pool with me in Bradenton, Florida. Notice that he's holding his pool cue backward to rub it in as he's about to sink the eightball for the win.

On graduation day at Franklin College immediately after completing my 30th year as a college professor.

Me at Franklin College.

The 2010s

54 68 65 20 32 30 31 30 73

In the spring of 2010, ROCMELIA invited our family to Taiwan for an eight-week stay. The primary purpose of our trip would be to record audio clips of English words, phrases, sentences, and paragraphs for use by the LATPAW system. All six of us would be participating in the recording sessions. Although we would be recording hundreds of new clips, we would also be re-recording a significant number of clips that needed redoing because of the relatively strong southern accents of the folks who recorded the clips originally. Evidently, such accents can be confusing to Chinese speakers trying to learn English for the first time. The secondary purpose of our trip would be for me to give some talks about my research at Mike's university.

Of course, it wouldn't be all work and no play. For us as a family, it was a once-in-a-lifetime chance to travel to the other side of the earth and experience the Chinese culture.

Before we left for our long trip, I got on the Internet to look for an English-speaking church we could attend while we lived in Kaohsiung. For some reason, I never heard back from the first church I contacted. But the second church I contacted, Bilingual Community Church, got back with me almost immediately. I told the pastor there, Dave, that my family and I were going to be in Kaohsiung for eight weeks and that we wanted to plug into a church right away when we got there.

I also told Pastor Dave that we would serve the church in whatever way they needed us. After our initial email exchange, I figured we'd be stuffing envelopes, setting up and taking down chairs, cleaning toilets, and so on. Honestly, anything was fine with me—as long as we were contributing to the church in *some* way. Pastor Dave was excited that we were coming, and he asked me if we could start by bringing some books and equipment they had purchased in the US for their upcoming summer English camps—which, of course, we were happy to do.

During a subsequent email exchange, I mentioned to Dave that we could also play live music if the need arose, since that's something my sons and I did a lot in the US. He was very interested in the idea that we had a band because the theme of the upcoming children's English camp at Bilingual Community Church was "Backstage with the Band." It seemed like our visit to Kaohsiung, our connection with BCC, our ability to provide a full band, and the theme and timing of the summer English camp was something God was orchestrating.

* * *

In June of 2010, Elizabeth, the boys, and I arrived in Kaohsiung, Taiwan for our eight-week stay. Shortly after arriving there, before the English camp rolled around, we all jumped into the process of helping put on a successful English camp. One of the first things we did was hand out flyers to children and their parents outside some of the local elementary schools.

When the English camp finally arrived, the boys and I led the music playing praise and worship songs on instruments the church already had in place.

We were *all* involved in the English classes that were taught each day as well. Depending on their ages, the boys either led or helped lead an English class for the kids, and Elizabeth and I taught English and American Culture classes to the parents of the campers in attendance. And finally, during the carnival at the end of the week, the boys and I played a full American rock concert for the campers, their parents, and everyone in the church.

While we were in Taiwan that summer, we also participated in two other English camps. One of them was at the Chung-Cheng Armed Forces Preparatory School, which was a high school for miliary-bound boys, and the other one was at Shu-Te University. At those camps, just like at Bilingual Community Church, the boys and I led the music and played an American rock concert at the end of the week. In addition, all six of us either taught or were part of the English classes that were offered.

The camps that summer were a great experience that God used to draw many children, young men, and college age men and women to himself. It was a beautiful thing to see and be a part of.

* * *

During our stay in Kaohsiung, a magical moment occurred in my life. On each of my three previous trips to Taiwan, Mike had taken me to the outskirts of Kaohsiung to visit with his mother-in-law and to see her beautiful fruit orchard. Mike's mother-in-law's house was on the side of a mountain, and behind her house, farther up the hill, was her orchard. Each time I stood in that orchard, I looked out across the valley toward a neighboring mountain on top of which was a 100-foot-tall golden Buddha. The colossal statue was located at the Fo Guan Shan Buddhist Monastery, which was a mile or so away from where I was standing. Every time I stood in that orchard, I imagined Elizabeth and the boys *someday* seeing what I was seeing.

Back then, of course, I thought that would never happen. But now, it *was* happening. On this trip, Mike took Elizabeth and the boys and me to visit with his mother-in-law and to see her fruit orchard—just like he had taken me three times before. At one point, as we all stood there in that orchard among the dragon fruit cacti, the lychee, and the lemon trees gazing across the valley toward the 100-foot-tall golden Buddha, it suddenly dawned on me that my past "visions" of standing there with my family had become a reality. It was one of the most magical moments of my life.

* * *

Living in Taiwan for almost two months was, of course, an amazing experience for all of us. But at the end of our time there, it was time to say our goodbyes. When we got back home to Indiana, I wrote a song that captures many of our favorite memories of the trip. The song is called *So Long Kaohsiung*.[16]

---

[16] You can listen to the song on SoundClick (https://www.soundclick.com/4thnormalformband), or you can see a cool video on YouTube (https://www.youtube.com/watch?v=DpfrJHxAXPg). I recommend

So Long Kaohsiung

Verse 1
All along YuCheng Road. Manic riders everywhere.
Makes me wonder to myself which ones aren't gonna get there.

Chorus
So long Kaohsiung.
Electric thoughts to think upon.
So long Kaohsiung.
In my mind you'll carry on.
zài jiàn (goodbye) Kaohsiung!

Verse 2
City streets. High-rise life. Traffic lights hypnotize me.
The Sanmin District is alive. I can feel the energy.

Verse 3
In a city that never sleeps. Night markets. The MRT.
No need for Fahrenheit. Symbols around that I can't read.

Bridge
The first few nights we stayed in the Song San Hotel. We celebrated my
14th birthday in the Kenting National Park. The climb up Monkey
Mountain. You know we really enjoyed the Love River. We spent a lot
of time in that coffee shop with our friends. Our week in the
ROCMELIA Center was a neat experience. The beautiful sight of
Frog Rock. Many, many monkeys! The smell of Jasmine in Bright River
Side Park. What about Bilingual Community Church?

* * *

One day, in the fall of 2010, I rode Franklin College's Segway home after work. The College had recently purchased the Segway for some

---

the video to see what Taiwan was like. We had the photos taken for use on our website and last CD.

reason, and I thought it would be fun to ride it home and let the boys give it a try. If you don't know what a Segway is, it's a scooter-like vehicle with a frame that contains its balancing technology and battery, two parallel wheels (one on each side of the frame), a steering column, a platform that you stand on, and a set of handlebars that you hold on to. To steer the Segway, you lean forward to move forward or speed up, you lean backward to slow down or move backward, and you shift your weight from one side to the other to turn right or left. One of the dumbest inventions ever.

Anyway, I contacted the woman in charge of the Segway, and she said I could use it anytime I wanted to. So, after my classes that day, she gave me a quick lesson on how to ride it—and off I went.

As I rode the Segway home that day, I slowly began to realize how truly ridiculous I looked. I started noticing people along the Greenways Trail looking at me and giggling as they pointed me out to their walking mates. There I was, dressed in tan dress pants and a pink dress shirt with a backpack on my back and a bike helmet on my head standing perfectly erect on a silly-looking scooter as if I were too lazy to walk or ride a bike. I was mortified. I looked like a complete dork. To make matters worse, I was too far into my ride home to turn around and cut my losses. So, I continued on. I couldn't wait to get home and get off that thing, and I hoped I could do so without my neighbors seeing me. Unfortunately, I had to ride the Segway back to campus the next day.

* * *

In January of 2011, I took on another software consultantship—this time for the director of the Metro Baptist Center in Indianapolis. The director, Tom, asked me if I would design and develop a software system that would help the MBC and the network of other inner-city churches and missions in the Indianapolis metropolitan area track the assistance they provide to the poor and homeless of the city.

After meeting with Tom on a cold January evening at a Starbucks in Greenwood, I agreed to design and develop the system for him. The name of the system would be the Urban Christian Assistance Network system. Although the original geographical scope of the UCAN system was the Indianapolis metropolitan area, it would eventually be used by churches and missions in several other cities and states.

* * *

Sometime in early 2011, I began feeling the urge to write a software engineering textbook. The textbook I had been using in my software engineering courses since 1995 (in its various editions) contained a lot of great topics, but I always felt like there were a number of concepts in the book that either didn't really matter that much or weren't clearly articulated. At the time, I was pretty reluctant to write a book like that because I knew such an endeavor would require an enormous amount of time and energy, and I knew if I started it, I wouldn't stop until it was done.

So, I prayed about it some, thinking that writing a college textbook was probably *not* something I wanted to get involved in. But for some reason, the urges resurfaced every once in a while. Don't ask me why, but the urges always seemed to manifest themselves when I was getting out of the shower in the morning. Weird, I know, but it's an interesting and noteworthy detail.

* * *

In June of 2011, we took a second trip to Taiwan as a family. This time, though, we only stayed for six weeks. We also only participated in the English camp for children at Bilingual Community Church. If I recall correctly, the other two camps were put on by another church in the city, so our services were not required.

I couldn't believe we were in Taiwan again. At the end of our first trip to Kaohsiung, several people had asked me if I thought we would ever come back to visit. Of course, being the realist I am, I told them that we almost certainly wouldn't. At the time, I thought that living in Taiwan was a once-in-a-lifetime experience. I couldn't imagine us ever doing that again, so I told them the honest truth. And besides, I didn't want to make that brutal trip again. Although I had thoroughly enjoyed being in Taiwan with Elizabeth and the boys, I hated the process of getting there. I mean, if I could've snapped my fingers, and we could've been magically transported there, I probably would've been fine with visiting there *every* year—kind of making it a thing.

Although Elizabeth had been advocating for another trip to Taiwan since shortly after we got home from our first trip, I resisted the idea. But after struggling internally with the idea for several months, I finally relented and said I would go. But under one condition. We had to take the shortest route possible. So, Elizabeth got online and found tickets that would take us from Indianapolis to San Fransisco to Taipei. Since we'd only be in an airplane for 18 hours or so, I felt a little better about the trip. Plus, the trip would be broken up by a four-hour layover in San Fransisco that would provide a break from the cramped airplane.

Unfortunately, when we got to the airport on the day of the trip, Elizabeth had left two of our passports on the printer at home. So, she called a friend in Franklin and asked her to get the passports off the printer and bring them to the airport. Despite her friend's best efforts, we didn't get the passports on time. We had missed our international flight.

Although we were quite anxious about missing our flight, the good people at American Airlines re-routed our trip, getting us on the next flight out of Indianapolis that would get us all to our final destination. Unfortunately, our new itinerary would be taking us to New York City to Vancouver to Hong Kong to Kaohsiung. A very *long* route.

When we got to Vancouver, they wouldn't let us off the plane. We sat in that hot and stuffy plane for probably three hours—even while the cleaning crew came in and did their jobs. I have no idea why they wouldn't let us off, but they didn't, and it was miserable. In total, we were on an airplane for close to 28 hours. Brutal. So, just in case it was lost on you, here's the irony: Although I had agreed to take the trip to Taiwan, as long as we could take the shortest route possible, it turned out to be an *especially* long and miserable trip.

* * *

Not much sticks out to me about that particular summer in Taiwan, except for this one thing that happened at church one Sunday morning. When church was over that morning, and everyone was milling about in the sanctuary and talking, I spotted someone that I recognized. The weird thing about it was that I immediately remembered his name— Warwick. I had met Warwick at the University of Illinois exactly 20 years earlier (in 1991) at an InterVarsity Christian Fellowship Graduate Chapter meeting, where he was the president of the chapter. The crazy thing was that I had only met him *once* because Elizabeth and I had decided to *not* join InterVarsity at the U of I and, instead, make a local church the focus of our Christian community while we lived in Urbana.

When I approached him and asked him if his name was Warwick, he looked surprised and told me it was. Of course, he didn't recognize *me* at all. I was *shocked* that I recognized his face and remembered his name after only meeting him once so long ago. I also remembered that he was a New Zealander and that he was a Ph.D. student in agricultural economics when he was at the University of Illinois. Although I was able to recall those details about him, I don't remember a single thing about our conversation that morning, like where he was living, what he was doing for work, why he was in Kaohsiung, or even what his last name was. Nothing. After that meeting, we went our separate ways—never to see each other again.

I've always wondered why I didn't get Warwick's phone number or email address or something. I mean, what are the odds of running into someone I met 20 years ago at a church on the other side of the earth at that exact time in history? Sometimes I think maybe it was a divine appointment that I neglected to take advantage of.

* * *

In July of 2012, Elizabeth and the boys and I drove to Florida to visit my mom, dad, sister, and other relatives who lived there. Although we had visited them many times before, the main purpose of our trip was to see my mom who had recently been diagnosed with stage four liver cancer. As usual, we had a great time with "Nanny" and "Poppy" and everyone. We all enjoyed talking with my mom, and the boys and I had a lot of fun with my dad—playing pool in the activity center and playing golf at the local executive golf course. We also had fun hanging out at the swimming pool and relaxing in the hot tub. Despite the great time we had in Florida for the two weeks we were there, we knew that my mom was very sick and that some of us might not see her again.

About seven months later, in February of 2013, my sister called to let me know that Mom was getting worse and that I should make plans to visit fairly soon if I wanted to see her again. Since Franklin College's Spring Break was coming up in late March, I bought a ticket to Florida for that week so I could see my mom one last time. Unfortunately, just two or three days before I was to travel to Bradenton, she passed away.

My dad told me that, even if I had made it there in time, she probably wouldn't have known I was there. Still, I wish I could've seen her and said goodbye. On a positive note, I was able to be with my dad during that difficult time in his life.

* * *

Before my mom passed away, I tried to visit my parents once a year by myself for a week. Whenever I was down at their place in Florida, my mom would always make us hazelnut coffee in the afternoon, and she and I would talk and watch cooking shows together. We had always enjoyed watching cooking shows together. In fact, we started watching them together when I was in the second grade. I still watch them on occasion—but usually in the form of short YouTube videos. Mom and I watched Graham Kerr, Julia Child, Wolfgang Puck, Rachael Ray, Justin Wilson, Emeril Lagasse, Jamie Oliver, and probably some lesser-known folks that I've forgotten about.

I still enjoy the time I get to spend with my dad. To this day, when I visit him, he and I usually play pool together down at the clubhouse where he lives. We used to golf when I visited, but we don't do that so much anymore. Dan and I always have a good time together, and he always makes me laugh. The stuff he comes up with and the stories he tells are priceless. He's always been one of the funniest people I know.

* * *

Sometime in the spring of 2013, after having thought and prayed about it for a couple of years, the urge to write a software engineering textbook became too strong to ignore. So, I decided to go for it. That decision marked a major shift in my academic career—at least in terms of my scholarly output.

Since 1991, I had been focusing on conducting empirical research and publishing the results in academic journals. It's interesting to look back at how my research interests evolved over the years. In graduate school, my research interests revolved around hypermedia design and development and energy and environmental engineering information systems. Then, they evolved from telecommuting to English language acquisition and American cultural literacy through online multimedia music study. And finally, they evolved from computational linguistics to student assessment.

So, when I finally decided to write a software engineering textbook, I began spending much less time conducting empirical research and almost all my time writing college textbooks.

* * *

In June of 2013, we took a third trip to Taiwan. This time, we stayed for seven weeks. As usual, we participated in the English camp for children at Bilingual Community Church. But we also participated in the English camp for high school age boys at the Chung-Cheng Armed Forces Preparatory School, and the English camp for college age men and women—this time at National Sun Yat-sen University.

* * *

At church, I met a professor whose research agenda was in student assessment. More specifically, he focused on "confidence weighting," where students indicate their confidence (low, medium, or high) in the individual answers they give to the multiple-choice questions on their quizzes and exams. I found his research very interesting, so I decided to utilize confidence weighting in my courses at Franklin College.

* * *

That summer, I started playing tennis—again. I had played a lot of tennis as a kid, pretty much up until I was 21 years old. But one day after losing in a local tournament in the very first round, a tournament that I thought I had a good chance of winning, I got so frustrated with *myself* that I quit playing tennis altogether—cold turkey. So, except for playing with my dad and my sons a few times over the years, I really didn't play tennis anymore. Instead, I played golf. I didn't play a lot of golf—just once in a while with my grandpa Jack, my dad, or my boys.

Anyway, a friend of mine at Bilingual Community Church, a guy whose English name was Mike, asked me if I knew how to play tennis. I told him I did, but I probably wasn't very good anymore. So, we went to Wenzao Ursuline University of Languages, a university not too far from BCC and played some tennis on a rooftop court. It was incredibly hot and humid in Taiwan in the summer, and there we were playing tennis on top of a five- or six-story building in the middle of the day. It was brutal! Although we were both soaked and worn out from the heat and humidity after about 45 minutes, I had a lot of fun, and, much to my surprise, felt the desire to start playing tennis again.

* * *

On all three of our trips to Taiwan, the boys and I often led worship during the youth group meetings on Saturday nights, and we frequently filled in for the regular band members at Bilingual Community Church when they were absent on a given Sunday morning. On all three trips, we visited Mike's mother-in-law and spent time in her fruit orchard. On a couple of our trips, Elizabeth and I spoke at church on occasion and led Sunday school classes on marriage and family. One summer, Elizabeth even planned and spoke at a one-day conference on the topic of homeschooling—something that many people there were interested in learning about and something that had only recently become legal.

* * *

As for me individually, when I wasn't doing something at Bilingual Community Church, working at an English camp, or doing things with family and friends, I often met with people for coffee at the Manhattan Coffee Shop, which was next door to the church. To me, the coffee shop was a very special place, where people from the church and the neighborhood would show up, order a drink, read a book, or engage others in conversation. Virtually every day, I would stop in there in the middle of the afternoon, have Derek (his English name) make me an Americano coffee, and talk with folks. It was a wonderful experience.

One of the interesting things about a lot of the shopkeepers in Kaohsiung is that they leave the doors to their shops wide open in the middle of the day while their air conditioners blast away in an attempt to keep their places of business cool. The first time I experienced this was at the coffee shop. Since leaving the door wide open with the air conditioner running was a *huge* waste of energy, it made me extremely uneasy. So, I would nonchalantly get up from my seat and discreetly close the door to keep the air conditioning in. However, a few minutes later, a customer would come in and leave the door wide open again, like it was nothing. So again, I would nonchalantly get up from my seat and discreetly close the door to keep the cool air in. This happened over and over, so I eventually asked Derek about it. He told me that shopkeepers in Taiwan leave their doors open because it makes their shops more welcoming. I didn't have the heart to tell him that it also makes their shops less profitable.

I also spent a good deal of time in the air-conditioned office above the coffee shop, where I worked on my assorted research and book-writing projects. Since the church was leasing the upstairs of the coffee shop, Pastor Dave gave me permission to use the office in it whenever I wanted. It was amazing sitting in the crisp air, watching the cars and scooters and people on the busy street below, and looking out toward the dozens of high-rise buildings in my line of sight. The view was so different from what I was used to in the town of Franklin.

* * *

During our trips to Taiwan, I also traveled with Mike (my long-time friend, not my friend from church) to various universities on occasion to meet with administrators, faculty, staff, and students—usually about my research or something they were doing.

This one time, when Mike was driving us back to Kaohsiung from Tianan, where I had just spoken with a group of people at Kun Shan University, I thought I'd try out some of my Chinese on him while we were in the car. Although I had learned to say "delicious" a few years earlier, I had recently learned how to say, "fried rice." So, in an effort to comment on our lunch that day, I thought I'd just combine the words into a sentence that Mike would understand in his native tongue. After practicing it in my head a few times, I thought I had it down pat. So, when I was ready to lay it on him, I said something to Mike like, "Chow fun hon how chur." What I was trying to say was, "The fried rice was delicious." As soon as I uttered the sentence, Mike looked at me half-shocked and half-laughing and said, "Oh! Don't say that until your Chinese is better!" Evidently, I had said something pretty bad.

I seemed to do that a lot in Taiwan. It seems like there were a lot of Chinese words, phrases, and sentences that I said incorrectly (usually because I used the wrong phonological tone) and that turned out to be curse words or insults. For example, one time I said, "Ni ma how ma" to Mike's wife, Susan, and it came across to her as "How's your horse?" What I meant to say was, "How's your mother?" The great thing about it was how gracious the Taiwanese people were when I did that kind of thing. They just laughed and acted thrilled that I was trying to speak with them in Chinese.

Another interesting thing about our summers in Taiwan was how we would often see a Chinese person who looked just like someone we knew back in the US—except he or she was Chinese. For example, there was a guy at church named Yu-min who looked very similar to my dad—except he was Chinese. There was also a guy on a "wanted" poster who looked almost identical to a guy on Zach's Franklin College soccer team—except he was Chinese. That guy was caught on camera breaking into washing machines and dryers at some local laundromats and stealing the money, so posters of him were plastered everywhere. I don't remember all the doppelgangers we saw, but there were several good ones.

Without a doubt, some of the very best memories of my life are of our trips to Taiwan as a family. It's still hard to believe that we made that trip three times together and that we lived on the other side of the earth in a completely different culture for several weeks at a time. We made many good friends there—many of whom we still keep in touch with. My long-time friend and colleague Mike and his family and our friends at Bilingual Community Church were what made our times in Kaohsiung so special. It was always difficult to say goodbye.

* * *

When we got back to the US, I began playing tennis regularly. These days, I usually play a few times per week in the summer, once or twice per week as the weather permits in the spring and fall, and once in a while indoors at the University of Indianapolis Tennis Bubble in the winter. The great thing about tennis is that you can play with people of just about any age. During the summer, I usually play in a Monday and Wednesday evening league in Franklin with junior high school and high school boys and girls, college men and women, tennis coaches, and men and women around my age. And on occasion, I will fill in for a player in a Tuesday and Thursday morning league in Greenwood that is made up of retired guys. Of course, sometimes, someone just wants to play, so we just set it up—spontaneous style.

So anyway, I was a tennis player again. In a sense, I wasted 30 years of my life playing golf—a sport that I never really liked and was never very good at. I mean, I enjoyed it in the sense that it was a game I could play with others once in a while. But, I love tennis, and I'm much better at it. For me, it's a great way to have fun *and* stay fit.

* * *

As for my newly acquired interest in confidence weighting, I found the manual scoring of confidence to be very tedious, time-consuming, and error-prone—especially since all my exams begin with 25 multiple-choice questions, and I sometimes have as many as 25 students in one class. That's 625 multiple-choice answers to grade and 625 associated confidence selections to factor in.

So, to solve that problem, I designed and developed a Web-based software system called Assessnik, where my students log in, select their answers to the individual multiple-choice questions on my exams, and then indicate their confidence in their answers. Assessnik not only makes grading their answers easy, but it also makes assessing their confidence in those answers effortless. Now, the multiple-choice parts of my exams are graded immediately and without error with the push of a button—before my students even leave the room.

Another nice thing about Assessnik is that it helps me discern when my students are guessing, when they fully understand a concept, when they don't understand a concept, and when they have a misconception about a concept. And since my students are rewarded with extra points for knowing what they *do* know and knowing what they *don't* know on an exam, they can earn extra credit.

* * *

A few years after the initial design and development of Assessnik, I added some functionality to the system. The new functionality permits my students to evaluate the presentations of their peers in real time—both quantitatively and qualitatively. I had gotten the idea for the new functionality after learning about the concepts of "crowdsourcing" and "the wisdom of the crowd" from my son, Zach, who was in graduate school at the time.

So, as a computing student is giving a presentation on the topic of Artificial Intelligence, for example, the other students in the class are logged in to the system and grading the presentation in real-time using a quantitative scoring rubric with assessment items and weightings like, *Clearly discussed any current applications of the topic (15 points), Clearly discussed any future applications of the topic (15 points)*, *Clearly discussed the potential ethical issues of the topic (if any) (10 points)*, and *Used proper grammar free of distracting habits (05 points)*.

In addition, the students evaluating the presentation are required to write responses to some open-ended prompts like, *Describe one thing the presenter did well and one thing the presenter could improve on*, *What were the three most important takeaways of the presentation?*, *What are two concepts related to the presentation that you might like to explore further and why?*, and *What is one issue of the topic that could emerge as a problem or challenge in the future and why?* Having my students respond to prompts like these permits me to hold them accountable for paying close attention to and learning from the presentation. Nice!

* * *

In 2014, I published my first software engineering textbook. For the sake of brevity, and for the sake of not having to talk about it again, I'll list the titles of all the textbooks I've written and will provide a brief description of each—for those who might be interested. I don't want to say too much about them for a couple of reasons. First, if you know something about software engineering, you can probably tell what the books are about by their titles. And second, if you know nothing about software engineering, none of it will make sense to you anyway.

- *Software Engineering: Activities and Tasks.* This book is rather small—only 135 pages. It is a brief overview of the System Development Life Cycle.
- *Software Engineering: Principles and Practices.* This book is by far the most significant work of my career. It is my magnum opus. It is an in-depth description of the System Development Life Cycle. I've published multiple editions of this book.
- *Web Application Construction with ASP.Net 4.6, C#.Net, SQL, Ajax, and JavaScript.* This book is about how to develop Web applications using Microsoft ASP.Net Framework. I've published multiple editions of this book as well.
- *Essential ASP.NET Web Forms Development: Full Stack Programming with C#.NET, SQL, Ajax, and JavaScript.* This

book is very similar to the previous book, except that it has a different publisher.

- *ASP.NET Core Razor Pages: Full Stack Web Development with C#.NET HTML, Bootstrap, CSS, JavaScript, and Entity Framework Core*. This book is about how to develop Web applications using Microsoft ASP.Net Core. I've published multiple editions of this book as well.

And there you have it. Just like I could never have imagined that I'd someday be a college professor, I never could have imagined that I'd someday write a college textbook—let alone several of them. But that's how life works when you eat your vegetables.

* * *

On Thanksgiving Day of that year, the boys and I decided to play racquetball in the Spurlock Center at Franklin College. Since it was a holiday, we had the whole place to ourselves, and we took turns playing each other in a round-robin-style tournament. Although I don't really care for racquetball that much, I was playing hard because I wanted to get a good workout. Plus, I wanted to win. The boys and I have always been competitive like that.

During a game with Nathan, as I aggressively moved to my right in an attempt to hit a ball back that he had just slapped against the front wall, I tripped over my feet and smashed into the side wall at full speed with my right elbow positioned directly next to my ribcage. I hit the wall so hard that it knocked the wind out of me. As I lay there on the floor gasping for breath, all four boys stopped what they were doing and rushed over to see if I was okay.

The look of deep concern on their faces was heartbreaking. In that moment, I felt like they were seeing me for the first time as someone who could be weak and in need of their help. I felt like I had shattered their perception of me as the one who could always be counted on to be strong. To be honest, I even felt a little embarrassed—like I was an old man who needed to be pitied instead of the man they used to think could beat up Superman.

Anyway, once I was able to breathe again, the boys carefully helped me up to my feet. But I knew something was wrong. I could tell that I had broken some ribs on the right side of my chest. I couldn't believe it. It was the fourth time in my life I had broken my ribs. What a klutz.

My injury came at a really bad time because the boys and I had a gig coming up at the Gear in Franklin in just two days. On the night of the show, I was still in a lot of pain, and I couldn't sing. So, I had to miss the gig. I was very disappointed. I couldn't even go and watch. It was the only 4th Normal Form Band gig that I ever missed. Fortunately, Nathan was able to sing lead vocals for me and play most of my guitar parts.

But believe it or not, there *is* a silver lining to that story. Before the accident, I had some *very* mild, yet chronic, stiffness on the right side of my neck. For years, I had tried to eliminate the stiffness through chiropractic adjustments, stretching, neck massages (from Elizabeth), and so on, but I could never shake it. But when I hit that racquetball court wall, I felt my cervical spine crack really well. My neck stiffness was gone, never to be heard from again! I was completely healed of it—just like that. A miracle really.

* * *

In July of 2017, I was approached by a friend of mine from church whose company, Mid America Health, Incorporated in Greenwood, was actively looking for someone to perform maintenance activities on a software system they were using called the Integrated Dental Data System. The IDDS was probably developed originally in the late 1990s or early 2000s, and its purpose was to record and report on the dental procedures performed on inmates in state prisons around the country. Since the system was old and had been modified by several people over the years, it had become unstable and full of bugs. So, they hired me as a consultant to track down the bugs and fix them as they arose.

From the looks of the code, I could tell that the system had been developed using a now-obsolete programming language that we now call Classic Active Server Pages. I could also tell that locating and fixing bugs in the system was going to be a complete nightmare—for a couple reasons.

First of all, there were no comments in the code that might help me understand what the code was actually doing. The man who developed the IDDS initially was clearly an intelligent person, but he either didn't know to add comments in his code, or he deliberately neglected to add them to ensure job security. I won't speculate, but if you want someone to hate you, don't add comments to your code.

And second, since the code of the IDDS was so outdated, I couldn't use Visual Studio, which is the software I use to design, develop, and test software systems, to isolate and correct bugs. Instead, I had to use Notepad as my code editor, and I had to display all my interim variable values on the Web page to see what was going wrong. That's sick—in a bad way. If you know what I'm talking about right now, you feel my pain and would probably give me a hug if I asked for one.

* * *

In 2018, I began a new phase of life. I became a father-in-law. That year, Zach married Camille Denise Rivera. Camille is from Orlando, Florida. The following year, Nathan married Abigail Rose Lepper who is from Greenwood, Indiana. The year after that, Isaac married Andrea Ester Davilla. Andrea is from Glendora, California. And the next year, Elijah married Jaycee Renee Smith who is from Whiteland, Indiana. So, in four short years, I had the privilege of becoming the father-in-law of four wonderful young women. I love having daughters-in-law. I love to sit with them and find out how they're doing. They've been a true blessing to me and our family.

* * *

Several months before Zach and Camille got married, I went with Elizabeth to shop for a dress that she could wear to the wedding. I'm not exactly sure why she needed to have a new one. I mean, she already had some dresses in her closet, and I liked most of them already. But, since this was the wedding of one of our sons, I guess she needed to have a new dress.

In an attempt to find the perfect "mother of the groom" dress, we went pretty much everywhere—from JC Penny to Macy's to Von Maur to Nordstrom. She tried on a ton of different dresses, and I must say, I was very patient. I really *did* try to enjoy the experience—after all, it was for a special occasion. For each dress that she tried on, I gave her my honest opinion—after first asking her what she thought about it, of course. A couple of the women who worked at the stores said I was a *saint* for going dress-shopping with my wife and sitting there patiently while she tried on so many dresses. Saint sounds good.

Another thing we did together in preparation for the wedding was take dancing lessons. I've never liked dancing because, when it comes to that particular activity, I have no rhythm, which is ironic because I actually have a lot of rhythm. I've also never liked dancing because it makes me feel uncomfortable when I do it in front of people—except for slow dancing. But even then…. Although I wasn't excited about taking the dancing lessons at first, I actually grew to enjoy them a little. To me, it was almost like a sport or something because it required a lot of coordination and teamwork. Plus, it was good exercise.

One of the dances we tried to learn was Salsa dancing. This type of dancing was important for us to learn because Camille's family is from Puerto Rico, and we knew there would be Salsa dancing at the wedding reception. So, I tried really hard to get it right, and I was pretty proud of myself. At the reception on the evening of the wedding, the salsa music started, and after dancing to a couple of songs with Elizabeth, I decided to ask Camille's mom to dance. It was a disaster. Although it looked like she was a great dancer and had danced that way her whole life, dancing together just didn't work. Evidently, she hadn't learned it right or something. Just kidding.

The 2020s

54 68 65 20 32 30 32 30 73

In January of 2020, I began yet another new phase of life. I became a grandfather for the first time. A grandfather? Was I really old enough to be someone's *grandfather*? And by the way, I've become a grandfather *many* more times since then. In fact, I'm swimming in grandchildren now. What a blessing.

I think the best part about having grandchildren is that you can just enjoy them—without the incessant responsibility of taking care of their needs. When they're very young, someone always has to feed them, change their diapers, put them in their car seats, give them baths, and put them to bed. Well…been there, done that. Of course, I do those things sometimes (except for changing diapers), and I love it. But I'm glad those things are no longer my job. So, when a baby I'm holding starts crying, I just hand him or her to one of their parents. Yes, being a grandfather is a blessing. As Proverbs 17:6 says, "Children's children are a crown to the aged…." God has been good to me.

The thing is, I don't feel old enough to be a grandfather. I mean, I don't have any aches and pains like you're supposed to have at this age. In fact, I feel as well as I did when I was 30 years old. Of course, I'm not as strong, springy, tough, resilient, or fast as I was back then, but I really don't feel my age. That's not something I take for granted by the way. It's a blessing from God, and I'm very grateful for it. It's only when I see myself in the mirror or in a photograph that I think, "Wow. What happened? I look like somebody's grandpa." But inside, it's still me.

* * *

Although I've told people many times that raising children was the best part of my life, those with grandchildren have almost always told me that grandparenting is even better. Well, as delightful as it is, I must say that, for me, nothing could ever compare to raising our four sons. In fact, if my entrance into heaven required that I forget every memory of my life except one, I would choose to remember the time Elizabeth and I spent raising our children.

One of my favorite memories of raising children was our morning devotions. From the time Elijah was old enough to sit still and listen, we had devotions as a family on weekday mornings. I think we met at 8 am, and the devotion lasted for 30 minutes or so. I don't remember everything we read and discussed, but I know we read and discussed some of the wisdom literature of the Bible, like the Book of Proverbs and Ecclesiastes. Although we usually read and discussed the Bible, we also read and discussed some great non-biblical literature, including the classic stories, essays, and poems collected and compiled into *The Book of Virtues* by William J. Bennett. That book is intended to help children develop character and understand moral issues. Our devotions were very rich.

But we didn't just read and discuss those great works of wisdom, we *reasoned* though them. Even when the boys were young, we talked through the implications of what we were reading. For example, one of the Ten Commandments says, "You shall not give false testimony against your neighbor" (Exodus 20:16). Instead of just having them memorize that commandment as some kind of rule to blindly follow without understanding how it could possibly be relevant in society, we discussed it in such a way that they understood the societal outcomes of such behavior if it were okay for people to lie in court. We tried to instill in them that the laws of God are not just *arbitrary* rules. They are *deliberately designed* commands to live by that (surprise) lead to social stability, personal blessing, and peace with God.

Elizabeth and I tried to take seriously our role as parents to cultivate in our children a genuine love for God. We tried to take seriously the passage in Deuteronomy 6:5-7 that says, "Love the Lord your God with all your heart and with all your soul and with all your strength. These commandments that I give you today are to be on your hearts.

Impress them on your children. Talk about them when you sit at home and when you walk along the road, when you lie down and when you get up." We also tried to take seriously our role as parents to instill in our children a love for others and a deep respect for the Bible as God's word.

As I write this, I'm reminded of Psalm 127:3-5 that says, "Children are a heritage from the Lord, offspring a reward from him. Like arrows in the hands of a warrior are children born in one's youth. Blessed is the man whose quiver is full of them." My quiver is indeed full.

* * *

In May of 2020, I handed Elijah his bachelor's degree diploma at Franklin College's annual commencement ceremony. For as long as I can remember, it has been an important tradition for FC's employees to present their children with their diplomas. Elijah's was my fourth. Back in 2015, I accepted Zach's diploma for him because he was still studying abroad in Germany for his last semester of college. The next year, I handed Isaac his diploma. And two years later, I handed Nathan his diploma. Of course, I was very proud of them—as any dad would be. After Elijah was done, and the next commencement ceremony was on everyone's mind, it became a bit of a joke around Old Main, where people would ask me if *another* Beasley boy would be graduating this year.

* * *

Sometime in the fall of 2020, I stopped riding my bicycle to work regularly. I still ride on occasion, but not very often. When I ride now, it's usually because it's a really nice day out or because Elizabeth needs the car. But for 23 years, I biked to work almost every day. Like I said earlier, I *even* rode in the winter. As long as it wasn't raining, or it wasn't too cold, I rode my bike. That was my normal mode of transportation.

There were several times when it wasn't raining when I left for work or left for home, but it started raining when I was part way there. When that happened, I usually just got a little damp. I only remember getting soaked a few times, and those times happened when I was on my way home. Of course, that was no big deal. I just changed my clothes when I got there.

In addition to that, there were a couple of times when it was entirely too cold to be riding a bike. Before I had a smart phone, where I could just check the temperature outside, I just opened up the front door and waved my hand around to determine whether or not it was too cold to ride. On both occasions, it didn't *seem* that cold when I stuck my hand out the door. But when I got about a quarter mile or so away from the house, my face began to ache. I knew I had made a big mistake. Despite that, I felt like I was too far into the ride to turn back. So, I kept going. Needless to say, I was relieved when I finally got to campus. When I got into my office and checked the temperature on my computer, I discovered that it was in the single digits outside.

As far as encounters with wild animals, I was attacked by Canadian Geese three times in the 23 years I rode my bike to work consistently. It was always the same scenario. I'd be riding along, minding my own business, when all of a sudden, one of the big ones would start hissing and running after me as it tried to bite my legs. It must have thought I was some kind of threat to the flock. They never did bite me, but it *was* scary. Beautiful birds, by the way. But filthy and disgusting.

* * *

Over the years, I often wondered how many miles I had traveled to and from work via my bicycle. I knew it had to be a lot because I had ridden my bike to work so consistently. But I never really got around to doing a serious estimate until I wrote this book. So true to form, I created a spreadsheet to produce an estimate.

In my estimate, I accounted for the round-trip distances from each of our houses in Franklin to Frankin College, the number of semesters we lived in each house, the number of semesters I was on sabbatical and thus didn't bike to campus at all,[17] and the number of weeks per semester that I *actually* biked to work.[18] Finally, I applied an adjustment factor of 80 percent, since I didn't ride to the College 100 percent of the time due to rain, cold, or something else.

As it turns out, I rode over 8,500 miles during that 23-year period. That's like riding a bicycle from Frankin to Los Angeles, California and back…twice…and then some. It's also like riding a bike from Franklin

---

[17] Although I've now had two sabbaticals, I only had one during that time period.
[18] I didn't bike to work during spring break or finals week.

to Anchorage, Alaska and back…and still having five hundred miles left over. Kind of wild if you ask me.

* * *

In February of 2021, I emailed my point-of-contact at Mid America Health and asked him if he would be interested in having me design and develop a new IDDS using the state-of-the-art Web development framework—ASP.NET Core. Since the old IDDS was still requiring a lot of bug fixes, he thought it was something we should discuss further. After hearing my rationale for replacing the old IDDS with a stable, user-friendly, and modernized IDDS, he asked me to put together an estimate of the project's cost. A few days after receiving my estimate, he gave me the okay to proceed. So, during the spring and summer of 2021, I designed and developed the new IDDS. Then, on September 1st, the old IDDS was retired and the new IDDS went live for use by the dental employees of Mid America Health.

* * *

Although I had taught my Inner-City Missions course pretty much every other year since 1999, I couldn't take Franklin College students to the city in January of 2022 because the Covid-19 Pandemic was still a thing. My students and I learned a lot about homelessness, addiction, lifestyle choices, and the uncertainties of life over those years. It was a life-changing experience for most of us—including my four sons and one future daughter-in-law who took the course when they were in college. Such missions work, however, wasn't completely new to my sons when they took the course because, when they were younger, I sometimes took them with me to serve at some of the same missions we worked at in the course.

Since I couldn't do the Inner-City Missions course that winter term, I designed and taught a course called Taiwan (Republic of China). The topics in the course included such things as Taiwan's natural resources, people, history, economy, political system, foreign affairs, relationship with China, science and technology, educational system, mass media, and tourism. A good amount of the course's content was generated by small teams of students who researched certain aspects of Taiwan and presented their findings to the class who used the Assessnik system to evaluate their presentations.

Since I wanted the course to be fun, we blind taste-tested Taiwanese foods and drinks, hosted three Chinese speakers (one in person and two in Taiwan via Zoom), role-played in a Taiwan-China history game, listened to traditional Chinese music, took a Google Earth Street View tour of the Sanmin District of Kaohsiung (where our family lived when we were there), and watched a Chinese movie.

The course really opened up the eyes of my students in terms of the current political conundrum and emotional heat between China and Taiwan. One time, one of my student's Chinese friend's father told my student to tell me that I shouldn't be teaching a course on Taiwan. The reason? There was no such thing as Taiwan.[19] My student relayed a few similar messages to me as well. I'm pretty sure my student wasn't on the side of his friend's dad or anything—at least from what I could tell. I think he would just talk to the guy about our class sometimes, and he would convey to me some of the political opinions the guy thought I should know. Still, I was a little worried that I might get assassinated or something.

* * *

In May of 2022, I hurt myself playing tennis. After having played on a United States Tennis Association team from Greenwood a couple of summers before, I was back to playing USTA tennis again. But this time, I was playing on a team from Franklin. Our team was practicing together for the first time trying to get ready for our USTA summer league that would have us traveling all around the Indianapolis area to play other USTA teams. That day, we were practicing on the courts at Custer Baker Intermediate School in Franklin.

Although I normally start playing tennis sometime in March, I was a little unmotivated to play that particular year, so it was my first time out on the courts. Before leaving the house that afternoon, Elizabeth told me to take it easy and not hurt myself. Truth be told, it wasn't my intention to go against her wise advice. I knew she was right. I was just going to go out there and take a few swings to get things in the groove.

---

[19] The relationship between China and Taiwan is complex. But basically, the Chinese Communist Party in China believes that Taiwan is just a part of China, whereas the Democratic Progressive Party in Taiwan believes that Taiwan is its own sovereign nation.

However, for whatever reason, this *one* time, I went a little too hard chasing a ball down. Somehow, I tripped over my own feet and crashed hard onto the green asphalt of the court. When I was a young guy, I could crash like that all day and walk away with a few scrapes. But now, I wasn't able to absorb such a fall with a smooth tuck and roll. Anyway, when I hit the ground, I landed on my left elbow and heard my spine crack, like when you get a chiropractic adjustment—except that the crack traveled up the *entire* length of my spine. It was very unusual and weird. My first thought was spinal injury. Fortunately, that wasn't the case.

When my teammates were finally able to get me up off the asphalt, I noticed that my left hand had started to swell up. Evidently, I had slapped my left hand on the asphalt in an attempt to break my fall. So, I took off my wedding ring right away so that the circulation in my ring finger wouldn't get cut off, and I'd have to have my ring cut off.

The next day, my hand was completely swollen and black and blue. But the worst part was, I had also broken some ribs on the left side of my chest. Can you believe it? This was the fifth time in my life that I had broken my ribs. At least I was always doing something active when it happened. And if you've played sports your entire life like I have, I guess you're bound to have some injuries now and then. But it's still odd to me because I've never been accident-prone. In fact, I've always been a relatively agile person. I think anyone who knows me would tell you that. But here I was—a five-time rib-breaker.

After that season I stopped playing USTA tennis altogether. Not because of my injury but because I decided that traveling to play tennis was just not necessary for me. I mean, I can play tennis in Franklin just about any time I want to, and I can be home in less than ten minutes.

* * *

Sometime in early 2023, I started playing the bass guitar regularly at church—about once a month. I didn't stop playing the drums. I just started playing the bass as well—when someone else wanted to play the drums. But unlike in college, when I only agreed to play the bass out of a willingness to serve and with no real interest in the instrument, I actually *wanted* to play the bass this time and found the instrument very fun to play. And unlike in college, when I just hit the root note of the chord, I now knew about chord inversions and how to use the bass to construct them to give the song more richness and soul.

Although my skills are pretty basic, I'm always improving—at least incrementally. Part of it is probably because I'm playing regularly, and part of it is probably because I enjoy it so much, which motivates me to learn. Plus, God gives gifts and talents and desires to people when he's good and ready. At least that's how it has gone down in my life.

So, as far as the bass guitar is concerned, I've sort of come full circle. I never thought I'd be a bass player—especially considering how I felt about the instrument in college when I first started playing it.

* * *

In the fall of 2023, I ran into a former student of mine at Franklin College's homecoming football game. He was an FC student way back in the late 1990s, and we probably hadn't spoken to each other since he graduated. We had a great time reminiscing about his college days and talking about some of the other guys back then who he still kept in contact with. It was nice getting updates on them.

At one point, he reminded me of the time he and some of his fellow graduating seniors in computing came to my house during finals week for a cookout. He said he would never forget playing basketball in my driveway and how I would do trick shots and slam dunk the basketball. I had *totally* forgotten about that! Evidently, I could still jump a little in my middle 30s. To tell you the truth, though, I'm pretty sure the rim in our driveway was only 9'9" high—three inches short of the standard rim height. But still…not too bad.

* * *

In January of 2024, I was contacted by someone at Mid America Health who was interested in having me design and develop a software system for another part of their company—School Smiles. The School Smiles arm of Mid America Health provides on-site dental services to hundreds of schools around the country.

At the time, the School Smiles staff was using a network hard drive with a hierarchy of folders and subfolders to organize the over 10,000 registration forms they receive each year from people requesting dental services for their children. Unfortunately, that particular approach was very tedious, time-consuming, and error-prone. Besides that, they had no way of knowing the percentage of registration forms in each status category (pending, data entered, insurance verified, ineligible, date of service pending, and patient scheduled) at any given moment in time. To help solve those problems, Mid America Health contacted me.

After discussing the details of the project with my point-of-contact, I sent her an estimate of the project's cost. A few days later, she gave me the okay to proceed. So, during the late winter and early spring of 2024, I designed and developed the Registration Tracking System. So now, I maintain both the IDDS and the RTS for Mid America Health.

* * *

On May 18th, 2024, at the end of Franklin College's commencement ceremony, I completed my 30th year as a college professor. That means I've been a college professor for a very long time. That also means I've attended a lot of commencement ceremonies. I still remember the very first commencement I participated in as a faculty member. It was at Union College in May of 1996.[20] The feeling was magical that day with all the wonderful pomp and circumstance. The formality. The music. The academic regalia. The proud families who were there to watch a loved one graduate.

I don't enjoy commencement ceremonies anymore, though. It's not like I hate them or anything. I mean, they *are* important and meaningful celebrations. But I *definitely* don't enjoy them like I used to. They're just too long and drawn out—especially when the commencement speaker gets long winded.

Since I've attended so many commencement ceremonies over the years, I'm entitled to posit a theory.[21] My theory is called "Beasley's Inverse Proportionality Theory of Commencement Speech Duration and Ceremony Enjoyment." Extremely catchy. My theory asserts that the length of a commencement address is inversely proportional to the enjoyment of the commencement ceremony. Pretty simple. So, if you ever find yourself making a commencement speech, keep it very short,

---

[20] I didn't attend commencement at East Carolina University in May of 1995. It wasn't on my radar for some reason.

[21] I'm also entitled to make up words as a long-time professor. And believe me, I have made some up.

and people will like the ceremony better—according to me. They will like you better too, so it's a double bonus.

Although the pomp and circumstance no longer evoke the magical feelings they did during my first commencement ceremony as a college professor, I do try to make the best of graduation day. I mean, I enjoy shaking the hands of my newly graduated students after the ceremony as they walk through the tunnel of clapping administrators, faculty, and staff—a tradition that was started at Franklin College several years ago. As I'm shaking their hands, I always congratulate them, wish them well, and encourage them to keep in touch. Once in a while, someone will even want me to meet their family or take a picture. The whole thing makes me feel like I've made a positive impact on their lives.

* * *

By the way, college professors are *required* to march in the faculty processional at commencement ceremonies unless they're excused by the dean of the faculty. I guess that explains why I've been to so many commencement ceremonies. In addition, we're required to dress in our full academic regalia—cap, gown, hood, all that.

When I graduated from the University of Illinois back in 1994, I *purchased* the academic regalia I wore during my own commencement ceremony. Since it was my intention to have a long career in academia, I bought my cap and gown instead of renting it. That was one of the best purchases I ever made. Although it was an expensive purchase for me in 1994, it turned out to be a great investment. Had I not purchased my regalia then, I would have had to rent regalia at least once a year. I'm sure my investment has paid for itself many times over.

* * *

With each passing academic year and with each cohort of retiring professors, I've watched myself slowly move closer and closer to the "senior end" of the faculty processional at the annual commencement ceremony. Now I'm a "front row" professor, which means that I sit in the front row of the faculty during the ceremony. It also means that I have gray hair.

When you line up for the faculty processional, you line up according to your seniority. In academia, seniority is tied to faculty rank, which requires many years to progress through. From least to most senior, the general levels of faculty rank at most colleges and universities in the US are lecturer, instructor, assistant professor, associate professor, and professor. And within each of those ranks, the most senior faculty member is the one who was tenured first or who achieved the rank first. As of now, I'm the fourth most senior faculty member at Franklin College. That's just hard for me to fathom.

These days, when I look at all the rows of professors behind me, it reminds me of all the years I've spent progressing through the ranks of academia to become one of the "sages" of the academy. And when I look at the rows of professors in the very back, it reminds me of the days when I was a much younger man—just beginning my career. But it hasn't just been my career. I think it has been my calling.

* * *

I've really enjoyed the courses I've taught at Franklin College. Since coming to FC in 1997, I've taught a number of undergraduate courses in software design and development. These are:

- CMP 130 (Introduction to Computing)
- CMP 230 (Management Information Systems)
- CMP 231 (Cobol I)
- CMP 232 (Cobol II)
- CMP 283 (Web Software Construction and Testing I)
- CMP 285 (Web Software Construction and Testing II)
- CMP 300 (Topics)
- CMP 330 (Computer Training Seminar)
- CMP 350 (Professional Development Seminar)
- CMP 362 (Systems Analysis and Design)
- CMP 370 (Database Design and Processing)
- CMP 385 (Software Engineering I: Analysis and Design)
- CMP 387 (Software Engineering II: Implementation and Maintenance)
- CMP 470 (Senior Software Maintenance Project)
- CMP 473 (Senior Software Development Project)
- CMP 499 (Senior Competency Practicum)

Some of the courses in that list have been discontinued (CMP 230, CMP 231, CMP 232, CMP 330, and CMP 350), but I still teach all the others regularly. As you can probably imagine, the courses I still teach have changed over the years because things in the field of computing have changed over the years—a lot. Plus, I'm always fine-tuning my courses. I'm always removing this and adding that, deemphasizing this and emphasizing that, and so on. I'm always trying to improve both my courses and my teaching.

* * *

Early in my career, I developed a philosophy of teaching to go along with my promotion and tenure materials. In my view, a good teacher possesses three main attributes. It's pretty simple really. First, you have to possess a thorough knowledge of the content being taught. Second, you have to possess an authentic concern for students. And third, you have to possess the ability to clearly articulate ideas. I think the last one is accomplished most effectively when both of the previous attributes are present and working together.

In practice, I employ a rather diverse set of teaching techniques that I refer to as my "teaching toolbox." I've never really subscribed to any particular method of teaching exclusively, and I've never been inclined to blindly jump on any avant-garde teaching techniques bandwagons. And believe me, there have been a lot of them. Sometimes I just roll my eyes. Oh, how I wish I could tell you about some of the dumb ideas I've seen. Just dumb. But I'm very determined to be kind in this book. Having said that, though, I do believe that many teaching techniques, old and new, *can* be useful in the right context. Thus, I try to maintain an open mind and utilize what seems to work best for my students— given the situation.

My teaching is also governed by two other beliefs. First, I believe in *teaching* the students in my 100-level, 200-level, and 300-level courses but *mentoring* the students in my 400-level courses. I try to make this distinction clear to the students in my CMP 470, CMP 473, and CMP 499 courses. That doesn't mean I *never* teach something new in those courses. But for the most part, since the concepts in the lower-level courses have already been taught, and they should have learned them, it's time for me to mentor my students in the real-world application of those concepts. And second, I believe in being completely fair. If I am nothing, I am fair. In terms of grading, there is no bias. Never. In all my years of teaching, I have never been accused of being unfair. Well, maybe a handful of times, but after I clarify with a student the meaning of the word "unfair," he or she usually says something like, "Well. I don't mean unfair…."

If anything, I'm pretty generous. For example, sometimes a student will come into my office to discuss an answer they gave on an exam that I marked as incorrect. If I can understand where they're coming from, or if I can understand what they were trying to say, I might give them a few extra points and then encourage them to improve their penmanship or express their thoughts more clearly in the future. Or, if their answer was indeed incorrect, I might even give them a few extra points just for making the effort to talk to me about it. Small things like that can go a long way in fostering rapport with students.

I'm no pushover, though. Far from it. Any of my students will tell you that I have high standards and that I require clear thinking. But if a student shows some initiative by coming to my office to discuss an issue with their exam or project, and they're respectful about it, I don't have a problem rewarding them for that.

And by the way, being right about something for the sake of being right has never been my style. I'm only interested in what is true and correct. For example, if I make a mistake grading someone's exam or project, or I miscount the points they earned on it, I don't feel the least bit threatened or embarrassed by it. In fact, I always tell my students that, although I graded their exam or project carefully, please let me know if they think I've made a mistake. If it was indeed a mistake, I just make it right. It's that simple.

But that's definitely not true about everyone. I had a colleague once (not in my department) who was always right—even when he wasn't. This one time, a student of mine provided a *correct* answer to a problem on one of my colleague's exams, but the answer had been marked as *incorrect*. So, my student went to my colleague's office to discuss the answer with him. Despite the presence of a clear computational error in the answer key, my colleague wouldn't budge. Not only that, but he gave my student a tongue-lashing for questioning him.

* * *

Despite developing a carefully thought-out philosophy of teaching, employing a somewhat diverse set of teaching techniques, utilizing an innovative teaching-to-mentoring instructional model, and fostering good rapport with my students, I've never won Franklin College's Faculty Teaching Award. Not that I think I deserve it or anything. The competition for that particular award at FC is especially high because we have a lot of exceptional teachers—and I don't put myself in the category of exceptional. To be honest, I'm fine with not winning the Faculty Teaching Award. I'd love to be recognized by my students and colleagues as a great teacher. Who wouldn't? But it will probably never happen. Nevertheless, I take my teaching very seriously, and I always try to improve.

I think my teaching really improved during the years my sons were in my classes. Since Isaac majored in organizational leadership and management, I only had him in one of my classes—Introduction to Computing. But I had Zach, Nathan, and Elijah in all or most of my classes, since the three of them majored in computer science, software engineering, or both. (Like his mom, Zach also majored in Applied Mathematics.)

During that time, my teaching improved for a couple of reasons. First, I wanted to make my sons proud of me for being good at what I did. Although I had always worked hard to improve my teaching (including my exams, projects, assignments, and other stuff), I worked harder at it because they were watching. And second, I wanted to do my best to pass down to them my knowledge of and skills in the fields of computer science and software engineering. It was kind of like I had a personal stake in them learning the concepts and skills of those fields the best that they could.

During that time, we had a lot of great discussions about the things we were studying in our computing classes. We talked about stuff like sort algorithms, data structures, cryptography, binary and hexadecimal numbering systems, and C# programming—you know, the good stuff. You probably think we all look like a bunch of nerds.

I really enjoyed those conversations with the boys, which usually occurred in our living room. Many times, though, someone who wasn't steeped in our specialized language and conceptual world would come into the living room while we were in the middle of a discussion, so I'd try to cut us off. I didn't want to be rude and exclude them from the conversation because I knew they didn't understand a word we were saying. Some of us still have conversations like that on occasion, and I still try to cut us off when someone unversed in the field of computing walks into the room.

* * *

Although I think I've evolved into a pretty good teacher, I believe my biggest vocational strength has been in the area of scholarship. As of now, I've authored five software engineering textbooks, contributed chapters to two books, published over 50 articles in refereed journals and conference proceedings, and delivered many conference speeches and keynote addresses.

In recognition of my scholarly record, my peers at Franklin College presented me with the Faculty Award for Excellence in Scholarship twice—once in 2007 and then again in 2015. That award recognizes outstanding *traditional* scholarship—like writing books and publishing research articles. Very few professors at FC have been given this award, and only two of us have won the award twice. Earning the Faculty Award for Excellence in Scholarship has been the greatest honor of my professional career because it means that my colleagues recognize and appreciate my hard work as a consistent and productive scholar over many years.

* * *

Although scholarship has always been important to me, students are my chief priority. But it wasn't always that way. While I was at the University of Illinois, it was all about the research for me. That's what I was being trained to do as a Ph.D. student. In *my* mind, I thought I'd graduate, get a job in academia as a researcher (primarily), and teach a class or two per semester. But a couple of years or so after graduating, my heart began to change, and my priorities began to shift. It's a good thing too because your first priority at a place like Franklin College has to be your students. They're our bread and butter.

I've enjoyed working with my students over the years. Most of them have been really good people who want to be successful in life, and it has been my pleasure to help them better their lives by assisting them in acquiring some truly useful concepts and skills.

* * *

During my career, I've been pretty careful about trying to be funny in the classroom—especially in my Introduction to Computing course. The majority of the students in that course are non-computing majors who don't know me from Adam and are just taking the course to fulfill their basic college math requirement. Most of them just want to get it over with and are, thus, in no mood to be entertained by some boring professor guy.

Of course, once in a while, I *will* say something funny in that class. When I *do* say something funny, it's usually something self-deprecating. For example, I will sometimes show a brief video in the classroom that illustrates a concept better than I ever could. So, when introducing my first video of the semester, I usually say, "I'm going to show a video now because, as the old saying goes, "Those that can, do. Those that can't, teach. And those that can't teach, show videos."[22] Of course, I only say that after they've seen some skills. Otherwise, they wouldn't know it was supposed to be funny.

Whenever I say something humorous in that class, I get two distinct reactions. The first reaction comes from the "good students" who are paying attention and are locked into the conversation. They will get the joke right away and will laugh. The second reaction comes from the "not-so-good students" who are *not* paying attention and are *not* locked into the conversation. They will *not* hear the joke and will *not* laugh. I recommend that the latter group pay attention in the classroom. That way, they'll get my jokes and will, thus, get their money's worth.

By the time my students are juniors and seniors, though, I can joke around with them some, which makes for a more enjoyable classroom environment. These students are computing majors that I've likely had in class before, so they get me and can tell when I'm joking. This one time, for example, after I had finished demonstrating a software system

---

[22] That joke is a slight alteration of Jack Black's line in *School of Rock* when he says, "Those that can't do, teach. And those that can't teach, teach gym."

that I had designed and developed for a client, someone commented on how professional the software looked. So, I was like, "Easy, guys. I put my pants on just like the rest of you—one leg at a time. Except, once my pants are on, I make great software." Most of them thought that was pretty funny, and some of them even got the reference to the *More Cowbell* skit on Saturday Night Live, where Christopher Walken plays the singer and studio producer Bruce Dickinson. Yes—*the* Bruce Dickenson.

* * *

Sometimes, a student will express interest in me as a person. Once in a while, someone will ask me a question like, "Do you have any plans for spring break?" or "Did you do any traveling over the summer?" I've also been asked (more than once) what I would have chosen as a career had I not chosen to be a professor of computing. I think my best answer has been systematic theologian. That might have been a good match because I've been interested in theology for most of my adult life. Over the years, I've taught Sunday school classes, led Bible studies, led men's study groups, led church study groups, and even brought a sermon on occasion.

I've also been asked many times by my students why I don't just do software consulting for a living, since the money is so much better. My response has always been the same. First, although I enjoy practicing software design and development, being a full-time consultant would probably be less stable than having a full-time job. As a consultant, I may have a contract—or I may not. I prefer to have a steady income and make some extra money on the side. And second, being a college professor permits me to *study* the *broad* field of computing, whereas being a software consultant would only permit me to *practice* a relatively *narrow* aspect of it. Being a professor of computing who is also an active software consultant permits me to have the best of both worlds.

One last thing about my students and their occasional interest in me on a personal level. Once in a while, someone will give me a small gift—usually at the end of the semester. It's usually a gift of chocolate or something else sweet. But sometimes, it's something they've made, or it's a card with some kind words and a few bucks on the inside.[23]

* * *

I've really enjoyed my career as a college professor. But the work has never been easy. During the school year, professors go a hundred miles an hour, and it can be very stressful to get done all the things that need doing. It's a huge exercise in time-management that I often liken to plate spinning, where a circus performer has to keep a dozen (or more) plates spinning simultaneously—without letting any of them fall to the ground and break. We have classes to prepare for and teach. We have quizzes and exams and projects to create and grade. We have students to meet with and advise. We have meetings and workshops and conferences to attend. We have committee work to complete. We have reading and studying to do. And we have research to conduct.

So, don't think because we're in the classroom 9 to 12 hours a week, we work 9 to 12 hours a week—as some who are *not* in the know might believe. Nope. It's a full-time job. If not for the time off we get each year, I think we would all get burned out pretty quickly.

But the lifestyle *has* been hard to beat. Having the summers off has given me time to slow down and clear my head. It has also given me time to focus on some of the things that are difficult to get to during the school year. For example, I've always stayed busy doing research, learning about advances in my field, writing books, or doing consulting work. In fact, it has usually been some combination of these. The truth is, I've never sat around doing nothing during the summer. I would be miserable doing that. Of course, having the summers off has also given me time to enjoy life—like traveling, visiting family, and staying active.

Another lifestyle perk has been the ability to take sabbatical leaves. When you take a sabbatical, you're relieved of your teaching and other responsibilities for a semester (or an academic year) *with pay* to engage in some kind of focused professional development. During my career at Franklin College, I've been granted two semester-long sabbaticals— one in 2006 and one in 2024. I am truly grateful for both of them. I still remember someone telling me when I was a young professor to

---

[23] Please tell me I don't have say I'm kidding about the money.

make sure to take advantage of that perk of the profession. I'm glad I took his advice.

But nothing in my career can compare to the experience of having my sons in my classes. Those memories will forever be the best of my career.

* * *

I've also enjoyed the people I've worked with over the years. As for my colleagues in the Department of Mathematics and Computing at Franklin College, they've been the best. I couldn't have asked for better colleagues. I think we as a department possess something special, and I think the other parts of campus view us as having something special as well. Over the years, we've cultivated and maintained a particularly collegial environment, where everyone works together, and no one has to have his or her own way all the time. And I can tell you that that kind of collaborative attitude is not all that common in academia. We truly value each other's input on things—like how to teach a particular topic, how to wordsmith a curriculum proposal, how to respond to a mandate from the administration, or how to help a failing student. We also have high standards and want our students to succeed.

I also couldn't have asked for a better computing colleague. Kerry came to Franklin College a year before I did, and he and I have been the only two full-time computing professors since I arrived at FC in 1997. Kerry and I have worked together very well over the years and have supported each other in so many ways. Since the very beginning, he's been in charge of the computer science program, and I've been in charge of the software engineering program. At the same time, though, we've worked together to ensure that *both* of our computing programs are kept up to date and serve our students well.

My colleagues in the other departments at Franklin College have been wonderful as well. I can't tell you how many times I've spoken with a colleague in another department when I've needed an expert's answer to something that falls directly within their area of expertise— be it English grammar, statistics, tax accounting, or WWII. Working in an organization full of intelligent and knowledgeable people has always felt very good to me.

I've also appreciated Franklin College's administration—especially the deans of the College. The deans that I've worked under have always been supportive of my endeavors. I don't think I've ever been denied funds when I've needed money for a research project or money for travel to an academic conference, whether it was in Indiana, another state in the US, or another country (Mexico, Germany, Ireland, and Taiwan). Deans have a tough job because they manage the faculty. I've heard it said that managing professors can be like herding cats.

And what can I say about Franklin College's staff? What a fantastic group of people. They've always been helpful and friendly when I've needed them. They keep the grounds and the buildings beautiful, and they make the business and technology aspects of the place work like a well-oiled machine. And whenever I've need something cleaned up or fixed in my office, it has always gotten done pronto. Really. They're *that* good.

The people of Franklin College are a special group of folks. They've always been a pleasure to work with. Yes, indeed. Franklin College has been a great place to work. And I've been blessed to be a part of it.

* * *

You know, it's hard to believe that a knucklehead kid like me could grow up to one day do the kind of work I've had the privilege of doing. Yeah, as a kid, I was pretty rough around the edges. Maybe most little boys are. But God took all of that stuff and *slowly* transformed me into someone he could use to expand his Kingdom by positively impacting the lives of others.

The last thing I want to say is, God has blessed me in many ways. I've been blessed with a wonderful family. I've been blessed with good health. I've been blessed with good friends and coworkers. And I've been blessed with a career that I enjoy and was well designed for. Make no mistake. Those things didn't come by accident. They've been a gift from God, and I take *nothing* for granted. I give God full credit for his blessings and direction in my life. I'm very grateful, and I acknowledge him for that.

Thanks

54 68 61 6E 6B 73

As with any writing project, it takes more than one person to make it happen. First, I'd like to thank Bailey Stamper for her creative book cover design. Bailey was a pleasure to work with.

Although I remembered most of the particulars of my stories on my own, I sometimes enlisted the help of others to help me fill in the details. So, I'd like to thank those who responded to one or two brief and out-of-the-blue texts when I needed help remembering some key dates and locations in my life.

I'd also like to thank my dad, Bob, and my sister, Dawn, for helping me remember the details of my early childhood, such as where we lived and when and why we moved from one location to another. It was a real pleasure visiting with them in Florida during my winter break in January of 2024 and reminiscing about old times. After that, I called and texted them so much that I bet they knew I was up to something.

I'd also like to thank my wife, Elizabeth, for helping me remember some of the details of how we met, our early relationship, and our life together as a married couple, parents, and grandparents. Elizabeth also helped me remember some of the stories I needed to tell in this book and provided invaluable editorial feedback on the entire manuscript.

And finally, I'd like to thank God for supplying the inspiration and motivation required to complete a writing project like this.

As with my editing process, it takes more than one person to make
happen. First, I'd like to thank Cathy Stamper for her creative book
cover design. It's always a pleasure to work with.

Although I can't mention most of the multitudes of people who help
on a daily basis, I want to acknowledge all of the team. Help me fill in the
details, so I'd like to name those who responded to one or two but
and one of the blue faces who all needed to present and enjoy some real
chats and focus until my fine.

I'd also like to thank my dad Bob, and my sister Dona, the helping
hand and my parents of support and love and in-laws in pro-

And to Ken and everybody who would carry and learned to advance in your
real pleasure visiting with them in Florida during twice their break, in
between coffee and remember to always not unless we all there being,
and it made them too much that I but that knew I was up to something.

I'd also like to thank my wife, for taking care in sharing more similar
some of these tribulations writing, our crazy relationship, not only the
together we came to laugh, persist, and stand update. I like both also
he, but the great array genre of writing, since I needed escape to the great
and professionalism editorial balance to the entire project.

And finally, I like to thank God for inspiring the inspiration and
motivation required to complete a writing project like this.

Appendix A

41 70 70 65 6E 64 69 78 20 41

This appendix lists all the songs the 4th Normal Form Band performed at one time or another. The two lists below should give you a good feel for the breadth of musical styles we played as a band. Yes. I kept *very* detailed records.

Song List 1. We typically played the songs in this list at state and county fairs, city festivals, coffee shops, and other events designed for general audiences.

- *A Rose by Any Other Name* (4NF Band)
- *All the Way Home* (4NF Band)
- *Blue on Black* (Kenny Wayne Shepherd Band)
- *Bringin' Me Down* (4NF Band)
- *Canon in D* (Pachelbel)
- *Carry On Wayward Son* (Kansas)
- *Cheap Sunglasses* (ZZ Top)
- *Crossfire* (Stevie Ray Vaughn and Double Trouble)
- *Dead or Alive* (Bon Jovi)
- *Deconstruction* (4NF Band)
- *Differently* (4NF Band)
- *Down from the Mountain* (4NF Band)
- *Earth, Wind, and Fire* (4NF Band)
- *Fly by Night* (Rush)
- *Free Bird* (Lynyrd Skynyrd)

- *Hard Way* (Scott Stapp)
- *Here Comes the Weather* (4NF Band)
- *Higher* (Creed)
- *Justify* (Scott Stapp)
- *Lights* (Journey)
- *Livin' in Indiana* (4NF Band)
- *Magnum Opus* (Kansas)
- *Margaritaville* (Jimmy Buffett)
- *More than a Feeling* (Boston)
- *More than Money* (4NF Band)
- *My Sacrifice* (Creed)
- *Mystery of the Seed* (4NF Band)
- *Number 70* (4NF Band)
- *One Last Breath* (Creed)
- *Peace of Mind* (Boston)
- *Poor Man* (4NF Band)
- *Portrait* (He Knew) (Kansas)
- *Red Barchetta* (Rush)
- *Remain with Me* (4NF Band)
- *Restless Evil* (4NF Band)
- *Risky* (4NF Band)
- *Save the Children* (4NF Band)
- *Seeds of Time* (4NF Band)
- *So Long Kaohsiung* (4NF Band)
- *Take Me Home Country Roads* (John Denver)
- *Taylorsville Angel* (Scott Coner)
- *The Distance* (4NF Band)
- *The Gambler* (Kenny Rogers)
- *The King of Cyberspace* (4NF Band)
- *The Rain is Falling* (4NF Band)
- *There Go I* (4NF Band)
- *Time to Fly Away* (4NF Band)

- *Undying Call* (4NF Band)
- *What Really Matters* (4NF Band)
- *With Arms Wide Open* (Creed)
- *You Can't Always Get What You Want* (Rolling Stones)

Song List 2. We typically played the songs in this list when leading worship in churches or when performing at special church events.

- *A New Hallelujah* (Michael W. Smith)
- *Amazing Love* (Chris Tomlin)
- *Ancient of Days* (Ron Kenoly)
- *Breathe* (Michael W. Smith)
- *Came to My Rescue* (Hillsong United)
- *Create in Me a Clean Heart* (Keith Green)
- *Deeper in Love with You* (Robert and Lea Sutanto)
- *Draw Me Close* (Kelly Carpenter)
- *Enough* (Chris Tomlin)
- *Ever Be* (Kalley Heiligenthal)
- *Everything with Breath* (4NF Band)
- *Fields of Clover* (Scott Coner)
- *God of Wonders* (Third Day)
- *God, You Reign* (Lincoln Brewster)
- *Grace by Which I Stand* (Keith Green)
- *He Knows My Name* (Tommy Walker)
- *He Reigns* (Newsboys)
- *Heart of Worship* (Matt Redman)
- *Holiness (Take My Life)* (Scott Underwood)
- *Holy is the Lord* (Chris Tomlin)
- *How Great is Our God* (Chris Tomlin)
- *In Christ Alone* (Keith Getty and Stuart Townend)
- *Jesus All the Way* (Scott Coner)
- *Jesus Messiah* (Chris Tomlin)
- *Just Like Me* (Sweet Comfort Band)

- *Lord, I Lift Your Name on High* (Petra)
- *Lord, I Need You* (Jesse Reeves, Kristian Stanfill, Matt Maher, Christy Nockels, and Daniel Carson)
- *Lord Reign in Me* (Brenton Brown)
- *Love the Lord* (Lincoln Brewster)
- *Mighty to Save* (Hillsong Worship)
- *My Deliverer* (The Ragamuffin Band)
- *O Praise Him* (David Crowder)
- *On the Road to Jericho* (Keith Green)
- *One Thing Remains (Your Love Never Fails)* (Brian Johnson, Jeremy Riddle, and Christa Black-Gifford)
- *Only King Forever* (Elevation Worship)
- *Quiet Love* (Whiteheart)
- *Ready for the Rain* (Steve Tarak)
- *Refiner's Fire* (Brian Doerksen)
- *Revelation Song* (Jennie Lee Riddle)
- *Rose Colored Stained Glass Windows* (Petra)
- *Sanctuary* (John Thompson and Randy Scruggs)
- *Searching for Diamonds* (4NF Band)
- *Shield Around Me* (4NF Band)
- *Shout to the Lord* (Darlene Zschech)
- *Somewhere in the World* (Wayne Watson)
- *Stand Back* (Scott Underwood)
- *The Lord is Righteous* (Bruce Thede)
- *The Power of Your Love* (Geoff Bullock)
- *Unfailing God* (Michael Rossback and Mitchel Schiff)
- *Walk on Water* (Audio Adrenaline)
- *Walk Toward the Light* (Greg X. Volz)
- *We Fall Down* (Chris Tomlin)
- *When You Walk into the Room* (Bryan and Katie Torwalt)
- *Whom Shall I Fear (God of Angel Armies)* (Chris Tomlin)
- *Worthy is the Lamb* (Darlene Zschech)
- *You are Good* (Israel Houghton)

- *You are Holy (Prince of Peace)* (Marc Imboden and Tammi Rhoton)
- *You Know I Know* (4NF Band)
- *You Never Let Go* (Matt Redman)
- *Your Grace is Enough* (Matt Maher)
- *Your Love Oh Lord* (Third Day)

Appendix B

41 70 70 65 6E 64 69 78 20 42

This appendix contains all the original songs of the 4th Normal Form Band. The music spans several different genres from folk to soft rock to blues to country to new country to hard rock, and the lyrics touch on an array of topics—sometimes with a biblical, cultural, historical, philosophical, political, or social subtext. I've put them in alphabetical order for quick reference. All of our songs can be heard on SoundClick at https://www.soundclick.com/4thnormalformband.

A Rose by Any Other Name © 2003 by Robert E. Beasley and Nathanael D. Beasley

Verse 1
She was a young girl who got on a bus
But was forced to take the rear. Her daddy's little dear.
And, at the diner, they refused to serve.
She was forced to leave with an unmet need.

Chorus
A rose by any other name is just as sweet.
A rose by any other term is as pure.
I dream of a day when one is judged
By the content of his character.

Verse 2
He was a young man with excellent marks

But was denied his choice. His mama's pride and joy.
And, at his work, they refused his rise.
He was left behind with no peace of mind.

All the Way Home © 2006 by Robert E. Beasley

Verse 1
We pulled into the circle of the elementary school.
He was strapped into that backpack and was sporting brand new shoes.
I felt both his excitement and his fear of the unknown.
And as I drove away, I realized my little boy…was on his own.

Chorus
Well, it seems like yesterday when he would reach to hold my hand.
When he thought I walked on water and could beat up Superman.
And although there's a sweetness to this bitter cup of letting go….
The memories of a baby boy made me smile…all the way home/
The memories of a little boy made me wonder…all the way home/
The memories of a little boy made me cry…all the way home.

Verse 2
I got home from the office as I do most every day.
Then I walked down to the cul-de-sac to see if I could play.
Though I played so many times before, I found I wasn't in demand.
He'd discovered friends as I was warned. He was becoming…his own man.

Verse 3
We pulled up to the college on that warm late-August day.
We moved his things and said goodbye and then we drove away.
As we sat there in the silence, we tried to fight the tears.
And we wondered in amazement at the passing…of those years.

Bringin' Me Down © 2003 by Robert E. Beasley

Verse 1
Well, my shoes don't fit. My shoes don't fit.

Yeah, my shoes don't fit. My shoes don't fit.
Well, my shoes don't fit, baby, and it's bringin' me down.

Verse 2
Well, my pants ain't right. My pants ain't right.
No, my pants ain't right. My pants ain't right.
Well, my pants ain't right, baby, and it's bringin' me down.

Verse 3
Well, my shirt ain't hip. My shirt ain't hip.
Yeah, my shirt ain't hip. My shirt ain't hip.
Well, my shirt ain't hip, baby, and it's bringin' me down.

Deconstruction © 2006 by Robert E. Beasley

Verse 1
Tainted thinking, darkened mind.
Grand delusions are what we find.
Eyes receiving, not perceiving.
Faint illusions of the ruling kind.

Chorus
Deconstruction interpretation.
Postmodern man is on the rise.
Deconstruction interpretation.
I can hear the Fathers' cries.

Verse 2
Twisted reason, shaded view.
Great confusions are sold as true.
Ears demanding, not understanding.
Weak conclusions of the gaveled few.

Differently © 2003 by Robert E. Beasley

Verse 1

I like the rain—a drink of water for the trees.
Some will complain, but it means life for you and for me.
Think about Mondays—for some it's a day that we must get through.
But it means we are able to work and begin our week anew.

Chorus
So, don't you think we should see things differently?
Through a lens of thankfulness, I see plain.
Woo, don't you think we should see things differently?
To count one's blessings is great gain.

Verse 2
I like the clouds—they help me appreciate those sunny days.
And when the thunder is loud, it means refreshing is on its way.
Consider the winter—for some it seems dismal and depressed.
But it means that in flowers the earth herself will soon be dressed.

Down from the Mountain © 2006 by Robert E. Beasley

Verse 1
Out in the cold in the city, it's time to go stand in the line.
There's a serious hunger within me, an ill-feeling that's hard to define.
As I stand by the doorway, I see all the others in need.
And then I stare as I wonder, how could this happen to me?

Chorus
I've looked down from the mountain. I've looked up from below.
I've known an unshackled spirit. I've known a desperate soul.
Looking back on the broken, picking up all the pieces
Was a hand that was caring and a heart that releases.

Verse 2
In the warmth of the mission, I take my seat in the room.
There are some baskets of clothing and some tables of donated food.
As I sit with the troubled, a woman calls out my name.
And then she shares of a future of hope and a heavenly rain.

Earth, Wind, and Fire © 2006 by Robert E. Beasley

Verse 1
Early in the morning, the sun awakes to take its place.
And in a sky of blue and gold, there's a smile upon its face.
Then a cool breeze whispers its soothing words of quiet peace.
And in a gentle still small voice, it speaks and then my worries cease.

Chorus
What a grand creation, Earth, wind, and fire.
Imagine my elation, Earth, wind, and fire.
A magic illustration, Earth, wind, and fire.
What a revelation, Earth, wind, and fire.

Verse 2
In a robe of purple, the mountain soars to dazzling heights.
And with its strength, it shades me and shows the power of its might.
What an awesome notion—a three-in-one that seems surreal.
The earth, the wind, the fire—a mystery to our minds revealed.

Everything with Breath © 2002 by Robert E. Beasley

Verse 1
Praise God in his sanctuary.
Praise him in the sky above.
Praise him for his might power.
Praise him for his acts of love.

Chorus
Let everything with breath praise the Lord.
Let everything with breath praise the Lord.

Verse 2
Praise him with the sound of horns.
Praise him with the strum of strings.

Praise him with the sound of drums.
Praise him with your everything.

Bridge
If his people remain silent, the rocks will sing his praise.
So, let's worship him in spirit and rejoice in all his ways.

Here Comes the Weather © 2006 by Robert E. Beasley

Verse 1
In the morning, the sky is red.
Getting ready for the storms ahead.
Nation and nation. Rumors of war.
Waiting for the tempest at the door.

Chorus
'Cause when the clouds start rollin' in, here comes the weather.
It's alright. Just a sign of the times. Here comes the weather.

Verse 2
In the distance, it's dark as night.
The sky is rumbling ready to ignite.
Kingdom and kingdom. Love grown cold.
Waiting for the story to unfold.

Livin' in Indiana © 2003 by Robert E. Beasley

Verse 1
In the springtime when the daffodils awake to the early morning sun,
Singing birds, the smell of fresh-cut grass. New life has indeed begun.

Chorus
I love livin' in Indiana, where the air I breathe is clean.
And I love all the changing seasons and all the friendly people that I meet.

Verse 2

In the summer when the fields have almost touched the periwinkle sky,
County fairs and playing basketball 'til the evening dark draws nigh.

Verse 3
In the autumn when the trees have dressed themselves in their colorful new hues,
Covered bridges and a homecoming queen and a school year that is new.

Verse 4
In the winter when the earth has wrapped herself in a blanket of pure white,
Shoveling the driveway, frozen fingers, and hot chocolate after a snowball fight.

More Than Money © 2002 by Robert E. Beasley

Verse 1
Working hard to move up. Time is flying by.
I can't waste a minute. Can't let my business lie.
Got to get there really early. Got to stay there really late.
Got to prove my dedication. Don't mean to make them wait.

Chorus
Time is my currency. Time to love that frees my soul.
Time means more than money. A life of love—that is my goal.
Time is my currency. Time to think that frees my mind.
Time means more than money. A life of peace you can find.

Verse 2
Working hard is noble. To excel can make one great.
But in vain you rise up early and in vain you retire late.
One handful with tranquility beats two handfuls with toil.
A handful with contentment than to burn the midnight oil.

Mystery of the Seed © 2006 by Robert E. Beasley

Verse 1
On the path, the seed gets snatched away.
Never understanding, I press on but lose the way.

And on the rocks, it never touches ground.
I only last awhile 'til trouble comes around.

Chorus
It's an enigma indeed this secret riddle that I read.
The kind of life that I lead is in the mystery of the seed.

Verse 2
In the thorns, the seed will suffocate.
The worries of my life distract and obviate.
But in the ground, it always multiplies.
Increasing understanding, I press on toward the prize.

Number Seventy © 2006 by Robert E. Beasley

Verse 1
He was amazed and in wonder when he first touched the writing for night.
He knew there was hope for the future for changing the darkness to light.
But one man spoke of his people as degraded condemned on the earth.
So many had never imagined their writing could be of much worth.

Chorus
He had a vision of love…Number 70.
He had a vision of love…how their lives could be.
He had a vision of love…Number 70.
Yes, a vision of love…a new world they see.

Verse 2
He was a kind-hearted teacher loaning to others for clothing and food.
Although infirm he would realize his life was to bring others good.
But they burned his books and his letters, and they tried to repress his ideas.
And punished were those who resisted, yet they pressed on despite all their fears.

Verse 3
As a child, he was scoffed at so cruelly, and his passing was mourned by few.
Yet he opened a new world for many that changed and expanded their view.

And now his ideas are imbedded in places that most don't perceive.
In our presence are magical letters that set the less fortunate free.

Poor Man © 2003 by Robert E. Beasley

Verse 1
Got my sights set high, lots of people to see.
Lots of money, lots of places to be.
Keeping an image so people can't see I'm a poor man.

Chorus
Poor in spirit, empty inside, poor in spirit, eyes open wide.
Looking for something that may satisfy this poor man.

Verse 2
Driving the best, putting on a show.
Living it up, I can't let it go.
Keeping an image so people don't know, I'm a poor man.

Verse 3
Look in the mirror, what do I see?
My aging eyes looking back at me.
Do the lines tell the truth? How can it be? I'm a poor man.

Remain with Me © 2006 by Robert E. Beasley

Verse 1
I've been doing some thinking about the way to charity.
To really care and to reach out in love. That's the man I want to be.
And I've been driving to get on the road to happiness.
To have a heart that reflects real joy and have a shining countenance.

Chorus
Remain with me. I'll remain with you.
Remain with me. I'll remain with you.
Remain with me. I'll remain with you.

Remain with me. I'll remain with you.

Verse 2
I've been striving to find it—that path to real tranquility.
To end the strife and to live in peace—a lasting warm civility.
Yes, I've been trying for too long to do it on my own.
So, I'll just remain with you 'cause that's when the fruit is grown.

Restless Evil © 2003 by Robert E. Beasley

Verse 1
One small bit in the mouth of a horse
Turns the whole creature and sets its course.
One small rudder in the aft of a ship
Steers the mighty craft and guides its trip.

Chorus
There is a restless evil—so small yet cannot be tamed.
I've seen a restless evil. Sets the course of one's life aflame.

Verse 2
One small spark in the heart of a wood
Begins a blaze that consumes all good.
One small part in the mouth of a man
Corrupts the whole person again and again.

Risky © 2003 by Robert E. Beasley

Verse 1
Some like to ride their motor bikes a hundred miles per hour.
Some like to drive in fast cars and feel the engine's power.
Some like to fly fighter jets and feel the g-force crunch.
Some like to ride roller coasters 'til they lose their lunch.

Chorus
But no, not me. I don't believe in that, Lord. I got too much to lose.

I don't want to end up six feet under, baby, and on my local news.
Because you know that. You know that's risky. You know that could hurt.
You know that's risky.

Verse 2
Some like to bungee jump and avoid that sudden stop.
Some like to climb really high until they reach the top.
Some like to walk a high wire without a safety net.
Some like to parachute as high as they can get.

Verse 3
Some like to beat the red light. That's insanity.
Some like to play Russian Roulette. Bad probability.
Some like to talk to strangers. That's gregarious.
Some like to play with matches. Pyromanious.

Save the Children © 2003 by Robert E. Beasley

Verse 1
In a desert country—no food to eat.
Cut off by politics. They die in the heat.

Chorus
Save the children.
Lord, save the children.

Verse 2
In the streets of Rio—no place to sleep.
Unwanted numbers. No one will keep.

Verse 3
In a big city 'hood—no one to guide.
They shoot each other. Nowhere to hide.

Verse 4
Inside a house—two grownups fight.

Inside they suffer. Inside they cry.

Searching for Diamonds © 2003 by Robert E. Beasley

Verse 1
Wisdom herself calls out in the streets.
She raises her voice out in the square.
At the entrance of the city, she makes her speech.
She sings her song in the open air.

Chorus
So, let's search for knowledge as searching for silver.
For understanding as searching for gold.
And let's search for wisdom as searching for diamonds.
As we've been told.

Verse 2
How long will we simple ones love our ways?
And just how long will we delight
In hating knowledge and loving lies?
In doing wrong and mocking right?

Seeds of Time © 2002 by Robert E. Beasley

Verse 1
One day when I wake up, my boys will be all grown.
Their memories of me will amount to the seeds that I have sown.
I don't want to be like those who wish they'd spent more time.
They're only children once—and that for a very short while.

Chorus
I'm not gonna be too busy. I'm not gonna be too late.
Gonna sow the seeds of time. My affairs—they can wait.
I'm not gonna be too busy. I'm not gonna be too late.
Gonna sow the seeds of time because the price is just so great.

Verse 2
My sons are a heritage entrusted to my care.
I'm gonna seize the moments and be a father who is there.
So, I'm gonna guard my time and mitigate the pull.
Because I'm a man who is blessed with a quiver that is full.

Shield Around Me © 2002 by Robert E. Beasley

Verse 1
Great is the Lord and most worthy of our praise.
Great is the Lord. I will praise him all my days.
Great is the Lord and most worthy of our praise.
Great is the Lord. I will laud all of His ways.

Chorus
You, oh Lord, are a shield around me.
You, oh Lord, have set this captive free.
You, oh Lord, are a shield around me.
You, oh Lord, have saved a man like me.

Verse 2
Oh Lord, our Lord, how majestic is your name.
Oh Lord, our Lord, you will always be the same.
Oh Lord, our Lord, how majestic is your name.
Oh Lord, our Lord, you have wiped away my shame.

Verse 3
Praise the Lord. Sing to him a brand-new song.
Praise the Lord. You are leading me along.
Praise the Lord. Sing to him a brand-new song.
Praise the Lord. Join in with the heavenly throng.

So Long Kaohsiung © 2010 by Robert E. Beasley

Verse 1
All along YuCheng Road. Manic riders everywhere.

Makes me wonder to myself which ones aren't gonna get there.

Chorus
So long Kaohsiung.
Electric thoughts to think upon.
So long Kaohsiung.
In my mind you'll carry on.
zài jiàn (goodbye) Kaohsiung!

Verse 2
City streets. High-rise life. Traffic lights hypnotize me.
The Sanmin District is alive. I can feel the energy.

Verse 3
In a city that never sleeps. Night markets. The MRT.
No need for Fahrenheit. Symbols around that I can't read.

Bridge
The first few nights we stayed in the Song San Hotel. We celebrated my 14th
birthday in the Kenting National Park. The climb up Monkey Mountain. You
know we really enjoyed the Love River. We spent a lot of time in that coffee shop
with our friends. Our week in the ROCMELIA Center was a neat experience.
The beautiful sight of Frog Rock. Many, many monkeys! The smell of Jasmine in
Bright River Side Park. What about the Bilingual Community Church?

The Distance © 2006 by Robert E. Beasley

Verse 1
At the L station on a muggy summer day,
A blind man plays for tips for those who walk his way.
She walks on by annoyed by his infirmity.
Thinks that he should get a job just like you and me.

Chorus
I hear the goats out in the distance.
I see a stranger standing near.

What you do to the least of my brothers....
A look around is all you need.
What you do to the least of these others....
You're doin' it to me.

Verse 2
On a Sunday morning on a sidewalk in the city,
A woman begs for change and hopes that someone will take pity.
He pretends he does not hear her plea to lend a hand.
Thinks it's time for folks like him to finally take a stand.

Bridge
I was hungering and thirsting.
I was a stranger that you let in.
I was naked with a sickness.
I was the captive you made a friend.

The King of Cyberspace © 2003 by Robert E. Beasley

Verse 1
His best friend is his computer.
It's something that he can adore.
It helps him expand his horizons.
To the world, it's his open door.

Verse 2
He's among the digerati.
Well versed in the knowledge of bytes.
He stays up late to battle
Other nerds who will fight.

Verse 3
His identity is clandestine.
Anonymity is his thing.
He loves to debate in the chatrooms.
In cyberspace, he is king.

The Rain is Falling © 2012 by Robert E. Beasley (Music by Nathan D. Beasley)

Verse 1
In the distance, I can hear the echo roll.
The night is grumbling awakening my soul.
And in the droning of a cloudy melody,
The river is rising, fighting to get free.

Chorus
The rain is falling. Been pouring for so long.
The rain is falling.
The rain is falling. Been pouring for so long.
The rain is falling.

Verse 2
From the heavens, I can see the train below.
Colored image of a figure we all know.
But in my mind's eye, that vision's turning gray.
'Cause when it gets here, I know it's gonna stay.

There Go I © 2002 by Robert E. Beasley

Verse 1
He stood in line at the mission. He looked a lot like me.
He ate wilted lettuce and day-old bread. He had no place to sleep.

Chorus
But for the grace of God, there go I.
But for the grace of God, there go I.
I'm blessed to live the life I see.
But for the grace of God, there go I.

Verse 2
He went to school, and he did really well and held a job for a while.

Then the lure set in, like a dear old friend. Now he'd sell his soul for a smile.

Verse 3
He had a family, a wife, and some boys. But he made a few mistakes.
In spite of all the warning signs, what a difference those choices make.

Time to Fly Away © 2003 by Robert E. Beasley

Verse 1
I know some who live to work
To accumulate more stuff.
You know, they'll labor well into the night.
But it will never be enough.

Chorus
But what will happen when it's time to fly away?
Will it be worth all the time?
And is it true that those with the most toys win?
Or will we leave it all behind?

Verse 2
Some of us are never satisfied.
Never pleased with what we hold.
Life is tough 'cause we can never get enough.
Amassing riches untold.

Bridge
Well, I know that naked we all enter.
And I know that we'll return the same.
The things we have will just be left to others.
We must return just as we came.

Undying Call © 2006 by Robert E. Beasley

Verse 1
He had a humble beginning but could somehow read and write.

He looked above for his vision and believed in a wrong and a right.
He was a man of ambition who made every effort to learn
The laws of an immature nation. To this labor he would not return.

Chorus
With malice toward none. With charity for all.
With firmness in right. Was his undying call.

Verse 2
They thought that his way would rob them and believed it was okay somehow
To wring their bread and their riches from the sweat of another man's brow.
And so, they drew up the papers to divide and create their own
A nation where one man would rule the lives in another man's home.

Verse 3
For years, he walked with the sleepless. He was tormented day and night
By the thought of a house separated and a war where so many had died.
He dreamed of a peaceful alliance. He knew all were fashioned alike.
But before his vision was realized, some conspired and ended his life.

What Really Matters © 2006 by Robert E. Beasley

Verse 1
Invented rules that close the door.
Condemning many by the score.
Releasing judgments so very bold.
Ideas that lead me to trust in gold.

Chorus
What really matters is justice and mercy.
I need some help in doing what's right.
What really matters is justice and mercy.
Together we can shine the light.

Verse 2
On the outside, clean and white.

Beautiful cover, virtuous sight.
Decorated, homage to pay.
On the inside, dead men lay.

You Know I Know © 2002 by Robert E. Beasley

Verse 1
Well, I heard a fellow talking just the other day 'bout how his chosen folks had been so blind.
They should have seen all the signs and all the wonders. It was out of sight, out of mind.

Chorus
But you know I know, if that was me, I would have been the very same way.
I would have turned away and shrunk in disbelief. It's by grace that I have faith.

Verse 2
As I read the holy book it seems so clear to me that the brothers should have been a lot more brave.
They should have seen all the signs and all the wonders. They should have followed to the grave.

Made in the USA
Monee, IL
08 October 2024

67454496R00157